Sudden Courage

ALSO BY RONALD C. ROSBOTTOM

When Paris Went Dark: The City of Light
Under German Occupation, 1940–1944

Sudden Courage

YOUTH IN FRANCE CONFRONT
THE GERMANS, 1940–1945

Ronald C. Rosbottom

ch.
CUSTOM
HOUSE

HarperCollins books may be purchased for educational, business, or sales promotional use. For information, please email the Special Markets Department at SPsales@harpercollins.com.

FIRST EDITION

Photo courtesy of Keystone / Stringer
Map of Vichy France by Rostislav Botev. Creative Commons Attribution-Share Alike 3.0 Unported. The spelling of "Rouen" and "Rhine" were corrected, and the city of Pau was added to the map. [https://creativecommons.org/licenses/by-sa/3.0/legalcode]

Library of Congress Cataloging-in-Publication Data has been applied for.

ISBN 978-0-06-247002-7

19 20 21 22 23 LSC 10 9 8 7 6 5 4 3 2 1

France Occupied by Axis Powers
1940–1944

A Selective Chronology

MAY 1940–JUNE 1941

- Germany invades France, Belgium, the Netherlands, and France in May; all nations have ceased combat by mid-June.

- Paris, an "open city," is taken peacefully by the Wehrmacht on June 14.

- The relatively "correct" Occupation of France begins; Germans are not yet at war with the Soviet Union.

- Although resistance activities are minor for the most part, there are German retaliations, including executions.

- Philippe Pétain's new government, L'État Français, is established in Vichy; its legislature passes unanimously and strict anti-Jewish ordinances are quickly imposed.

- Hitler cancels Operation Sea Lion, his plan for invading the British Isles.

- The Battle of Britain begins; Nazi air attacks against the United Kingdom (July–October 1940) are followed by the Blitz—the carpet-bombing of British cities that lasts until May 1941.

- It becomes obvious to all sides that the war and the Occupation of France will continue indefinitely.

- Prime Minister Pierre Laval is fired by Pétain in December.

JUNE–NOVEMBER 1941

- Germany's invasion of the Soviet Union offers a thin ray of hope that Hitler may have bitten off more than he can handle.

- The French Communist Party, previously neutral after the signing of the German-Soviet non-aggression pact of August 1939, becomes actively hostile to the German Occupation.

- Twenty-seven French hostages are executed at Châteaubriant on October 22, including Guy Môquet; a total of forty-eight hostages will be shot at Châteaubriant, Nantes, and Paris.

- The Reich is forced to demand increasing amounts of matériel and labor from occupied countries.

DECEMBER 1941–APRIL 1942

- Hitler declares war on the United States, after the Japanese attack on Pearl Harbor.

- The United States enters the war against the Axis powers.

- The Reich's first Russian campaign concludes indecisively.

- The first French Jews are deported from the Drancy camp outside of Paris on March 27, 1942, and sent to Auschwitz.

- Pierre Laval returns to the premiership in April.

JUNE–JULY 1942

- The policing of anti-German activities in France is transferred from the Wehrmacht to the SS and its Gestapo police.

- La Relève (roughly, the call-up): The Vichy government requests tens of thousands of volunteers for work in Germany in exchange for the better treatment and possible release of some French POWs.

- All Jews over the age of six are required to wear the yellow star in the Occupied Zone.

- The yellow star injunction is followed by a massive roundup of Jews, including French citizens, by French police, bringing more domestic opprobrium onto the Vichy government.

NOVEMBER 1942

- The Allies invade North Africa, where Vichy forces are defeated.

- The German Wehrmacht occupies the Zone "free" of France (previously administered solely by the Vichy government).

- After recalling its ambassador in May 1942, the United States breaks diplomatic relations with L'État Français.

JANUARY–JUNE 1943

- The Milice française, the soon-to-be-despised Vichy antiresistance police and paramilitary unit, is instituted.

- Because La Relève did not succeed, Laval institutes the STO (*Service du travail obligatoire*), a draft for required work in Germany.

- To avoid the STO, many young men either hide or join the Maquis.*

- The Wehrmacht's General Friedrich Paulus surrenders the encircled German forces at Stalingrad; many foresee a resolution of the war, whether Allied victory or armistice.

---

* Maquis (mah-kee) refers to the isolated camps throughout France, but mostly in the southwest and south-central parts of the country, where members of the underground hid out. The word comes from the low-lying, bristly, and impenetrable plants that grow wild in isolated areas of the Mediterranean region.

- Aloïs Brunner, an SS officer, takes command of the Drancy camp from the French police.

- Between March 1942 and August 1944, tens of thousands of Jews and other "undesirables" at Drancy, including thousands of children, are sent to death camps.

JUNE–AUGUST 1944

- The Allies invade France; the Battle of Normandy is launched on June 6.

- Paris is liberated by Free French forces on August 25.

SEPTEMBER 1944–MAY 1945

- The liberation of France continues, but at the end of the war, the Germans still hold a few besieged enclaves on the Atlantic coast.

Sudden Courage

Introduction

———

High school students are scary. We aren't cynical yet.

—JAY FAUK, 18, VIRGINIA HIGH SCHOOL SENIOR (2018)[1]

In times of war, we are brought abruptly to consider youth. While researching and writing my previous book, *When Paris Went Dark*, on daily life in Paris during the German Occupation of France, I took this truism for granted. On reflection after finishing that work, I realized that adolescents and youngsters played a much more important role in resisting the Germans than I had given them credit for. As early as the German invasion in May 1940, a substantial percentage of those few French citizens who "resisted" in some way or another, as well as immigrants from other European nations, were adolescents—young men and women between the ages of thirteen and twenty-five. After more research, I discovered that even though French historians, essayists, filmmakers, and novelists had paid some attention to the role of youth during World War II, there were few such studies, stories, or films in English, and the debate was still heated among historians of Europe about how crucial this age group had indeed been in the struggle against German fascism.

In general, Americans know little about the "French dilemma," namely, the fate of the only European nation to have signed a collaborative agreement with the Third Reich. That agreement allowed the Germans to maintain total control over a large section of France and permitted the establishment of a French government to administer the rest. In other nations, puppet governments were established by the Germans, led by domestic fascists and right-wingers,

but not one had signed a treaty that divided the country geographically, and then whose elected legislature voted for the end of their
previous government.

France was then, and is now, a highly patriotic country; it has always been proud of its history as the protector of the rights of man
and of citizens. Yet, unlike Germany's political and cultural self-
flagellation since 1945—a courageous and generous response to those
whom it terrorized for a decade and a half—many in France have felt
less urgency to apologize, for, they firmly observe, they too were vic-
timized by the Third Reich and by its Vichy minions.[*] They argue that
"France" was not involved in collaboration with the Occupying forces;
instead, they insist, the shadily established L'État Français (the Vichy
government), under the guiding hands of Chief of State Maréchal
Philippe Pétain and his prime minister, Pierre Laval, usurped the
Third Republic's legitimacy.[†] Many argued then, and still do, that
from the beginning of the defeat, London was the official site of "Free"
France—which included many of France's African colonies—and that
it was led by the indomitable Brigadier General Charles de Gaulle.

But the confusion remains, for many Frenchmen, especially the
French police, did assist the Germans in their repressions. For instance, more Jews were tracked and physically arrested by French
police than by the Gestapo. (The Germans simply did not have enough
available forces to occupy completely such a large country.) Further-
more, after the liberation of France in 1945, the politically astute de
Gaulle led the world to believe that most of his fellow citizens had followed his admonitions to resist passively and that only a minority of

---

[*] The official name of the government for the Unoccupied Zone was L'État
Français. But everyone—then and now—refers to that regime by its geographical
location in the spa town of Vichy in central France.

[†] On the contrary, not only did the Reich rely on the charade that "France" was
located in Vichy, but so did the United States, which maintained ambassadorial relations with Pétain's regime until late 1942.

ambitious and venal politicians, with orders from Vichy, had betrayed the values of *la France éternelle.*

This recurrent conceit continues to be manifest: during the 2017 French presidential election, the right-wing Front National candidate, Marine Le Pen, stated baldly, "I don't think France is responsible for the Vél d'Hiv. . . . I think that, generally speaking, if there are people responsible, it's those who were in power at the time. It's not France."[2] She was referring to the extensive roundup of Jews in Paris by the French police in July 1942 and their detention in the massive indoor stadium, the Vélodrome d'Hiver. Thousands of them, including many children, would later die in concentration camps. A while later, after the 2017 election, Jean-Luc Mélenchon, the passionate leader of the far-left La France Insoumise (Unbowed France), agreed with her:

> *To say that France, as a people, as a nation, is responsible for this crime is to agree to a . . . definition of our country which is totally unacceptable. France is none other than its Republic. At that time, the Republic had been abolished by the National Revolution of Maréchal Pétain. In that view of History, France, at that period, was in London with General de Gaulle, and wherever French were fighting against the Nazi occupation.*[3]

I do not intend this book to be a judgment against France for what happened between 1940 and 1945. Those who have not lived through the unpredictable events of a military occupation cannot fundamentally understand them: that is an adage with currency. My story is more focused: how much was the present reputation of the "Resistance" as a courageous force against the temptations of fascism built on the slim shoulders of adolescents, male and female, who often felt that they were standing for something larger even than their patriotic admiration for France?

The Germans and French were fighting their third war in less than a century, and in France there was a visceral suspicion, even hatred, of Germans. Prussia had decisively defeated the French military in the Franco-Prussian War (1870–1871), an embarrassment that some great-grandparents could still recall in 1939. And the horrors of the First World War—the Great War—were quite vivid in the collective memory of France; they had marked the youngest generation as well as their elders. News of French casualties of that murderous conflict had been brought home in photographs and newsreels, with the public listings of thousands of names of the wounded, the missing, and the dead—often including their ages. After the war the shattered bodies roaming the streets and byways of a mourning nation and monuments to the dead in every village kept the memories alive. All of this prevented survivors from ignoring how much promise, innocence, and vigor had disappeared in the space of a few years. And it was taken for granted that young people would not go again, sheeplike, to slaughter, or at least not without searing justifications. These memories created a major cultural shift in the formal and informal education of youth after 1918. The stories that emerged were doubtless heard with fascinated horror by young people facing another war with their cousins on the other side of the Rhine.*

||||||||||||||||||||||||

Recent events around the world have reminded us of how fervently youth can latch on to a cause or criticize their elders for creating a chaotic present. With their fervently held beliefs, they regard compromise as a moral failure rather than a strategy. They write their

---

* And lest we forget, a significant number of young Frenchmen were held, most for the whole war, in prisoner-of-war camps in Germany. There were those, of course, who resisted in their own way while imprisoned—by planning and effecting escapes, by communicating information to their free brothers and sisters—but effectively the great majority of trained young men were unavailable to the Free French or to the indigenous resistance for almost five years.

grievances across their culture, with billboard-large letters—in songs, in films, on websites, and in literature. We adults muse that, "well, when they grow up and see the world as it is, they'll change their tune." That does happen, but for a handful of brief years, they remind us that we might have compromised too much.

The association of these assumptions—moral passion and a distrust of authority—takes on much more credibility when placed within the context of war and military occupation. In any war, youth are the most immediately affected. The first to be drafted, they form the nucleus of armies, and for many of them a burgeoning career as a student is interrupted. Decisions made by them and by others on their behalf upset family plans, redefine their social circles, and put their affective relations on hold as they are pressured into rapid psychological maturation. Those not old enough to join the army may affiliate with less formal youth groups that emphasize patriotism, physical education, order, and hierarchy. The young are continuously under surveillance by their parents, their families, their friends, their mentors, and their teachers, priests, and rabbis, as well as by the forces of order constantly on the alert for any sign of social or political disruption. Moreover, adolescent motives for confronting, whether vigorously or passively, any stunning change in events may range widely.

In France during World War II, participation in resistance ran the gamut from the almost casual to the deeply committed. Role models became crucial; their examples and admonitions would often be just enough to encourage a young man or woman to make a stand for something larger than themselves, or to hold back or even side with the Occupier. The secularism—strict separation of organized religion and the state—that had been strongly supported by the Third Republic (1871–1940) had weakened the Catholic Church's political and moral influence since early in the twentieth century. But religious organizations and individuals still had a marked effect on this generation of adolescents. Protestant churches showed up first on the lines of resistance during the war, especially in protecting Jews and others from the laws passed by L'État Français and Germany. Protestants were also generous toward immigrants, including even communists. Although only 2 percent of the population, these Christians had an influence and set an example that far outweighed their numbers. The Catholic Church itself was split, as always, between its cautious episcopal leaders and the nuns and priests on the ground who lived with those most in need of succor and who often put themselves between the Occupiers and their victims.

The times had left many youngsters facing disruptions such as interrupted schooling, lack of employment, and the need to help out in one-parent families. Yet the temptation to be involved in a clandestine group, even for carrying out minor actions, was difficult to ignore, especially as the Occupation progressed. Many of the memoirs I have read and cite here, and the few participants I was able to interview, mentioned, in one way or another, the excitement of being involved in clandestinity. There was fear, of course, but gravitating toward an adventurous daily life always involves some trepidation. In turn, the most encouraging drug of all for these young people in wartime France was praise and respect from their mentors.

Until later in the game, these young people sometimes seemed oblivious that their casual actions might bring devastating consequences. I still remember a conversation with the mother of a friend, who told me how nervous she always was, not because she or her husband were in the Resistance (they were not), but because they might miss the last bus or the last metro and then have to walk home along empty streets after the curfew set arbitrarily by the Occupier. They knew, she told me, that being picked up by the police and spending the night in jail could suddenly become a death sentence should hostages be needed for German reprisals. The anxiety that settled like a smog over daily life in large cities during this period affected youngsters especially; they had not yet learned how unforgiving life could be, even when war was not raging. And of course, for the parents of these adolescent children, fearless as they often were, anxiety doubled.

Not all of the reasons for resisting the Occupation were social or sentimental; some were based on inescapable need. Jobs were available in Occupied France, but not everywhere, and not all were well paid. Many youngsters found themselves unemployable just as their families—and they—had to deal with restrictions, rationing, and inflation. (The disbanded French army provided scarce employment options, since it had been limited to 100,000 men by the German armistice agreement.) Resistance groups did not have salary standards, but some of them did have some modest funds to help members, so quite a few youngsters found themselves joining up just to have a few francs in their pockets or to help their destitute families. Joining in clandestine activity might have had a tinge of patriotism, but frequently this option was not one that a jobless boy found easy to ignore.

The French historian Alya Aglan has pointed out in her clever study *Le Temps de la Résistance* (Time in the Resistance) that to comprehend the Occupation of France and the reaction to it, we must understand the evolution over time of those who involved themselves in some sort of resistance.[4] Most French citizens found themselves living in an unpredictable present. Yet unlike their parents, or even their younger siblings, adolescents under the Occupation inevitably—and urgently—conflated the fundamental struggle to define themselves in relation to social convention and parental authority with the immediate demands of collaboration or complicity. They were seduced by images of a future that they might influence. Sources of information were believed or not according to one's commitment to changing the present; particular visions of future possibilities brightened, then faded, then brightened again. These adolescents were attempting to fathom a future that was both quasi-utopian (a better Europe could certainly emerge no matter who "won") and threatening (fascism was not the only totalitarian specter). As the French watched German newsreels in movie theaters, listened to the BBC on forbidden radios, and traded rumors from escaped POWs, news flowed like a brisk wind through the general population. And it affected teenage cognition powerfully. Most adolescents, as they learned about the French army's rout before a vigorous new Wehrmacht, demanded answers to questions about the sudden interruption of their lives. In doing so, not a few would conclude that there was only one option worthy of their passion for freedom—action.

The clock ticked. They were making the decisions that all adolescents must make—about breaking away, about establishing new friendships, about what to spend their time on—at the same moment as their security was uncertain. Adolescence has its own developmental time frame, but the unpredictable progress of the conflict in Europe kept interrupting it. Events were not providing youngsters with sufficient time to evolve intellectually, even while their bodies were evolving biologically. This tension is the one constant that unites all of the disparate memoirs, letters, and oral memories of those who lived during this period. Over almost five years, both the Occupational Authority and the resistance groups changed strategies several times, depending on events on other fronts. A ten-year-old in 1939 would have been fifteen in 1944. The intensity of that adolescent's focus on the world would have changed markedly during a war that coincided with the period of his own physical and mental maturation, and he would have reexamined and readjusted, at each momentous event, his attitudes about whether he should or not resist, and if so, how.

Generally haunting such decisions was another struggle—to understand the meaning of "patriotism," especially when one's nation had been divided by a wily German military occupation (see map). When ignited, patriotism is most effective as a call to arms; up until that moment, however, it is blandly taken for granted, as peace and prosperity weaken its most vivid colors. But what happens when such certainties suddenly crumble? What is more disorienting than seeing the retreating soldiers of a suddenly incompetent national army hiding among civilians to escape capture? Than seeing one's government suddenly move from Paris to Bordeaux and then fold overnight? Than having one's father suddenly become a prisoner of war? The realization at such moments that the flag symbolizes more than a casual pride and that history has imposed a vital responsibility on the nation and its citizens can be tonic.

ıııııııııııııııııı

What exactly is resistance in times of war or military occupation? Is passive opposition the same as resistance? What was more important, political ideology or patriotism? The parliamentary vote in July 1940 that abolished the venerable Third Republic in favor of the new État Français had troubled many. And for several other reasons—a sense of defeatism among the government, Pétain's famous handshake with Hitler in October 1940 at Montoire, the imposition of anti-Jewish laws, and the expressed desire to "cooperate" or "collaborate" with the Occupier—the Vichy government was increasingly seen by perspicacious youngsters as the enemy every bit as much as the foreign army that supported it. Young French conservatives too found themselves bounced around like pinballs as they decided to support a war hero, Philippe Pétain, then watched him sign an armistice they considered a surrender, and submit himself and his government to the whims of Adolf Hitler.

Is cooperation with a dominant authority collusion, collaboration, or anodyne cooperation? What is the difference between a police official who orders his men to arrest citizens who show lack of respect for the head of government and a civil engineer who works diligently at keeping public bridges and roadways intact, or the mines running? Is one collaborating and the other only cooperating? Such questions would not only influence opinion during the Occupation but roil the postwar process of *épuration*, or purification, during which many individuals were put on trial in an effort to parse their activities during the war, and thousands of unofficial executions occurred.*

And then there were those who did not have much choice in resisting the Germans or the Vichy government. For Jews especially, but also for undocumented immigrants and the sons and daughters of those who subscribed to suspect political ideologies—especially socialists or communists—there was little option but to act in some way to protect one's family and friends. Such actions did not need to be so bold as to draw attention, yet it was these youngsters who became couriers (many of their families had no telephones, so messages had to be conveyed by word of mouth), child-minders, and gatherers of provisions for families too nervous to go out. Soon, they would take bolder steps—joining combat groups, hiding Jewish children, helping others cross borders. Jewish adolescents especially were immediately drawn into the world of resistance. Their sudden courage was all the more remarkable considering that their gentile friends were able to take more time to decide whether to take the jump into an unclear future.

The first image or thought that comes to mind when we speak of "resistance" is the armed kind, which many assume would be the most effective at sowing uncertainty in the habits and psyches of occupying forces. But what might be called "soft" resistance can be just as effective. Soft resistance in Occupied France was neither pu-

---

* By the mid-1950s, most "collaborators" had been pardoned or had had their sentences commuted. Philippe Pétain himself was found guilty and exiled to the Ile d'Yeu, where he died in 1951 at the age of ninety-five. Laval, who had been prime minister twice during the Occupation (he was fired once by Pétain), was tried, found guilty, and executed in October 1945.

sillanimous nor inconsequential. To engage in it was to undermine the assumed control of the Occupier through repetitive propaganda; persistent, even if minor, sabotage; and the use of irony in the arts. In fact, we could argue that those who resisted the earliest used the same tools designed by the Nazis to control the citizens of all nations (including their own) where they had to keep populations quiescent. The Germans of course had radio broadcasts and films, but they too relied on denunciation, rumor, tracts, newspapers, posters, and signs, and so did the young French who resisted.

Despite political and ideological differences among its members, the Resistance as a whole was just that: patriotic French boys and girls, men and women, and freedom-seeking non-French refugees and immigrants, unwilling to accept the recent changes that had scarred the face of Europe. Picking up a rock or gun, or printing and distributing an anti-German leaflet, or hiding Jews or other "enemies of the state" were only the most familiar ways to resist. Breaking small ordinances, such as rules against jaywalking, making fun of a German in uniform, chattering at school with like-minded buddies, or laughing at a pompous professor supporting Vichy—all of these actions and more were, especially for the youngest, means of resisting. Of course, there was a "hard" resistance that included assassination, major sabotage, train derailments, theft and communication of intelligence, and it too was effective—to a point. It at least kept the Abwehr (the Wehrmacht's intelligence service) and the Gestapo busy. And it certainly aided the Allies during the first crucial weeks of the Normandy invasion, in June 1944. But in general most agree that armed resistance—which led to increased arrests and executions of suspected "terrorists," the arbitrary imposition of curfews, and the interruption of services—might have been as dangerous to the populace at large as to the Germans. Many Frenchmen in fact resented the acts of the "hard" resisters, especially in the last year or so of the war, for the German reactions were by then increasingly arbitrary and brutal. This book covers both "soft" and "hard" resisters. Some of the young people never carried a weapon; others shot and killed Germans and French police. The term "resistance" covered an impressive range of activities, but the copper thread that ran most consistently through these activities was a hatred of the Occupier and his minions and a pride in the myths that had created the image of France as a great nation.

These adolescents, in small bands or alone at first, made spontaneous decisions, empowered by a moral courage to do something. Tinged with a sense of adult adventurism, these activities persisted, becoming better organized, and thus more dangerous for the participants. While they were only modestly effective against the German forces, the activities of these resisters expressed a will to do something (*faire quelque chose*) and thereby resonated with many French citizens, who, slowly, would question a fait accompli. For these earliest of resisters, both adult and adolescent, withstanding the Occupation was not only an option, but a courageous duty.

Of course, most young people did not resist, or at least not at first. Some remained uninvolved, and not a few went to the other side and sought to join such early Vichy organizations as the Armée de l'Armistice (the 100,000-man force that the Germans allowed Vichy to keep under light arms), or later, in 1943, the paramilitary group known as the Milice française. Wearing dark blue, the Milice was supposed to put quietus to the increasing support for the Resistance. Many even joined the Third Reich's SS and fought in the Division Charlemagne in German uniforms on the Russian front.

One of the most successful young resisters, Jacques Lusseyran, estimated that as many as 75 percent of the French members of the early Resistance were under the age of thirty. More recent research has revealed that the average, or mean, age of those who joined the Free French forces in England was twenty-five in 1940 and had gone down to twenty-three by 1943.[5] Those older than thirty represented only 22 percent of the volunteers, while 34 percent were under twenty-one, the age of legal majority. Just under two thousand resisters were under the age of eighteen. It was definitely a masculine group: only about 3 percent were women.[*]

|||||||||||||||||||||

As I write, in democratic, less democratic, and authoritarian regimes worldwide, "resistance" has become a byword for the actions of those who believe themselves lacking the political, economic, or social means to lead their lives comfortably and freely, and who thus feel compelled to concoct actions—both violent and nonviolent—to force change. Sometimes these efforts are successful; mostly, they have modest short-term impacts. And frequently, they backfire, postponing the very change sought. As today's headlines remind us, youth everywhere are most often the first to fight against perceived governmental fecklessness, corruption, or oppression. Normal physical and psychological development from childhood to adulthood typically brings instability and confusion to youngsters. Imagine trying to navigate those shoals while worrying about your parents and your friends—those who are supposed to protect you. Imagine trying to become an adult while avoiding eye contact with strangers, keeping your voice low and your enthusiasms hidden. Yet so many did during the Occupation in France.

---

[*] By the end of August 1940, there were only about eleven thousand volunteers in de Gaulle's Free French army, a figure that would grow but still remain quite low during the war. This may be one of the reasons that he insisted so adamantly that the French be given responsibilities equal to the other large Allied armies, a stance he maintained until the end of the conflict. These Free French volunteers were not only young Frenchmen but also young Spaniards, Belgians, Poles, and even Russians.

The historian Timothy Snyder, in his provocative little book *On Tyranny*, speaks to civilian confrontation against a maleficent regime:

> *For resistance to succeed, two boundaries must be crossed. First, ideas about change must engage people of various backgrounds who do not agree about everything. Second, people must find themselves in places that are not their homes, and among groups who were not previously their friends. Protest can be organized through social media, but nothing is real that does not end on the streets. If tyrants feel no consequences for their actions in the three-dimensional world, nothing will change.*[6]

Youth recently have taken to the streets against authoritarianism in Russia, in Egypt, in Poland and Hungary, in Turkey and Algeria, and in the United States. And to our dismay, some also have carried bombs into arenas and churches and subways, often killing themselves in the process of terrorizing civilians. No age group is more ready to turn their almost innate sense of justice and fair play—no matter how inculcated—into action. In the diplomatic and political chaos of the 1930s, the only certainty was that every twelve months the year date would change. Instability became the norm: governments fell; new ideologies prevailed; the international economy imploded; technology—from airplanes to telecommunication—flourished. Sides were taken, sides changed, and anxieties floated beneath adolescent bombast. The imagination of a young girl or boy was infused with the noise and sights of wars not yet fought but being rehearsed all around them. They saw how the worries of their elders and their political, religious, and intellectual leaders grew, and how the news kept getting worse. Another massive war seemed possible, if not yet probable.

iiiiiiiiiiiiiiiiiiiii

Writing about this topic demands a certain amount of cautiousness on the part of a narrative historian. Dealing with such concepts as "youth" or "adolescence" is a parlous task. Biological definition of these terms only helps a bit; using puberty as the red line of designation is equally troublesome, for it is almost impossible to tell from the memoirs, letters, and accounts of individuals when such physiological change occurred. Youthfulness implies a future to be planned, of responsibilities to be assumed, of continuity. Disaster, war, and illness can displace these expectations with feelings of abandonment, a loss of confidence in protective institutions, and a search for safe shores. Youthfulness permits and encourages the imitation of adulthood, but when that imitation is suddenly and urgently replaced by a requirement to be an adult, anxiety informs all decisions.

Young people at that in-between age are in the process of trying to figure out where they fit into the world. They test themselves and their elders with their newfound sense of agency, tend to make mistakes, and, we hope, readjust after failure or embarrassment. "They [appropriate] and [engage] with the cultural scripts of the previous generation."[7] They seek the comfort of solidarity with their peers and frequently change attitudes and ideologies according to some dominant narrative of the groups they belong to or come into contact with. All of these qualities become especially meaningful in times of social crisis, such as civil conflict, economic chaos, or war. When their lives are disrupted, younger people have little to fall back on except their own inchoate sense of self and the contradictory messages of their elders and of the cultural environment in which they live. Today not much is different in the experience of adolescence, despite the striking changes in our world since the 1940s.

This book will bring to light, for American readers especially, the exploits of young French men and women (boys and girls) who left evidence of the anxiety of having to grow up fast during a war. For them, the question of time or timeliness was a major one, for the weight of the past, the pressure of the present, and the implications of the future affected these youngsters continuously and emotionally as they made decisions that they had never dreamed of making before September 1939. Using as examples the decisions, activities, and successes or failures of several youngsters whose compelling stories we know primarily from their own memoirs, but also from the memories of others who knew them, we can compose a suggestive history of the often underestimated influence of youth on the Occupation of France.

||||||||||||||||||||

As a teacher of young people for over fifty years, I recognize and admire the characteristics I have just outlined and will examine in this book. There is nothing more exhilarating, as one grows older, than to watch the intellectual maturation of youngsters as they physically become adults. An eagerness to know more, to question bromides, to speak out when the voices of their elders seem too moderate—these are tendencies that bemuse, frustrate, and often intimidate their seniors. But without the intellectual and moral energy of youth, our world would be colorless and morally bland, and our future would be less—deeply less—optimistic.

CHAPTER ONE

"Present!"

You can squeeze a bee in your hand until it suffocates. But it won't die
before stinging you. That's not so bad, you say, not bad at all. But if it
didn't sting you, bees would've disappeared a long time ago.

—JEAN PAULHAN

The story of young Guy Môquet is filled with nasty coincidences and
bad faith on the part of the Vichy and German authorities. Guy was
born in April 1924, in a middle-class section of Paris's fashionable seventeenth arrondissement. His father, Prosper, was a railroad worker
and an active member and labor organizer of the French Communist
Party (Parti communiste français, or PCF). In 1936, Prosper Môquet
was elected as a communist deputy in the Socialist Party (Section
française de l'Internationale ouvrière, or SFIO) victory that brought
Léon Blum, France's first Jewish leader, to power.* What followed was
a frenetically productive period in which France established social
policies that have lasted until today. What did not last, however, was

---

* The PCF was founded in 1920 and struggled for the next decade and a half to make
political use of, while differentiating itself from, other leftist parties, primarily the
Socialist Party. With the crisis of the Great Depression and Hitler's election in 1933,
the leftists in France, sometimes reluctantly, founded a "popular front" that would
govern France from 1936 to 1938. Communist support was crucial in that government's election, though no communists served as ministers.

Blum's progressive alliance. Eventually, after a brief return, he was pushed aside by a more conservative government.[1]

In August 1939, a non-aggression pact between Hitler and Stalin stunned French communists; immediately the Party had to forbid any anti-German demonstrations by its members and strongly promote neutrality in a pan-European war. Many followers resented such orders from Moscow, but officially toed its line. Unsurprisingly, the Third Republic did not trust the PCF and worried that it would provide a "fifth column" as Germany made threats against Poland, a French ally. As a result, the apprehensive legislature passed an act that outlawed the Party. Suddenly, thousands of French citizens were forced to go underground if they wished to continue political activities.

Then came Germany's invasion of Poland in September 1939, followed by the "Winter War" between the Soviet Union and Finland (1939–1940), with France supporting the Finns. French communists— who, per Party mandate, supported Stalin's invasion of Finland— were suddenly considered to be even more dangerous subversives. As a result, all French communist deputies were required to disassociate from the now-outlawed PCF or be immediately deprived of their parliamentary seat. About forty of them refused to resign from the Party (they still supported Stalin, though they were grievously frustrated at the turn of events that had suddenly made him an ally of Hitler), and were subsequently charged with aid to an enemy. Tried, they were found guilty of possible collusion with a foreign power and sentenced to up to five years in prison. As a result, Prosper Môquet was sent to prison in Algeria, where he remained until the Allies freed him in 1943, two years after the execution of his son.

Guy Môquet's mother later told researchers that her son had promised her that he would work to free his father. The teenager had comrades, the sons and daughters of these harassed French politicians, and they were among the first to resist—not the Germans, but a

French government that had suddenly turned ruthlessly against their parents' political allegiances. Though traumatic for Guy, the arrest of Prosper and his colleagues energized him to confront the obduracy and hypocrisy of the Third Republic. Starting in October 1939, at the age of fifteen, Guy and his cohort of young members of the Jeunesse communiste (JC)—also outlawed—printed and pasted *papillons* (little stickers) on walls, streetlamps, public urinals, kiosks, and even automobiles all over Paris, declaring the illegality of the arrest and imprisonment of French communist deputies, including Guy's father. After the German Occupation itself began in June 1940, they would take anti-Vichy tracts to cinemas, buy a ticket for the balcony, and then throw their leaflets down onto the spectators. Their messages declared the illegality of the arrest and imprisonment of French communist deputies. (They did not mention the German Occupier, as the Party had forbidden doing so.) At the same time, Guy openly wrote letters to the highest officers in the new Vichy government demanding the release of his father. Though these youngsters never attacked—directly or indirectly—the German authorities, they were a nuisance to the French police. It was risky activity, but they foresaw no drastic consequences. That was soon to change.

One of Môquet's fellow young communists, René Pignard, also composed and distributed leaflets demanding the release of other communist youth from Vichy prisons. The concierge of his building, in an effort to keep the French police from harassing her, pointed him out to the authorities, for she had seen him passing out the documents in her neighborhood. This set in motion a complex police surveillance effort to shadow everyone with whom Pignard had met or talked. During the early Occupation, the French police concentrated on communists and Freemasons and spent little time on the Germans' preoccupation with racial and ethnic groups. Later, the imagined power of the *"terroristes judéo-communistes"* would be a consistent propagandistic target of the Germans as well as the collaborative French. In that way, the Germans and their minions felt that they could separate the "bons Français" from unpatriotic communists and from ethnically inferior Jews, including French Jews.

A new police unit, the Brigades spéciales, created by the Vichy government especially to track communist activity, was soon feared by all resisters. The Brigades were recruited from the regular police and chosen because of their investigative experience, toughness, obedience to hierarchy, and hatred of Bolshevism. Their cohort tended to be older and were regularly recruited from the provinces, thought to be inherently more xenophobic. As the Occupation progressed, with capable candidates harder to come by, younger recruits were taken on, often lured by high salaries, promotions, or access to better lodging or food. Still, the pool of willing volunteers was shallow, and the men recruited later were less experienced, ideologically confused, and often more brutal.

The Brigades were geniuses at patience and disguise. They often dressed as *clochards*, or panhandlers, and would have no compunction about wearing yellow stars to camouflage their mission. Their most efficient tool, however, was the patient planning of what they called *filatures* ("shadowings" or "tailings"). They would sit for hours on stakeouts, yet never arrest a single suspect until they had the names of each member of his or her group. Watching their suspects, they would follow them, and follow them, and follow them again, for weeks, even months at a time; they would speak with neighbors and concierges, patronize bars and cafés in the neighborhood of the suspect, and familiarize themselves with all the exits of large apartment complexes and buildings nearby. Occasionally, after arresting most of a group's members, they would leave a few others free and then shadow them patiently until they either joined another group or started one of their own. They kept minute records, with precise physical descriptions of those they were tracking, including what they wore, down to the color of their socks. When subjects sensed they were being tailed, the unit would cancel its surveillance until their targets naively felt more secure again. After brutal interrogations—they were known especially for beatings—they might turn the poor resisters over to the Gestapo for another round of questioning. The German antiresistance offices relied on the Brigades to accomplish what they did not have the personnel to do themselves.

Between August 1941 and August 1944, the Brigades would arrest more than three thousand young clandestines. Over two hundred of these mostly young men would be executed at Mont-Valérien, a nineteenth-century fort right outside of Paris. No Occupation police unit—either German or Vichy—would be as effective in breaking up major resistance groups, especially in large cities, as these special teams of French civilian officers—and it was they who tracked down Guy and his friends.[2]

After diligently observing Pignard and his group for some time, the Brigades made simultaneous raids on all those who had associated with them. On October 13, 1940, Guy Môquet and Pignard were arrested in the Gare de l'Est—a huge train station in one of the poorest neighborhoods of Paris—handcuffed, and taken to jail. Through a sequence of unfortunate coincidences, Guy would not leave prison until his execution a year later. Given his age at arrest, sixteen, he was brought before a juvenile court, and since no evidence of communist activity had been found at his residence, he was found innocent and the French police were ordered to release him to the care of his parents. With his father incarcerated in Algeria, it was his mother who had this responsibility—which she would never be able to assume. Because his comrades had subtly implicated Guy so as to reduce their own sentences, the French police decided, against the court's order, to keep him in custody for a while longer. For still unclear reasons, he was removed from police jail and sent to the high-security prison at Fresnes, outside of Paris, then later taken back to another penitentiary in Paris, the infamous La Santé. Finally, again with no explanation, Guy was transferred to the "surveillance camp" of Choisel, near the town of Châteaubriant, in Brittany. While being moved from facility to facility, he continued to write to Vichy—not German—prosecutors and judges, asking why, if he had been found innocent, he was still a prisoner. Guy did not know that there were heated disagreements between the German Occupiers and the French police about how to treat members of the PCF, since the Third Reich was not yet at war with the Soviet Union. Thus, in Guy's case, the French appeared to be more fixated on the communist "menace" than were the Germans. The police rounded up hundreds of communist activists, even those for whom there was no evidence that they had participated in illegal activities; their "crime" was simply their membership in a still-outlawed Party. Guy Môquet was caught up in this bureaucratic imbroglio.

The Choisel holding camp was similar to a youth camp. Internees were free to wander around within its several-acre area and could receive visits from friends, relatives, and even spouses. (Cabins were set up for intimate visits.) In May 1941, it contained an estimated 641 "campers": 222 communists, 65 drug traffickers and pimps, and 354 *nomades* (itinerants, and probably some Roma).[3] It was the least unpleasant prison Guy had been in since his arrest. Courses were organized, and a variety of sports activities were offered; even the food was more plentiful than in other places of incarceration. The communists, always organizing, had set up a social committee that promised the camp warden and his officers that, if treated fairly, they would cause no trouble. And nearby, unbelievably, there was a camp for girls and women, which could be visited. All fared relatively well as Guy nervously waited for word on his legal problems. But bureaucratic inaction would seal his fate.

In October 1941, three young communists shot and killed Karl Hotz on a sidewalk in Nantes in full daylight. Hotz was a Wehrmacht lieutenant colonel in charge of Occupation troops in Nantes, a major port in Brittany. Learning of this attack, Hitler demanded that the Militärbefehlshaber in Frankreich (MBF), the Wehrmacht Occupying

Authority, take the most stringent measures against the "terrorists." In an attempt to assuage German outrage, the Vichy government did execute three communists, but Hitler remained adamant. He let it be known to the Wehrmacht general governing France that he "could accept the execution of three hostages only as a first and urgent act"; he insisted that "if the murderer is not delivered within a very short time, then [there should be] at least 50 further executions."[4]

The hostage policy—whereby a number of prisoners would be shot for any attempt against a German soldier—was focused consistently on set targets. From the beginning, Jews and communists, and occasionally Freemasons, were the authorities' first choice, if not the public's, for execution. This "hostage code" was officially promulgated among various police groups in September 1941, only a month before Hotz's assassination.*

1. Communists, insofar as we can identify them, . . . arrested for offenses against the Occupying Authority (for example, propaganda, distribution of tracts, etc.);

2. Jews, and especially known Jewish communists;

3. Ordinary French citizens, having committed serious crimes against the Occupying power (for example: illegal possession of arms, aggression or threats against members of the Wehrmacht), who are in prison or have been sentenced to long terms;

4. Gaullists, citizens who are known to be partisans of de Gaulle, and who have committed serious threats against the Wehrmacht.[5]

The most contentious debate among the various police authorities responsible for the maintenance of "order and security," both

---

* It is striking to see that "Gaullism" had become a crime only eighteen months after this unknown figure had made his first plea from London that all "free" French follow his lead.

German and French, was about the efficacy of executing innocent prisoners—that is, persons who may not have been themselves serious offenders, but who happened to be in jail at the wrong time.

Up until the German invasion of Russia, the MBF had relied primarily on the French police—which was nominally controlled by the Vichy state but substantially independent in large cities—to control unrest. However, it had become obvious that no matter how harsh their actions were, the French authorities were not as draconian as the Germans wished, whether in prison sentences, executions, or trial outcomes. The assassinations in the early and late autumn of 1941 brought the hostage debate—politically, legally, and militarily—to the forefront of German policy. Berlin felt that it had to send a powerful signal if it were to have a complacent France at its back while it fought the Russians in the east.

General Otto von Stülpnagel, commander of the MBF, was tactically opposed to this drastically repressive strategy, for he wanted to keep the French population as docile as possible. But his objections had no effect on Hitler or on General Wilhelm Keitel, the chief of staff of the German army. Keitel wrote to von Stülpnagel that "the Führer . . . has ordered that punishments should henceforth be the most energetic, in order to crush this movement [of communists] as quickly as possible. We can generally consider the death penalty be set at 50 to 100 communists as the appropriate punishment for the death of one German soldier."[6] Anything less, he continued, would not be a deterrent, would not terrorize the populace, and thus was not to be approved. And so the Wehrmacht general in charge of the Nantes area, where the attack against Hotz had occurred (only about forty miles from Châteaubriant and the Choisel camp), was ordered to find one hundred hostages and to submit their names.[*]

---

* As an afterthought, Hitler had relented enough to demand that "only" fifty hostages be shot first, and then, if the perpetrator(s) had still not been arrested, fifty

The prisoners of the Choisel camp were all considered hostages, and thus potential victims, but discussions between Vichy's minister of the interior and the MBF were splitting hairs as to what category of victims should be chosen: Communists? Gaullists? Jews? "bons Français" (that is, engineers, doctors, lawyers)? Of course, the answer was communists, and young Guy, though completely innocent of any of the violent attacks against German personnel, was an avowed communist.*

There were different barracks for different types of prisoners: communists, union leaders, professionals, minor criminals. When news arrived on October 21 of Hotz's assassination, the entire camp fell silent as they waited for the reaction—from both German and Vichy authorities. Rumors had already spread about the "hostage code," and a new barracks had just been built, number 19, where prominent communist prisoners were moved. They wondered—but the authorities knew—why this special accommodation was necessary: when condemned hostages were needed, the selection would begin with Barracks 19.

When the camp learned of the assassination, most of the preselected prisoners knew of their fate, but all were surprised when Guy and a few other quite young internees were selected to join them. Unfortunately for Guy, a survivor of the Nantes attack who had been walking with Hotz, a Captain Sieger, described what he had seen, in a report that read: "[The two German officers] were walking along,

---

more within forty-eight hours. Berlière and Liaigre argue that this reaction seemed extraordinarily harsh given the fact that so few German soldiers (four) had been killed in the six months since the invasion of the Soviet Union. But Berlin, increasingly wary of French rebels or "terrorists," both communist and noncommunist, still felt that a bloody response was strategically advantageous.

* This process of selecting hostages for execution is a major plot element of a long-running television series (2005–2017) *Un Village français* (created, directed, and produced by Frédéric Krivine, Philippe Tribout, and Emmanuel Dancé). It treats with subtlety the Occupation from 1940 to 1945, and its immediate aftermath.

talking, when two shots, apparently from the same pistol, sounded behind them. . . . Sieger turned around immediately and saw two men who were running, and were already yards away; they were wearing espadrilles, or sandals in rubber, and they appeared to be very young, and alert."[7]

Historians have surmised that Guy Môquet was selected, along with a half dozen other young boys, because they had characteristics of the described assassins, even though, considering their obvious alibi, they could not possibly have committed the crime. (Among the twenty-five hostages shot in Châteaubriant, several were quite young, including one who was the exact age as Guy, barely seventeen.) Môquet and the others were marched out to trucks where French police and SS soldiers awaited them.* Supposedly the French police guards had tears in their eyes at the sight of the condemned prisoners whom they had known and interacted with for months. The camp's other prisoners were held back by SS troops; a large machine gun had been trained on the barracks and their inmates to keep them under control, but shouts of "You can't shoot children!" and "Vive la France!" were heard from the crowd. "Au revoir, les copains!" (Until next time, buddies!) was another refrain that swept over the barbed wire as the condemned waited to be brought to the firing range.

Three trucks arrived and each took nine of the condemned plus their guards to a quarry, about a mile and a half from the camp. The posts against which the condemned would stand had already been set up. The priest accompanying the young man reported later that "Guy Môquet seemed moved by the proximity of his death; his attitude though was one of pride. He was not crying. Spoke little. He said

---

* The SS (Schutzstaffel, or "protection unit") was a Nazi paramilitary group that grew into a major organization tasked with maintaining order, rounding up and imprisoning Jews, and spreading terror among both German and occupied populations. Its leader was Heinrich Himmler, and its main police unit was the Gestapo.

to me: 'History's memory of me will be that I was the youngest of the condemned.'"[8] His prognostication would be fulfilled. Some reports have suggested that he fainted as he was being led to the stake and was killed before he revived. Others have disputed this notion. But the image of an unconscious boy, his limp body straining against the ropes that held him to the stake, then being shot, and afterward receiving the coup de grâce from the commanding SS officer, would resonate worldwide. From these rumors was formed the myth of Guy Môquet, which, as with all myths, sometimes competed with the facts.*

The PCF immediately appropriated the story, which spread almost immediately across France. Here was a young martyr to the promise of communism, a boy who loved his father and his Party equally, and who died honorably. The writer Louis Aragon, a communist and one of France's favorite writers, distributed his subtle poems of resistance across the nation through the clandestine press that he and his wife, Elsa Triolet, ran. He also wrote articles, as a quasi-journalist for underground papers, about such events as the one at the Choisel camp. One reads:

> But why call them hostages? Back in the days when there were still rules of warfare, hostages were prominent people named in advance to suffer the consequences of acts committed by their fellow citizens against the enemy. In [the Choisel] case, . . . the so-called hostages were chosen from among prisoners who had nothing to do with killing or plotting to kill a German officer. And they were handed over to the enemy by the Minister of the Interior of a government that calls itself French—a government that obligingly drew up a list of French men for the Germans to execute.[9]

---

* The myth of Môquet's execution continues to fascinate the French. As recently as 2011, the German director Volker Schlöndorff released a feature film, *La Mer à l'aube* (*Calm at Sea*), about the boy's last days at Châteaubriant.

Later, Aragon dramatized the reaction of other prisoners when the young Môquet's name was called in his barracks:

In Barrack 10, we learn from another [witness], the [SS] lieutenant "stood for a moment in the doorway, looked around with a sickly smile, then quickly uttered a single name: Guy Moquet [sic]. That name was like the blade of a guillotine on all our necks, like a bullet in all our hearts." Moquet, an overgrown, light-hearted boy of 17, was the most popular of all the prisoners.[10]

Whatever the truth, Guy became the martyr the communists hoped he would be, one who might have proclaimed the same sentiment as a young man in Aragon's poem "The Ballad of One Who Sang at the Stake": "If it had to be done all over / I would take this road again."[11] Throughout the Occupation, the communist propagandists would use Guy's execution to increase recruiting; many noncommunist groups did the same to increase their own cadres. In his study of Môquet's execution, the journalist and amateur historian Pierre-Louis Basse offers an explanation of the adolescent mind in the early days of the Occupation:

For Guy Môquet and a few of his buddies from [the Lycée] Carnot, the motivation [to resist an illegitimate government] came from deep within. Perhaps it originated from that worry that can be found strong in every young person, especially as he [or she] moves into adolescence, an awareness of an intoxicating disorder, capable also of creating the most courageous soldiers. [Guy and his companions] had that moral fiber. Politics were for grown-ups. But not honest feelings. These adolescents saw, perhaps through a confused anger, what others failed obstinately to see.[12]

With the mass execution of forty-eight hostages in three places (Nantes, Mont-Valérien outside of Paris, and Châteaubriant), the

Germans had hoped to shock the populace into helping them stop the attacks against their forces by the communists and the Gaullists. But the opposite happened: a few months later, Louis Aragon's manuscripts were smuggled out of France and were soon being read on British and French radio programs, originating from London. The outrage of everyone, from de Gaulle to Churchill to Roosevelt, became manifest in their speeches, published in the world's newspapers, and for the first time many in France—and abroad—had to accept the fact that the Occupation was no longer, if it had ever been, "correct," and that the Germans and the French police were not benefactors or protectors, but murderers of youth—youth who were carrying the spirit of "La Marseillaise" on their lips as they marched to their deaths. Four days after the executions, de Gaulle went on the BBC to declare that, "by shooting our martyrs, the enemy thought he would frighten France. France will show that it is not afraid of him." He called for five minutes of silence on Friday, October 31, from 4:00 to 4:05 p.m., throughout France. It is not clear how many participated, but perhaps as de Gaulle wished, his tactic put all the authorities on edge.

The benefits—and costs—of youthful resistance had become much higher.

To begin this book with the story of Guy Môquet is to enter into a historical briar patch. The controversy surrounding for whom or what Môquet had died came roaring back to French consciousness after the election of a center-right president, Nicolas Sarkozy, in the spring of 2007. His first public act was to instruct all schools and high schools to begin the 2007–2008 academic year with a reading of Môquet's last letter to his mother. The schools and the government would celebrate October 22 (the anniversary of the executions) with a full curriculum on Môquet and his companions' sacrifice.

A postage stamp featuring his handsome young face was released; government-produced pamphlets were handed out throughout France; and special celebrations were held at the metro stop and the street named after Guy in the seventeenth arrondissement where he was born and had lived. Sarkozy was accused of cynically appropriating a patriotic martyr for his own political ends; the communists were especially offended, as were writers and historians on the right who thought France was commemorating a kid who had *not* resisted the Germans. The events brought back many of the smoothed-over schisms of the late 1940s through the 1960s, but also, ironically, raised Môquet's notoriety to heights that even his most ardent admirers had never hoped to see.

Despite such debate (or perhaps because of it), Guy remains an example of a committed, morally certain young man who, without hesitation, began to resist the arbitrary anticommunism of the Third Republic. When L'État Français replaced that doddering government, he continued to write petitions requesting that he, and his father, be released from arbitrary imprisonment. He challenged the French who had closed their minds to any suggestions about how to govern from the political left. And it was this passion for justice that would fortify all of his young communist contemporaries, when the time came, to face an enemy even more vicious than those on the French political right.

Môquet—and his death at the hands of Nazi soldiers—became a symbol: a teenager, caught up in the complexities of politics and diplomacy of the late 1930s, deciding to confront those who sought to repress dissidence. And coincidentally, soon after his death, he stood as an example of resistance to many who had not known the details of his imprisonment, but only the fact of his execution by the hated Occupier. When, in September 1942, less than a year after Guy's execution, a group of young *màquisards* (members of the Maquis), near Besançon, bordering on the Jura Mountains, decided to establish

their own detachment, they insisted that it be named Le Détache-
ment Guy Mocquet (naively misspelling his name) "in the memory of
the youngest Frenchman assassinated by the Nazis at Châteaubriant,
and a student [as we are]."[13] This group of young irregulars carried
out several major attacks against the Germans, but were eventually
captured. Sixteen of them were executed on September 26, 1943, in
Besançon; remarkably, the condemned team was composed of both
members of the Jeunesse ouvrière chrétienne (JOC) (leftist Catholics) and their rivals, the Parti communiste français. Guy Môquet, the
"non-resister," had transcended his specifically communist origins to
become a model for all youngsters who would sacrifice themselves for
France.*

Before the end of the war, in December 1944, Charles de Gaulle
awarded Guy Môquet a posthumous Medal of Honor as well as the
Medal of the Resistance; in 1946, Môquet was named a Chevalier de la
Légion d'honneur, France's highest civilian award. Not only were a
street and metro stop named after him in 1946, but he was added to the
traditional roll of distinguished French men and women, the ordre de
la Nation. And the fiercely anticommunist de Gaulle, who recognized
several times that Guy was "mort si bravement et cruellement pour la
France" (dead so courageously and cruelly for France), was known to
have crossed the legislative amphitheater of the Chambre des députés
to shake the hand of Guy's father, Prosper Môquet, newly reseated
there.

As Maurice Druon, a well-known Gaullist resister and later per-

---

* The use of young martyrs for propagandistic effect had been a very long Republican tradition in France, beginning in 1793 with the separate deaths of two youngsters, Joseph Bara (age thirteen) and Joseph Viala (age fourteen), who had died in
struggles against royalists, one supposedly crying "Vive la République" before ex-
piring. Robespierre and others saw their usefulness immediately, and their stories
and images were soon spread across France in woodcuts and broadsheets. Both
these boys have been represented in paintings, drawings, sculpture, story, and song
for over two hundred years. Both have streets named after them in Paris.

manent secretary of the Académie française, wrote in 2007 about the brouhaha over Môquet's story: "Let's go back to that time: what was important, was to resist. It wasn't whether or not one was a communist or a Gaullist. We should recall, from time to time, for those youngsters who have forgotten, or who have never known, that if they live today in a Republic, it's thanks to boys like Guy Môquet."[14] Druon emphasizes what some have called the *précocité résistante* of many resisters: their sudden courage.

But if the life and afterlife of Guy Môquet is a good place to begin this book, we need to understand the circumstances under which he grew up, and why and how he and so many similar young people rose to combat the German Occupiers and those countrymen who assisted them. For this, we need to go back to the 1930s.

CHAPTER TWO

———

Coming of Age in the 1930s

———

[After World War I, French] patriotism . . . reflected an ever wearier,
ever more desperate search for impossible solutions to insoluble
problems.

—EUGEN WEBER

In France in the 1930s, the carnage of World War I—reflected in dead
or scarred fathers and uncles, brothers and sons—was never far from
memory. Portraits of the slaughtered, with black borders, were still
on mantelpieces in the homes of millions, and the memorials built
in every single village in France, often with repeated patronyms
from the same family, could not be ignored. November 11 (Armistice Day) and July 14 (Bastille Day) observances would feature the
French troops who had defeated the Germans, with little mention
of the British or American allies. The Tomb of the Unknown Soldier
was inaugurated in 1920, under the Arc de Triomphe at the top of the
Champs-Élysées in Paris. In northern and eastern France especially,
the fields had been permanently marred by shells and bombs, and not
a month passed without someone being killed or maimed because of
buried live shells. Towns and cities still bore the mark of massive air
and artillery bombardment. Huge cemeteries appeared near battlefields, where large numbers of the buried remained unidentified, and
the intermingled dead of both sides were buried in a huge mausoleum
outside Verdun, the site of one of the most prolonged artillery and

infantry struggles of the war. Widows in black, still mourning their fallen loved ones, were a common sight. Young boys and girls did not remember the war, but the older ones did, and like a tambour, its resonance beat softly in their imagination as they tried nervously to gauge the future.

Most of their Great War had been fought in northern France and Belgium, with little damage visited on German industry or its civilian population. During those four long years, 27 percent of the active French male population had been in uniform. About one and a half million men died, and almost two million were wounded. Many survived their wounds, thanks to remarkable advances in medical technology, but they had returned to their homes maimed, psychologically damaged, and unable to reinvigorate their nation. It is estimated that more than a million French babies were not born in the 1920s and 1930s because of the death or wounding of so many men.

One historian summarized the toll:

> The French had paid an obscene price for their 1918 pyrrhic victory. . . . [They] took twice as many casualties as Great Britain, three times as many as Germany, and sixty times as many as the United States. The Germans [had] sunk half of French merchant shipping; German artillery [had] destroyed 800,000 French buildings, thousands of bridges and 40,000 miles of roads. Five percent of France's total population of 40 million became casualties.[1]

A decade later, France was healing, and though not as debt-ridden as other nations, it would not avoid the worldwide depression. Consequently, the century's fourth decade began morosely. Though hatred of the war had empowered a strong and politically influential pacifist movement, there was still enough paranoia about a resurgent Germany to motivate war-conscious strategies.

Within those ten years, 1930 to 1939, a generation of boys and girls would grow from childhood to the cusp of adulthood, when another calamity would face them. Apprehensively, they witnessed the slow descent of the great nations of Europe into another international war. Still, they retained some confidence that France was perceptive and agile enough to withstand any incursions from the east. If there had to be a war, it would be fought in Germany this time, or in the same provinces of Belgian Flanders as the last one. Such complacency would be shattered in 1939–1940 by suddenly erupting belligerence that would stun French youth about how badly their elders, their friends, and they themselves had miscalculated. In his study of the same name, the historian Eugen Weber refers to the 1930s as "the hollow years" to describe a period of missed opportunities, government and financial failures, and diplomatic insufficiencies.

||||||||||||||||||||||

Every effort was being made to "fill" those hollow years, political and diplomatic anxieties notwithstanding. They were certainly not hollow when it came to introducing a multitude of newly invented conduits to feed information at ever greater speeds to an increasingly sophisticated public, which was becoming attuned to new sounds and even newer sights. There were moments of technological ebullience as an explosion of mechanical, architectural, and artistic inventions swept through Europe in the late 1920s and early 1930s. New images were also coming from the United States, especially from the near-fabulous New York City with its incessant construction of skyscrapers (*gratte-ciel*); these images sent a bold, confident message that reminded Europeans that they remained behind, but that also encouraged them to catch up. The Parisian cityscape was soon dominated at night by stunning light in the form of searchlights, neon signs, many thousands of automobile headlamps, and massive street lighting. Enhanced and controlled sound from loudspeakers and the honking and gear-shifting of automobiles provided sonic rhythms that George

Gershwin would brilliantly capture in *An American in Paris* (1928), a composition played over and over on the new "wireless" radios and phonographs now present in many homes. Even for those who lived far from a conurbation, the wireless brought modernity into the most modest of homes. Advertising, often mixed with ideological messages about class and wealth, used technology to dominate monuments, huge department stores, broad avenues, and even airspace. The spectacle of urban life was continuously changing and, with it, attention spans, desires, and social connections.

Beginning with the thrilling tales of the "knights of the air" during World War I, when men fought each other "honorably" in fragile flying machines, the fascination with the possibilities of air travel exploded onto the screens of movie houses. Hollywood had grasped audiences' desire to see these flyers in aerial combat, and other uses of air flight were being developed, most notably international mail delivery. The writer Antoine de Saint-Exupéry, an intrepid aviator himself, introduced a series of novels in the late 1920s and 1930s about the exaltation and exhaustion of flying, and he was especially eloquent on the loneliness of the solo aviator, who became a symbol for a new emphasis on virile courage. Women aviators were suddenly in the news as well, not intending to allow males to keep control of a new technology to themselves, as they had done in past centuries. Amelia Earhart became an international star and was almost as well known as her fellow American Charles Lindbergh. The French had been pioneers in aviation, with names such as Roland Garros and Louis Blériot (who had been the first aviator to fly across the Channel in 1909) known by all. "No other machine seemed to represent humankind's determined escape from age-old limitations to defy the power of gravity, and to obliterate the tyranny of time and space."[2] For the first time, as Lindbergh had so demonstratively shown in 1927 when he flew solo across the Atlantic, the "aeroplane" would provide a major military and commercial boon, and aeronautical engineering and production increased substantially. Today we may look back patronizingly at this fascination with the speed of change. But in nations where most of the population was barely educated beyond the age of fifteen, where agriculture was the major source of income and jobs, and where internal migration to urban areas was reconfiguring cities themselves, such change was indeed breathtaking.

During these interwar years, there was no advance in visual culture more powerful than the moving pictures. It has been estimated that between 1920 and 1938, monthly attendance at the cinema increased from 150,000 to 450,000. Paris itself had more than 22,000 seats, and there were 13,000 in provincial cities. Over two million tickets were sold in Paris alone in 1939. The increase was due to several factors, including the advent of sound films in 1929. Sound—the matching of the tones of a voice with the movements of an actor's body—taught many attentive moviegoers how to listen, how to interpret body language through dialogue. And soundtracks, with music that led the viewers to respond emotionally to what they were seeing, made going to the movie house a new intellectual experience, one that would be deftly used by political propagandists on both sides of the Rhine.

Films directed and produced in France that tried to entertain rather than to instruct competed in popularity with what Hollywood was sending abroad. For the first time, the French could watch a film where the actors spoke with the same provincial accents as the audience, but that also familiarized audiences with a variety of foreign tongues. At a time of wary isolationism, the cinema provided a template of recognition, if not tolerance, of "foreignness." There were war films of course, still reminding the French of the price they had paid for victory a decade before. But new films also were animated by a creative impulse to bring about international comity that might prevent further wars. The most popular film of that decade was Jean Renoir's *La Grande Illusion* (1937), which simultaneously emphasized the disappearance of class hierarchies (in this case, the weakening of international aristocratic camaraderie) and the possibility that "people-to-people" diplomacy could head off other disastrous wars. The movies offered a wider world and a variety of emotions and strategies to naive youngsters. An inexpensive form of entertainment—unlike the opera, symphony, or theater—films, for a while, brought social classes together in one place where status and background were temporarily hidden. And if for only a couple of hours, they assembled several generations, from the young to the old, in the same darkened room.

As cultural historians have pointed out, ideas of what constituted taste were massively and quickly changing during this period. Films that dealt with cops chasing robbers, and robbers chasing other robbers, proliferated. The detective story—both fictional and "true"—sold millions of copies of magazines and drew larger numbers to the movies. The wide-open spaces that had defined popular American westerns during the silent age were replaced with the fascinations of the labyrinthine city. Later, youngsters and others seemed to remember what they had seen on the screen during this period—escapes and evasions as good and not so good characters hid in a city, using its transportation, its commerce, its built environment, and its crowds to maneuver anonymously—when they took similar actions during the Occupation. The architectural environment, which had been taken for granted, would become an important asset for resistant denizens.

The movies also emphasized for audiences the role played by serendipity, coincidence, and social mishaps in the city. Unexpectedly encountering a stranger or a friend one does not want to see, hearing footsteps approach on the sidewalk, taking the wrong turn at an intersection, crossing the street haphazardly, navigating in a heavily populated environment—all were plot elements in horror and crime films and often in comedies as well. The unexpected—at the root of all comedy, physical and verbal—was shown in a myriad of representations and thereby raised the alertness of the city dweller. Such alertness would be invaluable to French citizens in the years to come. The cognitive changes evinced by film-going are not easy to judge, and no doubt most spectators did not leave the theater testing what they had learned while watching a movie. But memories of the speed, sounds, and images, and the variety of stories that movies brought to French (and European) screens, would have an effect during the war years, even with the idiosyncratic restriction of the authorities.

During the whole Occupation, movie attendance remained high and steady, despite the censorship of Vichy and German authorities. And where else would one find regularly a large group of adolescents in a public space? Tickets were cheap; parents were more lenient about moviegoing than the *bals* that their daughters wanted to attend; and there was, of course, protection for the least brave in a crowded, darkened space. Not coincidentally, as the Occupation began, the earliest repeated actions of adolescent resistance occurred in these darkened venues. Boys and girls would hoot at German-produced films, shout while newsreels bragged about the Reich's advances, and stand up to yell political platitudes in order to offend older audience members.

Social historians of the period have all agreed that moviegoing had a major effect on girls and women, theretofore marginalized members of French society. Women on the screen were depicted as witty, stubborn, canny, persistent, and secure in their environment. They adeptly worked out relationships with their elders. And diverse audiences found themselves sitting together, smiling, crying, and, at times, laughing out loud at the satirical representations of politicians and other leaders as they were outwitted by women and children. Movies tended to normalize transgressive thoughts and actions (and thus were repeatedly criticized by religious institutions). They offered a moment of social and cultural freedom that could be enjoyed, even by the most staid spectators.[3] And films about dark crimes "evoked a universe full of danger, mystery and insecurity, struggle and killing."[4] It was all illusion, but films would nonetheless have an impact well beyond the immediate experience of them when French moviegoers found themselves living cheek by jowl with the Germans.

If his family was fortunate enough to have a bit of disposable income, a youngster's main source of frequent and direct information about what was happening would be the TSF (*télégraphie sans fil*, or wireless radio). Radios were also prominently visible in cafés, and neighbors would invite friends over for the nightly news. Here, for the first time, boys and girls could listen to bulletins and hear directly the voices of leaders from all over Europe, uncensored by adults' judgments. Listening to news at noon and again at 8:00 p.m. soon became a family habit as ingrained as mealtime, and conversation always followed. In 1932, there were an estimated one million radios in France; by 1939, historians estimate, there were almost five million.[5] Though France trailed Britain and Germany in rural electrification (the "wireless" radios had to be plugged into a power source), its large cities received regular power, and this was where most radios could be found.

For the first time, beginning in the mid-1930s, arcane (for youngsters) French political struggles in Paris were widely reported on the wireless. Of course, there were hundreds of newspapers that reported the details, but adolescents might not have been ardent newspaper readers; the TSF made up for that deficit. For instance, in February 1934, there was breathless coverage of a near coup d'état of rightists against the Third Republic, with serious confrontations between the police and the Cagoulards, extremists who were vividly antisemitic, just at the same time as Hitler was chasing Jews from Germany. Suddenly, teens and their friends were asking their elders: "What is a Jew? Do we know any?" And though few Frenchmen had Jewish acquaintances (there were only about 300,000 Jews, both French and immigrant, in the nation), the increasingly vocal antisemitism often demanded a response pro or con. Political immigrants were also flooding into France, chased from Germany, Austria, and later Czechoslovakia. Some were well-off, but most were not. Paris was suddenly home to more recent immigrants than any other world metropolis, including New York City. If French citizens had not noticed this phenomenon, there were politicians and essayists who reminded them.

||||||||||||||||||||

Most French were certain that their nation was wise enough to stay out of unnecessary, treaty-imposed conflicts. They also benefited from the assurances of their leaders that they were safe from offensive warfare. Right after the end of the Great War, the French government and its military general staff began war-gaming how to protect themselves from a future German invasion from across the Rhine. After a decade of arguments that included debates over costs, engineering, and armaments (such as the appearance of newly developed weapons, especially airplanes and tanks), and bolstered with the confidence of a nation that thought it had essentially prevented German rearmament, the French decided to build, from the Alps in Switzerland to the English Channel, a series of massive forts that would form a permanent defensive border, with its own massive artillery directed unabashedly at their Teutonic neighbor. This would be the infamous Maginot Line.*

The debate raged within the French defense establishment in the 1920s and 1930s; some considered the extensive fortifications a useless panacea, while others dithered over how the next war would be fought. The Commission on the Territorial Defense even issued

---

* The economic and political arguments were made by André Maginot, minister in several governments during the period. After his untimely death at fifty-four in 1932, it was agreed that the line of forts should be named after him.

a warning to this effect: "A fortified position ... must not be seen as impregnable, and it is especially a bad idea to build a national strategy, especially defensive, on fortifications alone."[6] The still-living memory of the Franco-Prussian War, added to the lingering trauma of the Great War, seasoned these debates.

The desire to manifest a forceful and visible action against a resurgent Germany finally convinced the politicians that such a massive undertaking was economically and militarily justified. The primary justification of the French government for such a massive undertaking was demographic: so many young men had been killed or wounded in the Great War that it would be impossible to bring the French army up to its optimal manpower level before 1935. There simply would not be enough eighteen-year-olds to refresh an exhausted army. Thus was a massive fortification along the border with Germany, still the most populous nation in Europe, accepted as a rational military expenditure; the Maginot Line would act as a force multiplier for a depleted army. Still, many asked as the cost of such a "great wall" grew, if the 1914–1918 war had been the "war to end all wars"—*la der des ders* (the last of the last), as the French called it—then why prepare so desperately for another? Would not the effects of World War I last for generations, thereby precluding the need to raise massive armies, which might start another war on a flimsy basis?

For the military chiefs, the logic of such a project was much simpler. The line of forts, bunkers, and pillboxes would keep the putative surprise attacks at bay while the major part of the French army prepared itself. Importantly, they hoped that avoiding the Maginot Line would force the Germans to invade Belgium, an ally of Great Britain, thereby enabling the French army to focus on one front. This, it was believed, would bring the British into any future war, and less reluctantly than they had entered World War I. In effect, this enormous endeavor was conceived and built to buy time in case of a surprise attack from the east and to remain as a permanent barrier to future German incursions.

And so began a Brobdingnagian engineering and construction effort that, ironically, would be duplicated a decade later by the Germans themselves, on the western coast of France, with the Atlantic Wall. For most of the 1930s, the world marveled at the French military behemoth. Foreign rulers visited it, and military leaders from all over the world came to study it. It was the pride of a nation still recovering from the Depression, and it was supported even by many pacifists who saw defensive war as the only justifiable military activity. Marc Bloch, the historian and future *résistant*, suggested that its construction looked to the past of warfare, not to its future; but this did not deter the planners of the Maginot Line.

National and foreign newspapers and magazines, as well as government reports, were endlessly encouraging. In America, the magazine *Modern Mechanix* featured the following encomium in 1931:

FRANCE BUILDS WORLD'S GREATEST DEFENSE SYSTEM.

Not since the ancient Mongols erected the great Chinese Wall, more than 2000 years ago, has any nation conceived of so gigantic a system of defensive fortifications as is now under construction on the eastern frontier of Switzerland and Belgium.[7]

This wall, the experts kept repeating, would stop any army from overrunning France. Huge pillboxes could be hydraulically lifted and lowered for precision of fire and protection and were made of materials impervious—at least at first—to the strongest known artillery and tank armaments. The massive forts of reinforced concrete were connected by miles and miles of tunnels, with specially built railway lines connecting them. The air-conditioned barracks were roomy and comfortable—not like submarine accommodations—and there were huge galleys for food preparation, hospitals, and carefully designed sanitary facilities. All forts were interconnected by telephone and telegraph lines. (In fact, during the ensuing Battle of France, telecommunications were stronger up and down the Maginot Line than they were above on the battlefields.) France had sent a clear signal: we do not want war, but if war comes, we will meet the enemy with the most modern of preparations.

The result became what might be called a "white elephant." In May and June 1940, the Germans simply went around the Line, which was still unfinished at the outbreak of the war. Thousands of French soldiers and engineers were ordered to retreat, and many thousands were captured by the Germans. Numerous installations were sabotaged by the French command, but much of the Line remained in good enough order for the Germans themselves to make use of it, especially in the last months of the war in 1944–1945. Still today, a traveler in the fortified regions can see enormous pillboxes, bunkers, small forts, and other structures penetrating as deep as three or four stories underground, and almost all still indestructible. The Maginot Line has since entered the language of political and military symbolism as a perfect plan that disappointed its supporters and builders and failed to deliver on its promises. In the 1930s, the failure of the idea would have deleterious and immediate effects on the civilian population of beleaguered France.

||||||||||||||||||||

There was indeed a "lost generation" between the generation that died in the millions in the First World War and the one called on to govern and serve in the 1930s.* Youngsters in the late 1920s and 1930s saw this demographic divide, and many experienced it personally as

---

* It was most likely the inimitable American expatriate Gertrude Stein who coined this term, referring specifically to American writers, painters, and musicians who seemed at a loss to discover influences or create their own styles. The term was especially used, however, to define the generation that had been caught, still young, between the two world wars of the twentieth century.

fatherless orphans. Countless families were no longer nuclear but extended. With revolt and war surrounding their nation, the generation coming of age in the 1930s was even more than normally anxious about the future. With the civil wars in Russia, the colonial wars on several continents, and the territorial wars in eastern Europe making peace an illusion, they would be drawn to pacifism in their search for a more stable future, encouraged by the philosophical and moral backing of some of Europe's best-known writers and filmmakers.

For many, pacifism was a courageous, not a weak, choice, and though it would prove generally ineffective politically, its strong ethical voice in a nation still holding on to a myth of military greatness was heard persistently during this decade. The rather sudden eruption of a pacifist response to the near-defeat of 1918 had come as a surprise to the more conservative, traditionalist parties. Suddenly, these critics of the warrior class, and of the politicians who had failed miserably at diplomacy, were no longer seen as traitorous, but rather as a new type of patriot. Young people were now permitted to hear and discuss—in their classrooms, in their parents' conversations, via newspapers and the radio—the idea that war was not the apex of France's greatness, but its nadir. Many thought that such a belief made obvious sense.

One of the best known of Europe's pacifist philosophers and activists was a young Jewish woman, Simone Weil, whose family on her father's side had been French for generations. Since her death in 1943 of pneumonia, Weil's work has had an impressive resonance on behalf of a mystical pacifism, based on Christian doctrine. Her direct influence on curious youngsters of the late 1930s would not have been formative, as few of her writings appeared before she died, and those mostly in leftist or academic journals. But the passion that she evinced in an age barely recovering from a disastrous war makes her a good example here of the vigorous intellectual responses to another "Great War."

Weil would argue that not only the young but also the economically less fortunate suffered the most in wars, that war occurred within and reinforced a traditional class system, and that to be against war was to be against the deprivation that the working class had experienced for centuries. Surprisingly, Weil volunteered to go to Spain during that country's civil war, to stand with the Republicans in their fight against fascism, a movement she had been studying since the early 1930s, when she had traveled to Germany. In Spain, she saw that even those she admired most—the working class—could become killers with ease under the unforgiving technology of bombs and machine guns. And she heard too from Spanish intellectuals and soldiers in the field that sometimes the socially, politically, and culturally weak had no other option than violence in a system that only reluctantly recognized them.

In her biography of Simone Weil, Christiane Rancé describes succinctly that generation's quest for peaceful stability:

> *No matter their combat colors, they all [swore] to the same ambi-*
> *tion: to renew politics, to resist the rottenness of the current gov-*
> *ernment, to end parliamentary chaos. They all believe[d] that their*
> *very youth could do it, because the political and economic crisis*
> *was but a reflection of a deeper one that threatened the destiny of*
> *mankind, a spiritual crisis against which their youth immunized*
> *them.*[8]

The most significant aspect of Weil's passion for pacifism was that it was contingent upon her judgment about when violence was appropriate in the imposition of justice. She was not against violence per se, but rather against using war as a form of political will. As she is reported to have said at the time of the Munich crisis, why should an adolescent from her working-class Parisian neighborhood die defending Czechoslovakia? Let that state make the sacrifices necessary to preserve its own independence; should it be confronted by violence from another state, let it defend itself with appropriate force. The same pertained for France.[*]

By the mid-1930s in France and elsewhere, pacifism as a viable response to diplomatic emergencies had reached its peak, though many politicians felt that the times demanded a more muscular response to the increasing rise of fascism in Italy, Spain, and Germany. After the new chancellor of Germany, Adolf Hitler, made his first move to test the resolve of the French by reclaiming territory between the Rhine and France's borders, there was a strong call to send the much stronger French army to force the Germans to retreat. But there was no fervor for fighting another war with the Germans only seventeen years after the last. A satirical newspaper in Paris had joked that "the Germans are invading Germany," and everyone hoped that the nascent Wehrmacht would soon be scurrying back into the homeland, but they remained. The French Council of Ministers was split between those who wanted to show Hitler who was boss and those who had already decided that the Rhineland and its coal regions were not worth a nasty fight. One politician stated that a "tornado of pacifism" had surprised and intimidated the government.[9] We cannot help but wonder how the Nazis would have fared had Great Britain and France been less pusillanimous in their reactions to Hitler's repeated incursions during the late 1930s. After France's ignominious defeat in May and June of 1940, many citizens would remember this first sign of their government's cautious response to an aggressive dictator.

---

[*] Once she saw German troops rush through a town in France, she thought of nothing else but joining the resistance against military occupation. She died still begging the Free French in England to parachute her into France to resist the aggressive Nazi presence.

||||||||||||||||||||||

The intellectual, political, and social center for those adolescents who could afford a post-*lycée* education was, of course, the Latin Quarter. This area on the Left Bank of Paris—which runs roughly from the Jardin du Luxembourg north to the Seine and east to the Montagne Sainte-Geneviève and the Panthéon—was home to the major elite institutions of France: the Faculté de droit, the Faculté de médecine, the École des mines, the École normale supérieure, the Collège de France, and of course, the revered Université de la Sorbonne.

During the mid- to late 1930s, the Latin Quarter was the scene of dozens of mini-riots and loud propaganda from both sides of the political map. The Boulevard Saint-Michel (familiarly known as the "Boul'Mich'"), the central artery of the Latin Quarter running north to south, was filled on both sides with cafés, cheap restaurants, and bookstores. It soon became the scene for raucous verbal battles and occasional fisticuffs as both the leftists and the rightists tried to show that they had more support than their rivals. The student body and professoriate of the major schools and universities of the Latin Quarter tended to be conservative; higher education had not yet been universalized, so only well-off bourgeois continued studies after *lycée*. The Sorbonne and the École normale supérieure, however, were havens for leftist students, as were some of the larger *lycées*. In fact, the even-numbered side of the Boul'Mich' was the closely guarded territory of the right, while the odd-numbered side was the dominion of the left. "Neutral" pedestrians, bus riders, and automobile chauffeurs could often glimpse the opposing posters and flags and even hear the shouts of the two camps as they passed through this important thoroughfare. This was also one of the few places in Paris where communists rubbed elbows with leftist bourgeois from better-off backgrounds. They jostled each other playfully while saving their most boisterous conduct for encounters with the supporters of anticommunist and reactionary groups on the other side of the boulevard.[10]

Many of the tensions that made the Latin Quarter a site of so much political friction occurred after the events of February 1934, when right- and left-wing factions fought violently on the Place de la Concorde, across from the Chambre des députés. Heard on the radio as it was happening, this violence had shocked France. On top of this political discontent was a more serious and less easily rectified problem: by the 1930s, the Great Depression had finally reached France. It arrived later than in other industrialized nations, but it would last throughout the decade. The result was economic decline, unemployment, and reduced government support for those in need. Anxiety spread among the working class, and then among white-collar employees and business owners. When the father of a family lost his job or had his wages cut, there could be little support from the mother, since women were not, for the most part, offered high-paying jobs. When an adolescent reached fifteen, his family might not have been able to afford for him to continue in school, which up to then had been free, and would have to push him out the door to find a job to help the family. And in the background, the country itself seemed to be rudderless, for no government could address all of these events at once.

||||||||||||||||||||

On January 1, 1933, Adolf Hitler had become chancellor of Germany. Europe was fascinated. Here was a "man of the people," not a political regular, who had been elected head of a state that not only suffered massive losses in World War I but had to endure the economic consequences of military defeat and the political confusion that followed. Still, the German spirit and self-confidence, and the nation's eagerness to regain its position in the League of Nations, had prevailed.* Hitler's plans were not secret; indeed, it was only a year later that rightists, antirepublicans, monarchists, and antisemites in France began dreaming of a similar government—one that would sweep away dissonance and ethnic "invasions."

It soon became clear that the Nazis, though legally elected, would ignore the most basic democratic principles that had defined the Weimar Republic.† Hitler's rhetoric and use of cultural phenomena to influence his people were strongly influenced by Benito Mussolini, who had since 1922 led Europe's largest fascist state. In an effort to show the strength of his nation's newfound unity, Mussolini had ordered his armed forces to invade an independent African nation, Ethiopia. In newsreels and on the radio, Europeans saw and heard for the first time how the use of air power, mustard gas, and concentration camps could devastate a civilian, noncombatant population; it did not take a genius to see that the tactics employed by Mussolini's forces against African civilians could just as formidably be visited on their own nations. Robert Sudey, in his memoir of his years as a young *résistant*, recalls how news of impending war affected him: "What appeared to me unjust revolted me. I remember how, only ten years old, . . . the announcement of the Italian invasion of Ethiopia [in 1935] infuriated me. It seemed so incomprehensible to me, especially the idea that one nation could suddenly seek to enslave another!"[11]

With the confidence of someone who had read accurately the

---

* Founded in 1920, the League of Nations was the first international organization established to maintain world peace. Though effective in some areas, it was fundamentally weakened by the refusal of the United States to join, much to the disappointment of Woodrow Wilson. Of course, its greatest diplomatic failure was its inability to constrain the surge in fascism that began to dominate European politics in the 1920s.

† After the 1914–1918 war, the German state dissolved its empire and wrote a new democratic constitution in the city of Weimar. The new multiparty, democratic government lasted from 1919 until 1933, when Hitler assumed power.

political caution and diplomatic fecklessness of his neighbors, Chancellor Hitler was soon using "diplomatic" means to change the map of Europe that had evolved from the 1920 Versailles Treaty. In December 1935, the League of Nations returned to Germany the industrial region of the Saarland, which had been under French control since the end of World War I, and five months later, we have seen how Hitler's still weak army marched into the Rhineland, the last area of the Reich under occupation, as the French politely withdrew. (The provinces of Alsace and Lorraine had been formally returned to France after 1918.) These were relatively peaceful resolutions of international disputes, but the existence of only modest protests and no military resistance had encouraged Hitler to continue his dream of creating a larger Germany.

||||||||||||||||||||||

The French political left—a mixed group of far-left and moderate-left parties influenced by the increasingly well-organized French Communist Party—began to shape itself into a viable alternative to the nation's conservative right, which had ruled France under various guises since the end of the Revolution of 1789. In May 1936, surprisingly to many, a moderate-left consortium prevailed in legislative elections as the Front populaire (the People's Front). Led by Léon Blum, the first Jewish and first socialist prime minister of France, the Front had engineered the election of the first leftist government in Europe since the brief Paris Commune in 1871.

The French right was furious; those who had violently reacted in 1934 to the left's increasing influence were not calmed by this democratic change in political expectations. They believed that they had forestalled this drift through their public and often violent demonstrations. In fact, Blum had almost been killed in an attack scarcely four months before. By happenstance, his car had run into a demonstration of young rightists on the Boulevard Saint-Germain; when he was spotted, demonstrators attacked his car with paving stones and sticks. Blum was pulled from his vehicle, kicked, and beaten before eventually being rescued by the surprised police guarding him. Adolescents heard about this violence on the radio, as well as the vitriolic arguments on both sides that followed. Now many wondered if his election would lead to civil war. Might the army and police enable a coup against the Front populaire?

Blum moved fast. Though he would be in office for only a bit over a year (June 1936 to June 1937, then a month in early 1938; the legislative Party held power for almost two years), his government's legislation would permanently change the structures of French society: workers were given a two-week paid vacation and a substantial increase in the base hourly labor wage; admission fees to museums and for railroad tickets were reduced; free school was extended to age fourteen, and pathways to post-elementary schooling were made easier; generous subventions were offered to farmers hurt by the Depression; substantial changes in collective bargaining were imposed; massive investment supported social housing; weekly work hours were reduced from forty-eight to forty; a *code de travail* (worker's code) was established; and a Department of Sports and Leisure was created, to be dedicated to promoting the leisure time most French workers had never enjoyed before then.*

On the ground, individual freedom was suddenly expanded through the middle class's substantial increase in automobile ownership, although automobile ownership remained, if not so rare, something less than common. Now many families could move around throughout France without being tied to railroad schedules. The

---

* It is striking that such major social and economic adjustments were legislated in the middle of the Depression by a socialist government. Most of these changes remain in effect today, and are vigorously protected by French parties on both the right and the left.

popularity and increasing affordability of the automobile changed the land- and cityscapes of France:

> *For every automobile on the road in 1900 there were two hundred in 1920, seven hundred in 1930; there would be thirteen hundred in 1940. . . . January 1930 brought parking regulations, . . . paying parking lots, better circulation. In 1931 pedestrian crossings appeared; in 1932 luminous traffic lights. . . . In 1933 the last trams disappeared from the streets of Paris.*[12]

At the same time, advertising about automobiles emphasized the importance of speed, power, and individuality. Teenagers dreamed of having a car, or at least of their family being able to afford one.

The Front populaire government was especially focused on the physical well-being of France's youngest citizens. In a radio address in June 1936, Léo Lagrange, undersecretary of state for sport, leisure activities, and physical education, announced: "Our simple and humane aim is to enable all of French youth to find in the practice of sports, joy and good health, and to construct leisure opportunities so that workers can find a relaxing recompense for their hard labor."[13] Anxious youngsters might have perked up their ears; here, it seemed, was a chance to temporarily escape household chores and parental surveillance, if only for a few weeks. In her study of how post–World War I governments became fixated on the "re-virilization" of males, Joan Tumblety states unequivocally that "the Popular Front arguably did more to raise the profile of sport and physical education in France than any preceding government."[14] She notes that Lagrange had full authority to build hundreds of new sports fields, to introduce physical education into the school curricula, and to increase options for leisure for the working class—who, up to then, had never enjoyed the opportunities of the bourgeois to exercise beyond their labor. "The Popular Front also attempted to democratize activities such as aviation, tennis, and skiing that were previously the preserve of social élites."[15]

This new emphasis on reversing a perceived decline in virility by concentrating on developing physical activity in the next generation of male adults would create classes of adolescents who were adept at living and working in the out-of-doors, less dependent on their families for emotional support, comfortable working in groups of strangers from different social classes, and capable of performing in and interacting with gender-mixed groups. Their future eager participation in resistance activities during the Occupation was certainly prepared by the policies that focused on their physical as well as their patriotic development. Put another way, the insistence on controlling youthful imagination and energy, the establishment of hierarchical organizations, the search for leaders among adolescents, and indeed the very process of indoctrination not only served the purposes of governments but, in an ironic turn, gave youngsters the structures that would later make coordinated resistance possible against an aggressive Occupier.

||||||||||||||||||||||

Despite the turmoil created by rapid modernizations redefining daily life, and despite the knowledge of the turmoil that was roiling Italy, Spain, and Germany, France did not feel existentially threatened in the 1930s. Its most pressing problems were internal, created by the deep hatred between the major political parties on the right and left. Most adults believed that should an international war come, surely the French would unite to fight off an invading enemy, as they had done in a *Union sacrée* during World War I. (This was a public call to put all political divisiveness aside and to join together to defeat a much worse enemy than one's civic opponents.) On the other hand, some continued to argue that France had already lost, fatefully, a good deal of its resolve; that it had admitted too many foreign immigrants in the last two decades; that its respect for the teachings and organized activities of the Catholic Church had waned; and that what was needed now was a more virile younger generation, emboldened by a resurgent faith and ready to make France great again. Such were the outlines of what would be an even more fractured nation after the German invasion of 1940. But before then, France's attention was suddenly torn from the preoccupation with its own problems to a vicious civil war just across their Pyrenees border.

It had been the Great War's devastations, the terms of the Versailles Treaty, the hollowing out of royal families across Europe, and the Great Depression that had enabled the rise of fascist parties in Italy and Germany. Spain was next. The Spanish Civil War (1936–1939)—a revolt by the Spanish colonial army, led by General Francisco Franco, and resisted by a government of Republicans, socialists, communists, and anarchists against a fascist army attempting a coup d'état—was the most immediate conflict observed by French teenagers. Newsreels at movie houses showed massively effective new arms, while illustrated magazines and newspapers—increasingly attuned to the public's desire for vivid graphics—printed horrifying photographs of the devastation, including the bodies of women and children struck down by anonymous killers. Léon Blum's supporters pleaded with him to send French troops and matériel to Spain in support of another legitimate leftist government, but he refused. One reason was that influential members of his Socialist Party were passionate pacifists. Whether this was a smart tactical and political move is still debated today. Blum did facilitate the transfer of arms under the table. He argued without success that a stubborn Britain and others should join France in a united front against Francisco Franco and his fascists, and he allowed thousands of Spaniards to enter France as refugees. Nor did he stand in the way of young French men and women who wanted to enlist in the fight. But he never officially committed France to the protection of the Spanish Republic. Germany and Italy—that is, Hitler and Mussolini—were not timid in their support of Franco, the leader of the rebels; the air war over Spain was essentially led by their forces. The Soviet Union tried to aid the Republicans, but they were not on the same war footing as the fascists. The result was the defeat in 1939 of the Spanish Republic and Franco's ensuing dictatorship. France now had three fascist nations abutting its territory.

What shocked the French the most, however, and brought the apprehension of war to a higher level was the "strategic" bombing of Madrid and Barcelona, which, like Paris, were cultural centers of their nation. In April 1937, the horrible attack on the town of Guernica in the Basque region had already had its effect, but to see burning cities that looked like Paris and Lyon focused any apathetic attention. And journalists were now in the war zone, as they would be throughout the next great war, breathlessly broadcasting live radio reports while surrounded by screaming civilians. Finally, thousands of French men and women were crossing the Pyrenees to aid the Spanish Republic in its struggle against another form of fascism. Many of these volunteers would return to France as militants against the German Occupation a few years later.

Spanish Republicans defending an elected government against the simplistic solutions of fascism became real-life heroes to large numbers of youngsters in the late 1930s, and later during the Resistance, when they would fight side by side. Generational emulation was a key component of this political evolution, as youngsters watched their fathers, uncles, and older brothers support the Spanish Republic by hastily printing leaflets, raising money on the streets for orphans, helping fleeing Spaniards find safety in France, and even volunteering to fight. Among the lessons learned was that "spreading the word" could supplement the news coming over the "wireless" and thereby affect political reaction, a strategy that would be reincarnated during the Occupation. The Spanish Civil War radicalized moderate and left-leaning youth of France, especially those who were members of, or sympathetic to, the French Communist Party.

An example: Jean Lajournade was born in 1921. By the age of sixteen, living in Biarritz, he had already joined the Communist Party,
as much for social as for ideological reasons.* Living near the border
with the Basque country, in far southwestern France, he and his
friends were especially attuned to the war in Spain. "It sensitized
them," his daughter Michèle told me, "to the brutal nature of mil-
itaristic fascism." Some of Jean's friends had crossed the border to
offer assistance to the Basque Republicans, and Jean soon became
secretary of the regional Party (at age seventeen).

Young students were occasionally confused about political values,
but they believed that they understood good versus evil. They may
have agreed with the idea that military strength was needed and that
a willingness to go to war was part of a nation's heritage, and they
might have even been willing to serve their threatened nation. But the
indiscriminate killing of civilians they witnessed during the Spanish
Civil War, especially of children such as themselves, was a line, they
felt, that should never be crossed. The shock of having the earth turn
upside down demanded a cry from the heart, one that would soon justify breaking the laws of the Occupation, even if such action might
lead to imprisonment or death.

---

* This was not a rare phenomenon. We will meet many other young communists in
this book who had joined the PCF because it was well organized, because it admitted girls and women equally, because it allowed modest resistance during the year
when Germany and the Soviet Union were not at war, and because it had funds, both
from USSR coffers and from its own fund-raising. Ideology did attract many youngsters, but so did the possibility of solidarity with one's neighbors and friends and the
promise of action in a bewildered nation.

CHAPTER THREE

What the Hell Happened?

---

*It was the height of confusion for me. Where were our friends? Our
allies? Whom could we trust? Who?*

—A FOURTEEN-YEAR-OLD BOY WITNESSING FRANCE'S DEFEAT

Between September 1939 and May 1940, Europe's belligerent and
nonbelligerent nations warily watched each other. This cautious period, following Germany's invasion of Poland, came to be known as
the "phony war," the *drôle de guerre*, or the *Sitzkrieg*. In April 1940,
Germany succeeded in invading and occupying Denmark and Norway, thereby opening up German ports on the Baltic Sea so that its
navy could roam the North Atlantic. There was little resistance from
Britain and France, and what there was did not succeed. But France
was not too worried; after all, Britain's army might not be large or well
trained, but its navy was the strongest in the world, and its air force
had some of the world's most agile fighters and bombers. And France
had both a formidable navy and one of the largest standing armies in
Europe. Hitler could certainly be contained if he dared attack either
of these two nations or their colonies.

The wireless continued to assure the population that France was
fully prepared for war, in any form. "Passive defense" became the
general term for blackout shades, blue covers for automobile head-
lights, searchlights looking for German bombers, and admonitions
to be frugal with foodstuffs. Prompted by the devastation that had

been visited on Madrid and Barcelona in the late 1930s during the Spanish Civil War, air-raid shelters (*abris*) were created through-out France. Masterpieces were removed from the Louvre and other large museums to be hidden in the countryside. On newsreels at the cinema and on the radio, youngsters saw and heard of the relentless destruction of Warsaw by a merciless German invasion. As a con-sequence, they became anxious, searching their parents' faces for signs of assurance amid the confusion. Their fathers, uncles, and older brothers had been called up to military service; households were disrupted as mothers tried to compensate for the loss of fathers. Yet there was still no panic. Young folks continued to rely on the assurances that the French had a massive army, the support of the British, and the incomparable Maginot Line.

But surprising all, on May 10, 1940, German forces simultaneously attacked Luxembourg, Belgium, the Low Countries, and France. Their strategy was to make a feint that would pull the French army and the British Expeditionary Force north to Flanders (where World War I had ended in a stalemate). The Allied armies fell for the plan, al-lowing the soon-to-be renowned panzer divisions to sweep westward toward the Channel in order to cut off their enemy from reinforce-ments. Rushing through dense Ardennes forests and valley-pocked terrain faster than anyone had predicted, the Wehrmacht had sim-ply skirted the strongest parts of the Maginot Line, which stood im-mobile, guns facing eastward, waiting for a frontal attack that never came. Crossing the Meuse and moving with jaw-dropping speed, the Germans trapped the Allies, about 400,000 men, in a small pocket on the French-Belgian coast near the town of Dunkirk.*

---

* Amazingly, over 300,000 men and boys would escape from Dunkirk to England, thanks to a massive civilian effort that made use of yachts, fishing boats, ferries, pleasure boats, anything that could float and carry passengers. About 100,000 French and British soldiers were killed or captured during the defense of the Dunkirk evacuation point. Many French were evacuated by the British as well, but

Doubts resulted in an unfocused panic. Hundreds of thousands of French men, women, and children took to the roads of France, along with Dutch and Belgian refugees from the north, to escape the rapidly advancing Germans. The government had not given orders to evacuate, though only at the last minute had it declared Paris an "open city"—that is, one that would not be defended against military occupation in hopes that the conqueror would spare it from damage. Still, carts, wagons, automobiles, bicycles, and countless feet began an exodus toward an imaginary safe haven. (The term "exode," describing this short period of mass collective panic, still resonates with older generations.) Families were dispersed, thousands of children were separated from their parents, and elderly people died on the trek. Malicious German pilots would strafe crowds, justifying their attacks as preventing the retreat and regrouping of Allied troops. Crisscrossing multitudes often came to a standstill as machinery and automobiles broke down. And French citizens noticed something even more frightening than streams of noncombatants moving impassively toward the Loire River: mixed in among them were French soldiers in uniform and hundreds of others in mufti fleeing too. Rifles, helmets, and other gear were being discarded along the way. The tension between the civilians and the troops often ended with shouts and more physical outbursts of anger.

Early concerted efforts to resist total defeat began during this period of unpredictable turmoil. Downed Allied pilots were hidden and secretly moved to neutral borders; arms discarded by retreating soldiers were collected and buried for later use; occasionally, isolated German soldiers were attacked and even killed. The chaos was a problem not only for the French but for the German invaders as well—their success stunned them as much as their adversaries. Units separated

---

not as many as that nation thought should have been rescued, thus creating a thorn in the side of Anglo-French relations that would remain throughout the war.

from the main force became disoriented, and German soldiers were taken prisoner by the French and made to flee south with their temporary captors.

Looting and *vagabondage* increased during this period as youngsters discovered ways to find more food for themselves and those they sought to protect. Abandoned apartments and homes were robbed, in both cities and the countryside; even small thefts at shops and post offices occurred, not as a sign of opposition to the changed political atmosphere, but in reaction to the penury that had suddenly fallen on this previously wealthy country. (The massive scale of this juvenile delinquency would preoccupy the new Vichy government and result in strict regulations to control such unlawful activities, soon to become more serious than just looting.) Thousands of children simply disappeared, whether taken in by solicitous strangers, kidnapped, murdered, or killed along the way; newspaper ads and posters appeared throughout France, asking for news of missing children. Those adolescents who stayed close to their families suddenly became providers, protectors, and comforters well before they would have grown into these roles in normal times. It would take months for French citizens to return to their homes, even with the state's help, and more time still to forget the terror and embarrassment of suddenly being without leadership, home, or protection.

On arriving in any but the smallest villages, the Germans required mayors to accompany their officers to schools, pharmacies, rectories, and police stations in order to make clear to the populace that the Occupation had begun. School buildings were often requisitioned by the German army; they were ideal for dormitories, mess halls, and communication centers. Sometimes the Occupiers would allow classes to be held while the soldiers were in residence; most of the time, teachers and students were ordered to teach and learn elsewhere. For some youngsters, it was at first an adventure to have classes in barns or warehouses or large public halls. When the weather was clement, they learned their history and math outside—every student's favorite classroom. But they knew at the same time that their home lives and other habits had been interrupted by a foreign army that was stronger than their own and relentless in its imposition of order.

Évelyne Sullerot, a *résistante* and later a sociologist, compiled interviews with those who were children during the great exodus. Several of them commented on the weight of the memory of World War I as they found themselves confronting yet another invasion but two decades later.

> *The war [World War I] was often evoked in my family. More than a few times, I heard about the "Boches," heard "Courage! We'll beat them!," and "They shall not pass!"* In a six-volume work on the Great War that my father had bought, I had been able to see photographs of the destruction visited by the "Teutonic hordes," of trench warfare, of bayonet combat. Yes, at 13, I had been warned of "German barbarism."*[1]

Still, it often took a specific act of separation or of German violence to bring out the sudden courage that would be the hallmark of so many young *résistants*. A bomb falling nearby, Germans demanding the use of one's home, seeing someone struck or shot by Germans, watching one's parents break down in frustration, anger, and humiliation—such events often stunned youngsters, who would swear revenge. Of course, many were more cautious, trying to keep their lives—and their family's—whole in this unpredictable tempest. But the ones who had had enough began almost immediately hooting and giving uniformed

---

* These famous lines from the First World War showed a naive faith in an army that would not have succeeded had it not been for the fresh American troops who arrived in late 1917. "Boche" was a derogatory term for Germans whose utterance was forbidden in 1940 by authorities.

Germans the finger when they passed them. Still, remembered one of
Sullerot's sources:

> *The triumph of the German war machine had terrorized me; I*
> *couldn't see how England—a secondary military power—would ever*
> *be able to undertake, even if it escaped an invasion, the re-conquest*
> *of a continent. The United States was far away, and little disposed to*
> *intervene. . . . I began then thinking of a very long German occupa-*
> *tion, where I would have to inscribe my own life. I would have to work*
> *stubbornly, to fool them, to stand quietly, to submit while grinding my*
> *teeth, and perhaps to perish.*[2]

Time was being adjusted as this young man's world turned upside
down. "When will this all end?" would be one of the determining
factors of youthful participation in the Resistance. As another interviewee remembered: "The violent entrance of History into our familial atmosphere was starting to upset our whole system of values."[3]

The rapidity of the Wehrmacht's maneuvers dumbfounded those
who had believed years of propaganda about how well protected
France was from invasion from the east. Suddenly, without announcement, the French government moved southward from Paris
to Tours, at the Loire River, the historical geographical divider of
France, and then much farther south to Bordeaux. Such precipitous
action startled the British. Winston Churchill, who had just become
prime minister on May 10, could not believe his ears when French
leader Paul Reynaud called to tell him that Britain's key ally was
in retreat. He flew over to France five times between mid-May and
mid-June—not insignificant actions—to check for himself, only to
find each visit that the situation had worsened even more than he
had imagined. The success of the Dunkirk evacuation probably saved
Churchill's premiership, which in turn would later provide Charles

de Gaulle with an important political ally and a base for his Free French armed forces.

The French Third Republic was disintegrating. On May 17, a week after the invasion, hoping for a miracle, Prime Minister Paul Reynaud named Maréchal Philippe Pétain to his government, calling him from his ambassadorship in Madrid, the capital of Franco's Spain. (Also named to a subordinate defense post was an unknown brigadier general named de Gaulle.) The news was met with relief in the newspapers and on the air waves, which were attempting to keep up with the rapid progress of major events. The prospect of relief from what seemed a disaster abounded. After all, Pétain was the hero of Verdun.* Surely, he would know how to contain and defeat the Germans. The hard-liners' argument was simple: if we fight, we will send a message to Hitler and Mussolini that they had better not try to export their ideologies by force, that France would stand forcefully against them. But well before joining the government, Pétain had decided that the war was lost; he believed that the politicians' lack of focused preparation had bored like termites into the French army, leaving a hollowed-out military. For weeks Pétain pleaded with Reynaud's cabinet for a temporary cessation of hostilities, but to no avail.†

Then, on June 14, the "open city" of Paris was occupied, without a shot being fired in its defense. Finally, Reynaud resigned his government, and Philippe Pétain was named, in his place, *président du conseil des ministres,* or prime minister. The day after, on June 17, on the radio, the eighty-four-year-old marshal announced to his nation

---

* The battle for the forts at Verdun on France's eastern border was the longest of the First World War, lasting eleven months, from February 1916 to January 1917. Casualties on both sides were massive, but in the end Pétain's troops defended and counterattacked, finally forcing the Germans to give up.

† For the rest of his long life, Reynaud would regret inviting Pétain into his war cabinet.

that hostilities must cease, and ordered the French armed forces to stand down:

> *It is with a heavy heart that I tell you today that we must stop fighting. I spoke to the enemy tonight to ask whether he is ready to search with me, soldier to soldier, after this struggle, and honorably, the means to put an end to hostilities. Let all French citizens group around the government I preside over during these hardships, and silence their anguish, obeying only their faith in the destiny of their country.*

Commentators on all sides remarked that he spoke with the vocal tremor of an elderly man, a grandfather assuring his grandchildren that all would work out, for now he was in charge. The public's reaction ranged from exhausted relief ("Thank God, our men can come home now, and the bombing and strafing will stop") to hesitant acceptance ("He seems like an old-timer, but he does know the military") to deep anger ("How could he stop fighting when our army is still holding off the Germans?").

But all was illusion, and as the Germans rolled into Biarritz, not far from the Spanish border, in the late spring of 1940, young communists immediately went into action to undermine the new Vichy regime. Wrote Jean Lajournade in his unpublished journal:

> *We decided to print tracts ... against Pétain and his government, who were fooling people, and pushing them to collaborate.*
>
> *We had found an old mimeograph machine, in bad shape, but good enough to print somewhat readable leaflets. We hid it in the Anglican church's sacristy, which was no longer in use. . . . We distributed them any way we could. We took bikes to the exit gates of the Boucau foundry [the area's biggest employer]. As the workers left, we would mix with them, and then throw our leaflets in the air before disappearing.*[4]

Thus was French resistance almost simultaneous with the defeat of their nation.

||||||||||||||||||||

One of the most compelling contemporary reports we have of this massive defeat comes from Marc Bloch, who served in several French military headquarters as French forces maneuvered through northern France and Flanders. Written in 1940, just months after the German victory, *L'Étrange défaite* (Strange Defeat) was not published until 1946, two years after Bloch had been executed by the Germans for his resistance activities (and his ethnic background). It offers a remarkable account of these events and of the reasons for the quick defeat of the French armies by the German Wehrmacht. Bloch's argument is simple, and supported by dozens of anecdotes he heard and conversations he had with other officers after the armistice: France lost because of the lack of imagination of its officer class—"the incapacity of command."[5]

The French military establishment had not forgotten 1914–1918, and were confident that they could win as they had then: through a persistent toe-to-toe confrontation, preferably in Belgium. They had not understood, as Bloch so aptly noted, that "the Germans conducted a war for today, under the sign of speed. . . . We did not want to know or did not want to understand that [this new rhythm], due to the vibrations of a new epoch, was theirs."[6] In Bloch's view, far too many French senior officers held memories that were too vivid, and too rigidly fixed, of the successes and failures of the Great War. Yet, most of the younger soldiers on the line knew only the misty tales of those sacrifices that had been passed down. Bloch believed that this disconnection between the generations was a major reason for the rapid disintegration of the French army's tactics. (Such an observation was, of course, verified in the subsequent appointment of an eighty-four-year-old military man, Pétain, to be leader of the new

French state.) For Bloch, a combination of arrogance, intellectual laziness, and organizational rigidity made the defeat of the French military effort predictable.

Competing theories regarding the brief Battle of France have continued to be published for almost eight decades as military historians attempt to explain a defeat that was due as much to human failure as to the strategic performance of the Wehrmacht. Yet Bloch's thesis remains compelling. For instance, the American military historian John Mosier has worried for decades over this apparently incongruous conflict—how had a powerful and well-mechanized French army failed so remarkably and so quickly before a newer, still-developing German force? He writes, in line with Bloch's thesis, that the defeat was not caused by Germany's superiority in mechanized vehicles, especially tanks, nor by a superior air force. France had both, and many of its armaments were better designed. But "Germany possessed a much larger cadre of experienced officers and noncommissioned officers than did its opponents, and its methods of training were much more efficient.... The German army was ... the least mechanized of the major armies, but it was the most mobile, not because of its vehicles but because of its brains."[7]

The failure of leadership would be a dominant preoccupation of the French during the entire war. One of the reasons for the obscure Charles de Gaulle's quick rise to the top of public attention was the determined leadership he exuded. His strong, incomparably confident voice soon became an antidote to the repeated bromides of the older general, Pétain. And the stories told in this book are, in many ways, tales of young persons seeking, defining, and eventually obeying strong voices, no matter their military heritage, their political experience, or their age. Bloch's *L'Étrange défaite* remains one of the few on-the-spot analyses by a professional historian whose reasons for the resounding defeat of France in six weeks in the spring of 1940 still have the ring of certainty.

De Gaulle wanted desperately and quickly to establish a unified command of all French citizens who opposed the Occupation of his nation. This included those living in the French colonies of Africa, Asia, and the Middle East, as well as those who managed to get to England to join his nascent military forces. Eventually, he became identified as "Free France," and by using his personality and a diplomacy supported by Winston Churchill, he slowly built the idea of a nation that had never surrendered. This was a remarkable achievement. The reigning monarchs and elected leaders of other occupied countries—Poland, the Netherlands, Norway, Czechoslovakia—had left their nations and settled in England, "the last island" refuge. By contrast, de Gaulle, cashiered and condemned to death by the Vichy government, was a mysterious figure to many French, barely on the horizon of much better known politicians and military leaders.[8] There were those who at first saw him as a weak reflection of Pétain, his mentor: conservative, Catholic, military, arrogant, hierarchical. Why should he be speaking in the name of a defeated nation when the *Maréchal* had selflessly offered to lead France through this awkward time?

The word of an armistice, based on reports from retreating soldiers, had spread quickly by radio—more quickly even than communications within the military. Before an official agreement had been signed with the Germans, units of the French army had already been preemptively surrendering. The day following Pétain's speech, on June 18, de Gaulle, still a member of the last cabinet of the Third Republic, gave his own radio address from London; though heard by few, it would often be repeated in print and on the air over the next few months. De Gaulle rejected the armistice signed by Pétain and called on all "free" Frenchmen to continue to fight the Nazi war machine. "Whatever may happen," he said, "the flame of French resistance must not go out; it shall not go out." A few days later, on another broadcast, he reiterated that "honor, common sense, patriotism demand that all free Frenchmen continue the struggle wherever they are and however they might."[9]

We must recall that events were moving so fast that the French did not know how decisively their army had been routed, and many believed there that was still time for a number of options. Just as there was a strong pacifist element that thought an armistice was a good idea, there was an equally strong *belliciste* contingent who thought that the war should be continued, all the way to the Mediterranean and beyond. Other questions were repeated throughout France. Should the Republic continue as it was, or should a new, Fourth Republic be established? What about abandoning the whole idea of a republic and turning to a monarchical or authoritarian form of government? Was Pétain to be trusted? Yes, he was France's greatest living war hero, but he had signed an armistice agreement that handed three-fifths of the country over to the Germans. Was that a brilliant tactic or the decision of a mentally weakened old man? The armistice had not resolved doubts into certainties.

Recalling years later his reaction as a teenager to the immediate fact of France's sudden military incapacity in May 1940, Jean Fragne struggled to explain how soul-shattering it was. Standing alongside a road leading away from the front—which was changing more rapidly than even the wireless could keep up with—he saw a large column of French troops, unarmed, moving along slowly, while guarded lackadaisically by a few German soldiers who were only a few years older than he. With a friend, he shouted at the exhausted prisoners, "Run! Escape!" But with a few hand gestures, the French officers signaled the boys to keep it down: they did not want to alert the guards, so as to avoid reprisals. "Go home," they soon shouted at the youngsters. Fragne continues: "That spectacle of giving up [was] incomprehensible for us adolescents, but it did clarify something. We had lost everything. . . . The wound I felt will never heal. And we were only in the first half of 1940!"[10]

||||||||||||||||||||

The armistice, initialed by a joyful Hitler outside of Paris in the same rail car where the 1918 armistice ending World War I had been signed, had left much unclear. What type of government would Pétain permit? Who was de Gaulle, and what were his chances?*[11] France's morale was in the doldrums as returning soldiers—those who had not been captured—limped home, disconsolate, embarrassed, living witnesses of France's failures. To add insult to a great injury, almost two million French POWs had not been released. From the earliest days of the armistice agreement, their continued incarceration would infect the collaboration between the new French state and the Third Reich. As well, another question kept the French up at night: who and where were their allies? The nation felt an acute sense of abandonment. Had not the English first taken their own troops away from Dunkirk before loading the French soldiers? Had not the British fleet attacked the French navy at Mers-el-Kébir in Algeria in early July, killing 1,300 French sailors?† Where was the United States? Did the Americans not see what was happening?

The absence of American intervention particularly dismayed the French. Prime Minister Reynaud had written several times to President Franklin Roosevelt, asking for counsel and, especially, material aid. Roosevelt, in the midst of his third campaign for the presidency, did not want to run as a war president, so he put off any suggestions of intervention in the European war. In addition, the pro-German and anti-European war movements in America were vibrant and loud. The

---

* Once like father to son, Pétain now felt completely betrayed by his former protégé, "that viper I nourished in my bosom."

† Churchill was afraid that the Germans might capture the fleet and thus have substantial control of the Mediterranean. Mixed signals caused the British to fire on the French navy before negotiations for surrender could be finished.

president of the America First Movement, Charles Lindbergh, had made well-publicized trips to Germany, where he became convinced that the Third Reich was the side to be on, or at least to be neutral toward. This was also an especially difficult time for America's closest ally, Great Britain, as it anxiously counted the days until a German invasion after Hitler's expected victory over Europe's largest army. Only after the passage of the Lend-Lease Agreement in early 1941, a year after the German attacks on France, did the United States become more involved in helping the British. The agreement permitted the shipment of matériel, including destroyers, to the United Kingdom (and to the Soviet Union and, later, Free France) in exchange for bases in British-held territories in Canada and Bermuda. From then on, Roosevelt fulfilled his promise that the United States would be the "arsenal of democracy," but it was too late for France and Britain in the late spring of 1940.

Confusion paralyzed what remained of the French government. According to the well-designed armistice agreement, France would be divided into seven zones; parts of its northern provinces would be joined to Belgium; its whole Atlantic seacoast would be forbidden to civilians, though the Mediterranean coast would remain in the hands of the Vichy government; the Italians would control small sections of southeastern France, while the rest was demilitarized; and in the east, Alsace and Moselle, part of Lorraine, would return to German control, having been rejoined to France after World War I. There would be no French standing army, only 100,000 lightly armed troops, but the fleet and the colonies would remain under the umbrella of the Vichy government.*

---

* By September 1940, the Vichy government had established new regulations and new sanctions in the portion of France it had been allowed to govern, the so-called "Free" Zone. The Germans were anxious that the large population of France not become too resistant to its presence; consequently, it kept a gimlet eye on the machinations of the Vichy government, essentially managing the new État Français through the offices of the German ambassador in Paris, Otto Abetz.

On October 24, 1940, only four months after the Occupation had begun and L'État Français had been in power, an event occurred that
would mark the rest of the war, in ways completely unintended and
unexpected by the participants. At the urging of Pierre Laval, both
Hitler and the elderly Maréchal Pétain agreed to meet in a train station at Montoire, in central France, a small town on the rail route
between the southwest and Germany. Hitler may have agreed in
part because he would be returning from a meeting with Francisco
Franco, near Spain.*

When he descended from the train to meet Pétain, Hitler politely
smiled, but rather than salute another soldier, he offered his hand.
This handshake was minutely analyzed by nervous European leaders
when it was reported on radio and in newspapers (with photos). Here
was a *Maréchal* of France, the victor of Verdun, shaking hands with
Corporal Hitler, a member of Kaiser Wilhelm's defeated army. The
moment was endlessly examined by French citizens: how could Pétain
have recognized such a *petit homme*, who should have saluted, not offered his hand? Pétain assured his nation, after the news had spread,
that "I went freely to the meeting, at the invitation of the Führer. I was
under no 'Diktat,' no pressure. A collaboration was planned between
our two countries. I accepted the principle of it."[12] Many thought this
was a good sign. The term "collaboration" had not yet attained its
highly negative connotation of moorless morals, greed, and warped
patriotism. Most French, including pacifists, read the encounter as a

---

* The chancellor was probably in a sour mood as he crossed France to meet Pétain,
for his interchange with Franco had been unfruitful. Despite the material aid from
Germany and Italy during his coup, Franco refused to join the Axis powers and forbade German U-boats and other vessels to use ports in Spain or in its North African
colonies. Though ideologically close to Hitler, Franco was wily enough to know that
his army was too weak to withstand attacks from or a blockade by Great Britain.

brilliant tactical move, as Pétain diplomatically outsmarting Hitler. Such an agreement meant that POWs might be coming home soon, that France would become whole again, and that the nation had been fortunate to have had such a wily leader assume the position of chief of state. But there were others who felt the opposite; they believed that Pétain and his entourage had been duped, and that the Vichy government's obsequiousness was repellent. "Collaboration" soon came to be seen as collusion with the very forces that had humiliated a proud nation. Those who had held on to the idea that Pétain could withstand the demands of the Germans were profoundly affected by this event, in which the hero of Verdun had appeared to be a supplicant. The Montoire spectacle, as with another one that Laval would orchestrate two months later—the return to Paris of the ashes of Napoleon's son from his burial vault in Vienna—would haunt Vichy for the remainder of the war.[13] Adolescents saw this panoply of subservience as yet another reason to look elsewhere for leadership.

CHAPTER FOUR

A Blind Resistance

In a happy land, children never stop being children.

—JACQUES LUSSEYRAN

The green-turned brass bell outside the school building rang decisively, and the seven- and eight-year-old boys, ignoring their instructor's admonitions, ran pell-mell toward the classroom door. Little Jacques Lusseyran, wearing eyeglasses for his myopia, forced his way toward the middle of the group of pumping legs and waving arms, only to suddenly stumble when one of his classmates nudged him out of the way. Unable to catch himself in time, his right temple hit the edge of the teacher's desk, and while crashing to the floor, he felt one of the arms of his glasses puncture his right eyeball, almost removing it. Bandaged and frightened, the little boy was immediately carried to his nearby home.

While attempting to calm his screaming, his parents heard from a visiting ophthalmologist that the boy's right eye would have to be removed. His mother and father consoled seven-year-old Jacques, telling him that he would get along just fine in life with one eye. But within twelve hours, his "good" eye (whose retina had been torn in the accident) sympathetically went sightless and was removed as well. Within two days, a boy who had loved so much the visual world was without sight, able to perceive only a fuzzy whiteness. Yet soon young Jacques would prove to be brilliantly resilient. "Blinded on May 3

[1932], by the end of the month I was walking again, clinging to the hand of my father or mother, of course, but still walking and without any difficulty. In June, I begin learning to read in Braille."[1]

So began the remarkable story of a child's courageous adjustment to what most would consider a permanent, mind-numbing tragedy. How do you run, freely and with abandon, as a child and a teenager when you are blind? And yet Jacques Lusseyran ran fearlessly, along paths, in woods, and over unpredictable terrain thanks to the ever-present support of a close friend. Jean Besnié never took his blind friend's arm, but on occasion, Lusseyran would grab Jean's arm or shoulder; Jean, who had grown up in the same Parisian neighborhood as Jacques, knew to give his companion his own space, his own tempo, but unobtrusively, and compassionately. This combination of a secure friendship and a carefully learned independence would produce an imaginative and courageous young man who would never take the Occupation of his nation for granted.

When it was time for Lusseyran to enter a *collège* (middle school), and later the *lycée*, his parents made, for the era, a quite courageous choice. Paris had—and still has—a prestigious and world-renowned school for the blind, and its social and physical scientists have for more than two centuries been in the forefront of treating the un-sighted. It was natural then, when Jacques lost his sight, that he would go to the esteemed Institut national des jeunes aveugles on the Boulevard des Invalides in Paris's distinguished seventh arrondisse-ment. But a quick visit to the school with his mother resulted in her decision, partially at his request, that he not be sequestered among the "handicapped" but be given instead the regular education of any young, intelligent boy. This decision was providential, for it is almost certain that his later resistance activities would have been impossi-ble in such a specialized school, one that saw regimented adjustment to the sighted world for its students as its most important mission.

Lusseyran's memoir *And There Was Light* has three interlocking tiers: growing up as an adolescent in a damaged nation, coping with blindness, and becoming the leader of a successful resistance group. He recounts these imbricated narratives with attention to detail, but in a style filled with wonder at how he balanced on a high wire while blind. Later, in a collection of essays, *Against the Pollution of the I*, Lusseyran developed at length his theories on the psychological dimensions of blindness, arguing that the ego is a selfish and greedy manipulator of the very senses that we trust without question. Firmly—and incorrectly—holding to the idea that our identity depends on the fables these working senses create for us, we believe ourselves permanently diminished when one or more of those senses are lost. In his introduction to these essays, Christopher Bamford, a researcher in Western spiritualism, explains that "Lusseyran . . . began to understand that there was a world beyond the ordinary auditory sense, where everything had its own sound."[2] Here was the young man's first resistance: he refused to allow the absence of sight to identify him, morally or physically.*

He never made excuses to his companions for his handicap. His exquisite attention to the natural world, sightless as it may have been, was evident, even fascinating, to them. This heightened reliance on "hearing" and "seeing" the world more acutely than his peers almost certainly attracted those looking for answers in a world at war, where their parents were apprehensively off balance. Lusseyran believed, and argued, that blind persons have to face imaginatively the challenge of not being sighted, and that they soon learn to recognize certain "pressures" that the sighted do not. They possess a tactile hypersensitivity that allows them to "read" signals from objects—buildings,

---

* Reading these observations, which Lusseyran delivered in lectures throughout the 1950s and 1960s, one notices how much he uses his experiences as a young resister against the Occupation and his survival of almost two years in Buchenwald as touchstones for his belief in a different mode of cognition, developed because of his blindness.

furniture, spaces—that others ignore and also to perceive an infinite number of signals that the human body emits to those whose perceptions have not been subverted by the powerful, but superficial, sense of sight. It is perhaps a universal wish of all young people to possess a "sixth sense" to help them as they endure the transition to adulthood. Jacques Lusseyran believed that his blindness effectively provided him with a set of intuitions and sensitivities barely felt by those not "diminished" by blindness. For an example, he recounts that moving to Paris from the countryside, where his parents had taken him immediately after his accident, had not been easy:

> *The [city] street was a labyrinth of noises. Each sound, repeated many times by the walls of the houses, the awnings of the stores, the grills over the sewers, the dense mass of the trucks, the scaffolding and the lampposts, created false images.*[3]

Yet by developing a new sentient arsenal and learning to interpret the world confidently with his four remaining senses, he could determine the "true" images. (He even asserts that he could "smell" moral order and interpret "moral voices"—capabilities that would serve him well during his leadership of young *résistants*.) Counterintuitively, this talent to see beyond appearances was especially useful in a metropolitan environment, where the noise that urbanites produce might be expected to confuse and frustrate the blind. But in Paris, and especially where normal interactions had been disrupted, Lusseyran discovered, for example, that walls "produce a sound":

> *Is it really a sound that I perceive in placing my attention on the wall? I'm not completely certain. But it is, if you wish, a shaking, something very light, but something repeated endlessly. I would say that it repeats as long as the wall stays behind me, exerting some force on my body.*[4]

He had no inkling that this new form of cognition would become crucial in his later activities.

Rather than encourage him to move deeper into the silent world of blindness, the military debacle of May–June 1940 and the subsequent Occupation would ignite in him the ability to focus an even more uncanny attention on the changes affecting those around him. To "see," Lusseyran had needed to develop a new, enhanced sense of "touch"; what better incentive and aid to have when living in a world where nothing was as it should be?

Those in occupied territories who migrated to the clandestine world—that is, who performed acts that demanded subterfuge, disguise, and secrecy—speak of the "extra" sense they soon developed that allowed them to move through an increasingly suspicious environment. While they did not examine it as thoroughly as Lusseyran did—he was on his way to becoming one of the most important mid-twentieth-century proponents of anthroposophy, the belief that the spiritual domain can be objectively and rationally understood—members of the underground were well aware of the unfamiliar nature of living an extended clandestine life.* Whether from paranoia, fear, anticipation, or simply palpable excitement, resistance fighters described such a hypersensitivity almost as if it were a sine qua non of the clandestine life. But Lusseyran analyzed this phenomenon physiologically and logically; he almost certainly would have discussed his conclusions with his closest friends, who realized that they were in the presence of an extraordinarily talented person, a leader. Lusseyran recounts that his friends, when "lost" in the labyrinth of Parisian streets, would turn to him, the "blind guy," to find their way home.

---

* The books Lusseyran published during his short life are still consulted by those who have suffered similar sensorial handicaps. "Attention," a crucial word for Lusseyran, comes up repeatedly in his writings; it emphasizes the presence of an almost tactile otherness unavailable to those who rely solely and simply on sight.

His blindness was increasingly accepted by his friends as a "special power," one that set him apart and that encouraged them to follow him. When he joined up with these classmates in the Jardin du Luxembourg en route to their high school, the group would follow Jacques, never passing him or going before him. The band would grow, and the sound of the chattering laughter that accompanied them would soon reach the ears of the school's attendant, who would say: "Well, well, so it's the Lusseyran parade." [5] This respectful, admiring procession would form the core of the Volontaires de la Liberté, one of the most respected early resistance groups of Occupied Paris.

Jacques went to the best *lycées*, intimidating the unimaginative administrators with his prodigious memory and his brilliant use of Braille as an aid in reading; a noisy Braille typewriter become a sonorous sign of the extraordinary young man in their midst. He was always at the top of his classes. Though often intellectually bored, he knew that he had to do what others did, only better, if he was to rise to a profession as a scholar and teacher, a goal that seemed to come to him naturally. He also learned the kinds of friends he could rely on. He was able quickly to decide how to ignore those who were scornful of him or who pitied his situation. "My real friends always belonged to that special race of children, the seekers, the tireless ones, the ones we will call enthusiasts as young men." [6] His comfortable ability to read this "race" of adolescents would also contribute immeasurably to his later success as a leader.

Leaving aside for a moment Lusseyran's "impairment," we return to the question: why did such young men, often with full freedom to make any choice, decide to risk their careers, their reputations, their families, and themselves in order to show their frustration with the Occupation? In Lusseyran's case, he knew Germany and Hitler more deeply than his fellows. He had decided in his early teens to study German, primarily because his father's business caused him to travel there frequently, and Jacques became fascinated with the voice and promises of Germany's new leader. (One area where his blindness did not separate him from sighted people was listening to the radio.) The sudden explosion of the wireless as a rather inexpensive addition to a household, and Hitler's use of the radio waves, brought the threat of war and revolution even closer to those huddled around it during the traumatic years of the ascent of Mussolini in Italy, the rise of the Nazi Party in Germany, and the vicious Spanish Civil War. Lusseyran spent hours a day perfecting his German (a skill that would probably save his life later). Tuned to Stuttgart radio, he learned what fascism meant and thus grasped earlier than his cohort that the Germans were running circles around European diplomacy in the 1930s. When he learned over the airwaves in 1938 of the Anschluss, Hitler's annexation of Austria into the Third Reich, he was almost overwhelmed: "My thirteen-year-old imagination wants to stand up to the shock, but it is too great, coming all at once. History hurls itself on me, wearing the face of the murderers."[7]

As the news became more dire, the pusillanimity of his nation's political leadership catalyzed a larger realization:

> *Most grown-ups seemed to be either imbeciles or cowards. They never stopped telling us children that we must prepare for life, in other words, for the kind of life they were leading, because it was the only good and right one, of that they were certain. No, thank you. To live in the fumes of poison gas on the roads in Abyssinia, at Guernica, on the Ebro front [in Spain], in Vienna, at Nuremberg, in Munich, the Sudetenland and then Prague. What a prospect!*
>
> *I was no longer a child. . . . What attracted me and terrified me on the German radio was the fact that it was in the process of destroying my childhood.*[8]

And then the Germans were in Paris. Lusseyran recounts how subtle yet insidious the Occupation was at first. His friends told him about the omnipresence of Germans in uniform and the prevalence of

German street and directional signs. Life seemed to go on as before—except, of course, for Jews and anti-Nazi German immigrants.

> *If I didn't know yet precisely what the Occupation was, that was be-cause it was too important, and, after all, almost invisible. The Nazis had perfected a new way of inserting themselves into the body of Europe. They held themselves in rigid order, at attention quite cor-rectly, at least in France. They stole from us, looted us, . . . but they didn't talk about it, or hardly ever. They never made threats. They were satisfied with signing requisitions.*[9]

This initial hesitation to respond to the Occupier makes sense: most people avoid a confrontation until they understand the ethical reason for doing so. These early months were defined on all sides by nothing if not by uncertainty. And for youngsters desperate to know what was going on but not privy to the fast-changing effects of a military occu-pation, it must have been dispiriting.

Like his classmates, Jacques was, for a short time, depressed, anx-ious, and befuddled by the turn of events. And his mental state was not assuaged by the plaintive excuses and bromides of his parents and teachers, themselves in a state of shock over recent events. He mused that "during the first months of the Occupation, I experienced something like a second blindness."[10] This was a stunning metaphor for the effect that the defeat of France and the German Occupation had on most of the nation's citizens. Lusseyran then recounted, matter-of-factly and modestly, as if he were joining his school's Latin club, how he decided to found a resistance group among his cohort. Given the debates that were swirling around schools, in clubs, and at home, it seemed purposeful to do something that would maintain French integrity. The teenager began to conceive of a template for a clandestine organization that would last as long as the Occupation.

Most of the professoriate of the middle and high schools of France were known to be quite progressive, even socialist. A large percentage were still pacifists, and not a few were communist; they had served in the trenches of World War I and thus against Germany's persistent warmongering. A good number of these teachers would join in resistance activities early in the Occupation. Yet others were Vichy patriots who continued to believe that Pétain had done the right thing in saving France from the devastation of all-out war. They despised the Germans, but were even more worried about the communists. And there were those instructors who insisted on instilling in their pupils a different patriotism, one that reminded them of the legacy of the French Revolution and of the nation's struggle to be a guarantor of human rights.

"Almost all the boys my age [sixteen] were worried. Those who weren't were fools, and we dropped them," Lusseyran recalled.[11] Indeed, his *lycée*, like all of them, had students who were not as bothered about the German presence as others. Some were viscerally pro-Pétain and even admired the German army. They and their parents had been among those most vocally against France's brief reign of socialism in the mid-1930s; perhaps a good dose of rigorous attention from a new government to a foundering nation, especially one so decisively defeated, was just what was needed for a brighter future. (Suffice it to say that the fate of France's Jews was not of much concern to those espousing this view.) Arguments and even fights erupted daily in the schools of France early in the war. More often than not, a student's sympathies were well known by all of his classmates.

The historian and political philosopher Annie Kriegel writes in her memoir:

School was not an island apart from the real world. Tensions, political opposition and conflict [could easily] become violent between professors and administrations, among professors themselves, between professors and students, among students. And the climate of course was even more tense in boys' schools than in the girls'.[12]

When Kriegel's school reopened in September 1940, most of the teachers who were communists, Freemasons, or Jews had been fired and replaced with new, younger instructors (not necessarily supporters of the Vichy regime, but certainly not Jewish or communist). As a result of the purge, boys had female instructors in their classes for the first time since their earliest years. Soon the students began to notice a nervousness among those teachers who had remained, for teachers were not trusted by L'État Français. The German Occupation Authority was not overly concerned with the education of youngsters and left that aspect of daily life to the reactionary Vichy government. Of course, some German bureaucrats paid attention to the curricula and to the texts that dealt with recent history, but in general it was the Vichy regime that obsessed—but to little avail—about the preparation of the next generation of Frenchmen (not Frenchwomen, for girls were expected to become good mothers and housekeepers). No matter the number of young Pétainistes or even pro-German students in a school ("It was a period when some crossed the [school's] threshold raising their fists, while others raised their arms"), the teaching cohort remained generally pacifist, neutral, or quietly pro-Republican.[13]

Soon after the partition of France, orders had been sent down from the Ministry of Education to cease instruction in the post-1918 history of the nation. But Lusseyran's favorite history teacher would close the door and continue class after hours for those who wanted to stay (and all but two in the class always did) to hear about the 1920s and the 1930s and how Germany had fallen for a charlatan. He would talk about *Mein Kampf* and Goebbels and even the racial characteristics of Nazi ideology. At one point, he shouted at his students: "Young gentlemen, this is not a war of nations. There will be no more wars of that sort. Get that into your heads! The world is one. That may be uncomfortable, but it is a fact. And every nationalist is behind the times, just an old stick-in-the-mud."[14] Most likely a secret communist, this teacher and his comrades would eventually also be fired by the Vichy government. Yet their effect on these highly moralistic youngsters, whether quiet or less so, was impressive and lasting.

Two of the nation's most prestigious *lycées*, Louis-le-Grand and Henri-IV, stand on the hill in the Latin Quarter above the Sorbonne, sited around the Panthéon, the burial place of France's great thinkers and leaders. Rivals then as now, they were the training ground for the nation's intellectual elite.* It was in the courtyards and libraries of these two schools, and in the cafés between them, that Jacques first began to discuss the moral imperative that he believed his generation should follow. In his knowledgeable and perceptive novel about Lusseyran, *Le Voyant* (The Seer), Jérôme Garcin captures the adolescents who were on the cusp of changing their lives forever: "Strange little adults, their upper lips coiffed with peach fuzz, and fingers still marked with the ink of the classroom, who still had not known the bittersweet taste of a woman's delicious skin."[15] Events began to more noticeably touch these youngsters as they learned from their parents, and their own experience, how the Occupiers were slowly but inexorably making daily life a grinding affair. It was difficult to ignore the fact that Germans were now living comfortably in Paris, and elsewhere in France, while most of the French were not.

||||||||||||||||||||||

By the spring of 1941, the Nazis had been in Paris for ten months. The first school year under foreign military occupation was about to end, and one could sense an increasing impatience among middle and high school boys and girls as the enormity of the war intruded

---

* No women were enrolled in these *lycées* then; as a consequence, it was almost impossible for women to enter the top ranks of government or finance before the 1950s. This would change, especially because of the influential role that girls and young women had played in the Resistance.

into their young lives. (Lusseyran noted that "our uneasiness was more intense than the uneasiness of people fully grown."[16]) Boys were offended at the sight of German signs, of the bright red, white, and black swastika flag hanging from official buildings, at notices of *"Wir sprechen Deutsch"* outside the best shops and restaurants, at German police directing traffic. And from family, visiting adults, and their professors they heard daily about the desperate situation of their beloved France. The uneasiness, frustration, and anger of their parents—an amalgam of helplessness—further sowed confusion among uncertain adolescents.

Interactions with the Occupier were often no more than signals given, on both sides, of a banal disrespect. For example, confident adolescents in these first tentative months of German control were annoyed when stopped and asked for their *Papieren*. One youngster even floored the accelerator of her car after a German guard asked for ID, speeding away with her parents in the backseat. *Why should I show ID in my own country? Who do these Boches think they are?* The young German soldier was left behind with his mouth open. And to add insult to injury, those sentries at identity checkpoints were often not much older than the youngsters they were trying to control.

Public transportation was curtailed. Gatherings of more than a few friends were deemed suspicious; ID checks and curfews were stepped up. And word slowly spread of arrests of Jews and of other youth who had joined an incipient resistance by making fun of German soldiers or even more dangerously, cutting electric wires or smashing windows. All of this news was passed through whispers and later by way of leaflets, clandestinely printed and distributed. These events became as important a subject for adolescent conversation as dating or parties.

In May 1941, a small group of adolescent boys, aged fifteen to eighteen, met in the apartment where Jacques lived with his parents, situated only a subway stop away from Montparnasse, the center of

American expatriate intellectual and social life in the 1930s. It was not far from the Lycée Louis-le-Grand across from the Sorbonne, Jacques's high school. The door to the apartment house was located between a drugstore and a candy shop, and the building was comfortably sited in the heart of bourgeois Paris, across the street from one of the city's best-known maternity hospitals. On the fourth floor of this building was the Lusseyran dwelling. Jacques's parents had given him two rooms at the back of the residence where he might study in peace—and where the noise of his constantly used Braille typewriter would be muted. The privacy of Jacques's rooms made them an ideal location for a bunch of boys who wanted to plot. (The naive obliviousness of these youngsters to the possibility that such meetings might attract the attention of the German or French police still amazes, but in this case their luck held.)*

At their first meeting in Jacques's apartment, they spoke seriously about creating an organization that might put their ideas for resisting the Occupation into action. To his surprise, his friends told Jacques that they all expected him to be the leader, and they were willing to follow his instructions. Lusseyran was at first stunned: *Why me? Why a blind boy?* The answers were what we now know to have been expected: his character had been made clear through his lucid response to sightlessness in middle and high school. His good humor, intelligence, and loyalty were all factors in his comrades' faith in him.

Once the subject was broached, it took passionate form, but it quickly became clear to Lusseyran and his most trusted accomplices that there were important steps that preceded direct confrontation with an increasingly suspicious enemy, both the Germans and their

---

* One of the most frequently used excuses by older French *résistants* for not having teenagers in their midst was their conviction that they were notoriously unable to keep secrets. On the contrary, there probably has never been such a closed-mouthed group of young people as those who offered their services to the Resistance. But the popular belief in their tendency to chatter remained strong throughout the war.

allies, the French police. The boys needed to recruit and organize, then contain the undirected energy of their eager cadre. They needed to coordinate activities. One close friend immediately asked several important questions: "What kind of people do you want to get in touch with? How many? When will you need money and how much? Where are you going to put the headquarters of your movement? What sort of discipline are you thinking of using to keep the activities of the members under control? When are you going to tell London about your existence?"[*][17] Lusseyran later recalled how quickly he and his friends moved from an idea to a plan of action; he also suddenly realized that he was not at all trained to be a leader of an energetic bunch of intelligent youngsters taking on the mission of confronting the continent's most successful military forces. "I had thought of everything but the danger."[18]

Years after that moment, Lusseyran wrote that "blindness is a state of perception which . . . is capable of increasing many faculties sorely needed in every intellectual and organizational activity."[19] His prodigious memory (and thus lack of a need to write anything down), talent for making logical connections among disparate bits of information, and ability to pay close attention to even the smallest detail, as well as, frankly, the common perception of him as deficient because of his blindness—all of these advantages made him an ideal resistance leader. Never once, he reminds us, in the two years that he led the group did anyone question his decisions or insinuate that they could not trust the instincts of a blind man.

Still, he hesitated. A second meeting was called, this time in the family apartment of Jean Besnié, his best friend. Each member of

---

* By this point, the boys had concluded that they wanted to be affiliated with de Gaulle and the Free French, headquartered in London under Winston Churchill's protection. Seeking, as they almost always were, clarity of purpose, they easily rejected the other anti-Vichy resistance movements, whose many divisions they found overly subtle.

the initial group had been tasked with identifying a few interested youngsters. More than fifty eager high school students and some university students had heard about the meeting and showed up. As they sat on the floor, listening to Jacques's presentation, there was growing excitement at the unfolding of a cool adventure. But Jacques was not smiling—this is not a game, he warned. They were about to embark, he explained, on a serious project, one for which they had no experience. They had no one to consult for advice, especially not their parents, teachers, or priests. They had no printing presses, no more than pocket money, no arms (and this group would never become armed), and no experience. Up to now, skipping the occasional class or having someone else do their homework had been their most serious offense, and those transgressions certainly were not punishable by imprisonment, deportation, or death. All of that would now change.

The roomful of boys became somber, but no one raised timorous questions, and all agreed to search for and find even more classmates who might become part of this grand project. Jacques's role as their leader continued to be unquestioned. In his memoir, he interrupts this narrative of the founding of the Volontaires de la Liberté to relate a detail that seems completely off-subject: he asked Besnié to take dancing classes with him. He explained that this was not an idle decision, that he needed to train his body to handle the new feelings of being "grown-up" enough to lead a passionate revolt against violent adults. "The seething of my mind, transmitted to my body, gave me a strength which I would be at a loss to call by name.... There was in me such a train of forces preparing themselves for deeds that all roads had to be cleared at once to allow them to pass."[20] After his lessons, he felt that dancing with girls the energetic waltz, the rhumba, the foxtrot, and, especially, the forbidden "swing" gave an erotic edge to the dangers he had yet to fully comprehend. As he writes, dance helped chase the "devils" away—his own, and his new enemy.

||||||||||||||||||||

Le jazz. If there was a cultural meme in France in the 1930s that competed with American films by Busby Berkeley, it was the music of
Louis Armstrong and Benny Goodman. Tradition has it that the first
notes of American jazz were heard in 1917 in the Atlantic port of Brest,
played by the Harlem Hellfighters, the 369th Infantry Regiment from
New York City. The regiment carried with it a forty-four-piece jazz
band led by James Reese Europe (appropriately enough). As soon as
they disembarked, they played. A reporter described the reaction of
war-weary Frenchmen: "The first thing that Jim Europe's outfit did
when it got ashore wasn't to eat. It wanted France to know that it was
present, so it blew some plain ordinary jazz over the town. . . . As soon
as Europe had got to work, that part of France could see that hope was
not entirely dead."[21]

This gift to the twentieth century from New Orleans and Chicago
took Europe by storm. Whenever a cultural phenomenon appears
too quickly, then is instantly adopted by "vulnerable" youth, moral,
political, and cultural establishments tend to criticize it, to frighten
the larger public about its odious influences, even to ban it. Jazz—as
would rock and roll in the United States in the 1950s and hip-hop in
the 1980s and 1990s—was continuously put through such prudish
"moral analysis." Its rhythms and origins were deemed foreign, even
"savage"; its musicians were unfamiliar, meaning black. Jazz was
noisy and urban, metropolitan and invasive; in other words, it entered
into all social strata. But its audience was especially the young, who
discovered a sexy rhythm that spoke to their desire to differentiate
themselves from the staid world of their parents.* Jazz was certainly

---

* In the twenty-first century, conservative nations on all continents are searching
desperately for means to stop the spread, through the internet, of what they judge
to be "degenerate" cultural production (for example, hip-hop). Attitudes regarding

not French (though some Vichy critics tried in the 1940s to argue that it came directly from the popular songs of French peasants!). Jazz singers and players were often multinational—black, Jewish, or Gypsy (the common term for the Roma; the greatest of all Romani-French jazz guitarists was Django Reinhardt, who drew German audiences to the Saint-Germain quarter of Paris during the Occupation). Adolescents snapped to it when jazz was played on the radio, in films (after sound movies became common), and on the phonograph; the bands that played at the *bals* they frequented with friends often sneaked jazz into their repertoires.

Soon the word "swing" came to be used as a general, though often misapplied, synonym for jazz. Beyond being a new term, it was also a code word that identified such bands as temporary outsiders (*Je suis swing*), to the point that some bold gentile youngsters would later on, in solidarity with their Jewish brothers and sisters, wear yellow stars with "swing" instead of "Juif" printed on them. And swing also definitely caused ethical guardians to fret. The music and the dancing encouraged young bodies to touch, embrace, and sweat. Girls were dancing with as much vigor as their male counterparts, clothing was looser, and touching was often intimate.

Predictably, when the fascist nations began forbidding swing and jazz as degenerate, "unmanning," dark, and ethnic, it only drew adolescents closer to the line that separated their cultural desires from authorities, be they parents or the government.* The attempts by patriarchal governments to direct adolescent passion into athletics, gymnastics, or quasi-military activities were only partially successful.

---

jazz and its dance equivalent, swing, were no different across Europe during the 1930s and early 1940s.

* Shown throughout the Reich in 1937, Goebbels's famous exhibition of modernist painting, music, and graphics, *Entartete Kunst* (degenerate art), had codified the Nazi obsession with cultural degeneration, ethnic intermarriage, and racial superiority.

Youth wanted to party to their own rhythms, be they musical or beliefs in progress. Being "swing" was a seemingly innocuous way of ignoring the imposition of moral codes and political strictures, a form of
"resistance" that preceded the official moralism of the Vichy government. Younger French would later use swing to recognize the hypocrisy of their conquerors, who never banned jazz in France during the
Occupation and who themselves, as German youngsters, had loved it.

As the journalist Mike Zwerin writes, somewhat ecstatically, in his
analysis of swing under the Nazis:

> *Jazz [and its derived dance variation, "swing"] was . . . a system of*
> *latitudes, . . . of integral bonds between an individual and a group. As*
> *such it became perhaps the best metaphor for liberty that any culture*
> *has ever come up with. . . . It became the quintessential allegory for*
> *the pluralism of opportunities within which anyone who knows how*
> *to use an instrument and contribute to a common sound can make a*
> *statement about what he believes is beautiful and true.*[22]

The historian Jeffrey Jackson explains the explosion of jazz in
France between the wars as an effect of "mobility," or what we call today "globalization." National identity, some conservatives feared, was
being overwhelmed by "foreign" influence—for example, *l'art nègre*.
Traditional French customs and manners had been infected by the
Americans and immigrants from French colonies. Encouraged by the
engines of mass consumption—advertising, for instance—the masses
were introduced to the world of leisure theretofore closed to them by
the upper bourgeoisie and aristocracy.[23] This rebellion at seventy-
eight revolutions per minute was not hidden away in dance halls and
living rooms.

In the late 1930s, another social and cultural phenomenon suddenly appeared in large metropolitan areas of France that only a few
years later would become an important meme for both sides in the

resistance struggle during the Occupation. It was a behavioral and vestiary style known as *zazou*. The term was derived, supposedly, from scat syllables used by American jazz singers in the 1920s, and it described a small, but visible, sliver of the adolescent demographic in the late 1930s and early 1940s. For the most part, the *Zazous* were children of the wealthy, for being *zazou* was not cheap—you could not hold a job if you acted like a precious dandy; you needed money to spend hours every day in cafés and dance clubs; and you had to be able to afford the outlandish style of dress and coiffure that both genders affected. The *Zazous* were nonviolent agitators: not overtly critical of politics, they were loud, funny, and crazy-acting. Johnny Hess, a major figure in French jazz during the 1930s and 1940s and the composer of two immensely popular songs, "Je suis swing" (1938) and "Ils sont zazous" (1942), popularized both the concept and the name. He remembers:

> *I was definitely zazou. . . . The Zazous came from nowhere. I must have said the word one day in an act. Zazous, swing, these were spontaneous reactions, a way to piss off the Occupier [even though Zazous had strutted before the war too]. I wore my hair a bit long, sunglasses. The collaborationist press insulted us, which amused us no end. . . . It was a provocation, of course. . . . Everything I did was a provocation. . . . I even sang in cabarets where you'd find Germans— not in uniform, in mufti. I understand German perfectly, since I was born in German-speaking Switzerland. Between songs, I'd hear them say "We should lock that guy up, that weirdo."* [24]

The *Zazous* were not among the most daring of those who resisted the Germans and their collaborators, but they were countercultural, and they were quite brave at times, first in standing up against the right-wing punks who would bully them in the late 1930s, and later against the Vichy and German moral police, who felt that they were, in some way, making fun of the myth of purity and virility so cherished by the Reich and L'État Français. The girls dressed with hints of masculinity, the boys with hints of femininity, and such playfulness with gender categories drove conservatives of various stripes to anger, if not violence. These young rebels wore loud colors and pegged pants and used their pompadour haircuts to offend. The young men also carried large umbrellas, called *Chamberlains*, after the feckless British prime minister. They loved swing music and were seen dancing everywhere it was played. And while they affected a disdain, a *je m'en foutisme* (don't-give-a-damn attitude), rather than anger, the *Zazous* nonetheless stood as quite visible critics of a restrictive and arrogant system.

Jacques Lusseyran's experiment with dance, though brief, placed him well within the mildly rebellious atmosphere that defines all teenagers and proved once again that what sighted kids could do, he could do too.

||||||||||||||||||||||

Wisely, Lusseyran's tight group decided to meet somewhere besides their parents' apartments. They found, as others would over the next three years, a dilapidated building, this particular one on the southern borders of Paris; filled with transients and foreigners, it was watched over by a complacent concierge. The comings and goings of itinerant tenants would serve as cover for the occasional presence of a bunch of teenagers. Next, they became precise in recruitment; inviting just anyone to join was a sure path to exposure. Already word of the presence of this "new group" had gotten around too casually, so the original team started over, this time through a system of interviewing that would have no equal during the Resistance. Interested adolescents, even those who had been at the first meetings, had to "go see the blind guy." His co-conspirators had agreed that Jacques would be the only recruiter, the one person who could say yes or no to a postulant. This was a completely counterintuitive vote of confidence in their blind friend: did not one need to see in order to recognize danger, to be able to look directly at those so eager to become warriors for liberty? But at the time, the choice was quick and unanimous; no other peer was as trusted and as respected as Jacques.

His friends eventually claimed that he had "the sense of human beings."[25] In his later publications, Lusseyran detailed how this sense was manifest to him, if not at first to others. To begin, he had learned to forget that he was blind, but his interlocutors could not, which gave him initially a strategic advantage. Next, we recall that he felt he had a tactile connection to the world that was not solely limited to the sense of touch, but that extended to the energy that emanated from persons or objects. "When the voice of a man reaches me, I immediately perceive his figure, his rhythm, and most of his intentions."[26] He called this his "immediate cognition," and he considered it his most powerful interpretative tool to understand a world closed to the sighted.[27]

The rules of recruitment of young *résistants* were quickly established by the "Central Committee" of Volontaires de la Liberté. Without Jacques's say-so, no one could join their group. Not only did this decision give him confidence, but it also helped him to accept without guilt the fact that he could not participate in clandestine acts as other members did, such as following someone, distributing newspapers, carrying arms, or passing notes in the street or on the metro. His usefulness was intellectual and perceptive, and no one criticized him for his inability to act physically against the Occupier.

Here is how it worked: Jacques (whose name was unknown to most of the later postulants) would answer a coded knock at his apartment's door; he would welcome the young man (still no women), ask his name, then lead him down a somber hallway, into his darkened room, spartanly furnished, with two facing chairs in its center.* At first, Jacques's blindness was discomfiting for the postulant, an advantage for his interlocutor. Lusseyran would ask his interviewee to take a seat facing him, and then would begin an innocuous conversation, about anything except the purpose of the interview: school, courses, the weather, or the interviewee's family. There would be no direct questions such as, "How do you feel about the Vichy government?" or, "Are your parents communists?"

The stranger would be anxious to talk about joining the resistance group, to assure his interviewer of his discretion and commitment, but Jacques would patiently wait until he had a sense of his interlocutor's bodily movements, tone of voice, and command of the moment. How did the visitor phrase his sentences? Was he nervous? If so, could he be made to relax? Did he shake his leg or rub his hands on his trousers? Was there the odor of sweat? None of these indicators immediately chilled an applicant's chances, but his ability to relax, to speak with unpretentious confidence, and to explain his own moral values would weigh heavily in the final decision.

After this initial questioning, Jacques would pose a few subtle questions about how the Occupation might be affecting his candidate, how his family might respond to his becoming a member of a clandestine group. He might ask about the interviewee's friends, or his favorite professors, or the books he read. Eventually, Jacques would end the interview. The young recruit would be led again through the long hall to the door, where, as it slowly closed, he would be thanked for having come and admonished about letting anyone know of this meeting. The young would-be *résistant*, of course, would have hoped

---

* The apartment in southern Paris was used by the planners, but not for interviews. The Central Committee did not want to reveal their hiding place. It is still remarkable that Jacques used his parents' apartment for his encounters. Such adolescent naïveté often coexisted with the cunning needed to resist.

for a brevet of acceptance, but no commitment had been made, no future meeting set.

At first, younger boys—ages seventeen to nineteen—and then older ones, mostly university students, began to show up to meet Jacques Lusseyran. "They were scholars from the colleges of letters, science, medicine, pharmacy, law, the schools of advanced agronomy, chemistry, physics. The Movement was growing at the pace of a living cell."[28] After each interview, Jacques would discuss the potential recruit with his closest advisers (the Central Committee). What he had gleaned from the interview was not solely biographical or philosophical or political information, but what he would have called "moral" information. He was brilliantly astute at probing, sightlessly, the signs a person gives when trying to hide secrets, or to impress, or to shade the truth, even to lie. Lusseyran tells us that he interviewed about six hundred youngsters during his two years as leader of the group. This is an almost inconceivable number, but it is entirely credible. The number of adolescents who sought to aggressively resist, whether out of personal commitment, in emulation of their peers, or for unknown intimate reasons, grew steadily, and volunteers wanted to join Lusseyran's increasingly respected organization. This was Jacques's major responsibility, and he was brilliant at it.

His ability to remember even the smallest detail was phenomenal; he carried hundreds of names, phone numbers, and addresses in his head, another advantage for those now obsessed with secrecy. His honesty, his integrity (true integrity: the wholeness of his actions, words, and sentiments was manifest), and his intelligence reassured the frequently nervous youngsters whom he led. And when he said "no," "no" it stood. Occasionally, a would-be volunteer was accepted on probation, then watched carefully by others until he had proved his bona fides. Jacques would make only one mistake in these hundreds of interviews—but it would be a deadly one.

The *Volontaires* considered their primary job "to get the news out" (as they put it). What news? All that the Occupation Authority did not see fit to print. "The French people were completely ignorant of the war, and because of this they had only instincts to rely on," Lusseyran concluded.[29] They understood that the confusion and despair caused by the Great Defeat was quickly turning to apathy, a most advantageous quality for the Occupier working to loot and thereby neutralize France. The youngsters' mission to reenergize a depressed nation gained force, slowly at first, but persistently. They would collect rumors, send coded messages to group leaders, and reprint what they had heard—illegally—on London and Swiss radio programs. Calling others to action, and to reaction, they encouraged their readers to hold out for a better future, not only for France but for Europe too. They questioned the premises of the armistice that Pétain had signed, showed how the Vichy government was but a hand-servant to the Nazis, and sang the praises of those who were carrying on the fight throughout the world, especially in its colonies.

It is hard to know how effective such nonviolent action could have been, but those who have studied in detail the French Resistance during the Occupation argue that such "moral" resistance resonated among the populace. Violent resistance, which the *Volontaires* eschewed, had its place, but it often had disastrous repercussions for those who happened to live in the areas or neighborhoods where the actions took place. There was sympathy, however, for a group of nonviolent, fast-running boys. The communist historian Albert Ouzoulias is precise in describing how often ordinary citizens helped the rapscallions who were driving the authorities to distraction: "With cool courage, the shopkeepers, artisans, and concierges of the neighborhood help the patriots. Curtains have been pulled, apartment house entrances closed. Then our running comrades, followed by German soldiers, miraculously find doors open, then immediately close behind them."[30]

As Lusseyran explains, each step his group took to "resist" created a tactical problem: it was much more difficult to coordinate effective resistance than they had imagined. Soon, citizens in large cities and small towns began to look forward to grabbing one of the dozens of "newspapers" that were seeding a burgeoning confidence in the future. Yet putting together just two pages, recto and verso of one sheet, required punctilious, punctual, and continuous labor. It called for coordination, information-gathering, and more technical skills than some of these boys had. Where could they find *ronéotypes* (mimeograph machines), ink, and paper, especially paper? Where could they print so that the noise could not be heard? How were they to maintain regular editions and distribution? How exactly should they distribute the newsletters? And most important, where would they find the funds to continue these activities? Materials were available in the black market, but that was an expensive place to shop. Being a new group composed of students, they received no money from established resistance networks. For this need, the boys soon began taking up collections as surreptitiously as they had passed out tracts or plastered the walls with small bits of paper calling Frenchmen to resist.

Lusseyran's ambitions went beyond printing *Le Tigre*, the first name of the paper, which would later be called *Défense de la France.*[*] He wanted to establish a complex intelligence movement, one that not only printed the "news" but helped all those who were resisting, no matter the manner—those who hid downed Allied pilots and transported them across borders; those who worked in sensitive places and received information that London and de Gaulle desperately needed. Who better than an adolescent to do this type of work?[†]

---

[*] The first paper was named after Georges Clemenceau, the best-known prime minister of France during and right after World War I. Newspapers of the day soon named him "the Tiger" because of his fierce persistence in trying to solve what seemed like insurmountable problems, especially at the end of the conflict.

[†] Of course, all such groups relied on the same strategy, using their youth as a disguise for undercover work. The Vichy government was alert to the problem of "delinquent" youth for this very reason.

Young as we were, we could easily go everywhere, pretend to be playing games, or making foolish talk, wander around whistling with our hands in our pockets, outside factories, near barracks or German convoys, hang about kitchens and on sidewalks, climb over walls. Everything would be on our side, even help from the girls [when they could be recruited].[31]

The success of the printing and distribution of their newspaper, as well as their other clandestine activities, soon took its toll on young Jacques. As commander of the *Volontaires*, he had no one to turn to for advice on how to continue at the pace that his movement was growing, no one to confide in about his own anxieties. He found a professor or two who would give him a pat on the back, or some suggestions, but what he needed was another *combattant*, someone who knew the special nature of relentless resistance.

Through one of his closest colleagues, Lusseyran met Philippe Viannay, an "adult" of twenty-six years who had begun another movement in Paris and the north of France, called Défense de la France. Jacques and his acolytes knew this group's newspaper well; in fact, they had helped distribute it along with their own. They had been impressed that this journal was printed, not mimeographed, on paper of first-rate quality and now had a circulation of about twenty thousand. Viannay told Jacques that not only did his group have printing presses and several places to print, but they had arms too, including machine guns (hidden in tunnels and sewers under Paris), specialists and machines that could print forged identity papers, and a radio transmitter—a direct channel to de Gaulle and the Free French in London. They also had young, though experienced, agents working in Paris, north of Paris, and in Burgundy. For Jacques, the difference between his *Volontaires* and Viannay's group was that between a Boy Scout troop and a paramilitary organization. He immediately trusted Viannay (who would become one of postwar France's most influential journalists) and decided to urge his own troops to join Défense de la France. Most agreed, and Jacques became a member of its executive committee, which had three female members as well.

Soon the combined networks were printing and then distributing thousands and thousands of copies of their newspaper in apartment buildings, on café terraces, in metros, on buses, outside church services—wherever they could pass quickly through or mingle in large crowds. The editorial board, concomitant with the executive committee, insisted that the paper and the network be as apolitical as possible—that is, that it not support a single ideological group— and thus avoid the struggle to have dominance over other resistance groups or their outcomes. Many members were still unsure as to how France should be governed once the Germans had left and L'État Français was abolished; members included communists, socialists, rightists, even monarchists, those who were anti–de Gaulle, and those who supported him. Neither Viannay nor Lusseyran wanted their energies to be wasted on intramural bickering, or worse.[*]

Défense de la France grew rapidly, and after the Germans occupied the whole of the country, pursuant to the Allied invasion of North Africa in November 1942, it could count cells in the former "Free" Zone as well. Women and girls became increasingly important to the movement's clandestine activities. How pervasive was made clear on July 14, 1942—Bastille Day, the French national holiday. The Germans had forbidden parades or any show of French patriotism in the Occupied Zone, with little success. Lusseyran describes what happened with unembarrassed pride:

---

[*] This attempt to be apolitical was admirable, but it rarely prevailed outside the narrow confines of the group's editorial management. Political alliances and differences would haunt the Resistance and its memory until well after the war.

*Forty squads of ten members each passed out [a total of] seventy
thousand copies of the paper between eight o'clock in the morning and five in the afternoon on the subway cars, publicly, calmly,
from one passenger to the next, and smiling as though it were the
most natural thing in the world. Soldiers and officers of the German
army, not to mention spies in plain clothes who could not be identified, turned astonished eyes on the object that had just been handed
to them.*[32]

It was an unmitigated success: no violence, no arrests, and no one
denouncing any of the four hundred youngsters who participated.
Jacques and the executive committee of the network were elated. It
was the high-water mark of Défense de la France (and its assimilated
Volontaires de la Liberté) while Lusseyran was still one of its leaders.

||||||||||||||||||||||

Meanwhile, as he worked clandestinely, Lusseyran's personal life
continued. He was still living with his parents, not hiding in an abandoned apartment; he was still going to classes. He was, after all, an
excellent student, and he continued preparing for the major examinations that would allow him to go to the best schools in France (the
grandes écoles), especially the École normale supérieure in Paris,
where all the country's most accomplished and respected professors
of the humanities and social sciences had been students. Lusseyran
had an excellent chance of passing the entrance exam with honors;
he had finished near the top of his *prépa* (preparation) courses, the
most rigorous of pre-university curricula. He knew that his blindness
might cause him problems, especially since the Vichy government
had published a law that forbade handicapped, or "deformed," persons from holding governmental positions. (The most remunerative
and respected teaching positions in France were government-paid.)
Nevertheless, he had letters from sixteen professors, who had sent

them to the Education Ministry, and he had finally been awarded an exemption by that office.

But on the June morning when he showed up with his Braille typewriter for the examination, the proctors refused him a seat. He argued that the ministry had given him an exemption, but he was shown another letter from the minister himself that forbade his entrance. Lusseyran was furious. Although he could not say it, he wanted to: *I've organized and led a large resistance group as a young blind man; I can certainly take an examination!* Jacques suddenly realized that he *was* "handicapped," at least in the eyes of the French government, and that no matter how much he tried to show that he was independent, there would always be those who found him deficient. He was not being forbidden to take the examinations because he was on some secret list or being followed by the Vichy police. It was because he had been blinded at the age of seven. These were not innocent judgments: "For me it was not an examination, not even a competition which was at stake. It was my whole future in the social system in my own country."[33] Yet Jacques had never indulged in self-pity; nor did he have time to reflect morosely on his academic situation. He still had a large organization to help run. The first rumors of a resurgent Russian military during the second year (1942) of the German invasion of the Soviet Union were reinvigorating even the most reluctant Frenchman, let alone the passionate young *Volontaires*.

At the beginning of his clandestine activities, Jacques had confided his involvement to his parents, assuring them that, if anything, his blindness would protect him from being harassed by the police. "They had courageously silenced their fears. They had given me their full support, but we were agreed that from now on I should not tell them anything. What good would it do to multiply the risks? They were putting their apartment at our disposal, and that already was dangerous enough."[34] But when more sophisticated plans had to be made

as the enterprise began to expand, gatherings in the Lusseyran family apartment on the Boulevard du Port-Royal had become frequent.
Jacques decided to find another place to meet, interview recruits, and
develop strategy.*

Lusseyran selected one of the group's hideouts in the Marais, a
primarily working-class—and Jewish—neighborhood on the Right
Bank, across the Seine from where he lived and attended school.
However, on July 20, 1942, before he could make that move permanent, there was a knock at his parents' door at five o'clock in the
morning, the Gestapo's favorite time to surprise their suspects. He
had been betrayed. His father's nervousness at the presence of police in his home was so obvious to Jacques that it calmed his own
nerves and reminded him that his first task was to protect his parents. There were six Germans in the room, four soldiers and two
plainclothesmen. Jacques sensed that they were surprised to find
that he was blind; when they searched his room, they found nothing
but hundreds of sheets of Braille. Fortunately, he had given a packet
of false IDs and a cache of tear gas devices (fountain pens that could
shoot gas) to Jean Besnié the night before, so nothing immediately
incriminated him or his parents or younger brother, who was not
implicated in Jacques's clandestine activities.

Who had betrayed him? We now know that his Judas was Émile
Marongin, code-named Élio by the Germans. Jacques had interviewed him quickly, as the new alliance of the Volontaires de la Liberté and Défense de la France was revving up. He told his friends

---

* His parents were never arrested, nor even detained. This was not true of some
young resisters who, besides having to worry about themselves being imprisoned,
also had to worry about their parents, not a few of whom were also sent away. See
especially Charles Kaiser's compelling *The Cost of Courage* (New York: Other Press,
2015), about a family of six, three of whom were clandestines. These three were
supported by their older sibling and their parents, who would die in German prison
camps while the *résistants* survived.

that he had not liked Élio's handshake or the tone of his voice, but he did not say no, and this would be devastating, for Élio was working for one of the most notorious French black-market groups in Paris—the Bonny-Lafont gang—close associates with the Gestapo, so close they were referred to as the *"Gestapo française."* Primarily hustlers and black-marketers, the gang had been given much leeway by the Gestapo to arrest, torture, and turn over suspected "terrorists." For this duty, they were generally left alone by the Germans while they pursued their other nefarious activities. Jacques Lusseyran's mission as a leader of hundreds of young *résistants* was over.[*]

|||||||||||||||||||||

For six months, from July 1942 to January 1943, Jacques Lusseyran was held in France's largest prison, Fresnes, where he was interrogated almost daily, or else taken into Paris to the Gestapo headquarters on Rue des Saussaies, down the street from the Élysée Palace. He never revealed whether or how much he was tortured, but he does reveal that he struggled mightily to keep from thinking about what might happen to him. The Germans did not learn for a long time that he was fluent in their language, and they were chary of interrogating a blind boy who might or might not be important. The confidence that he had built up as a bulwark against the sighted was threatened by the uncertainty of what was intended for him. Jacques explains his rambling thoughts: "I had been betrayed so meticulously, and this was revealed to me so fast, detail after detail, that I didn't even have time to get angry, nor time to understand or suffer. The only thing that counted was to fix in my memory all that they knew."[35] That extraordinary memory would allow him to recall what they had asked during each interrogation,

---

[*] After the war, Marongin would be arrested, tried, and executed by the new government. At his trial, he apologized to Lusseyran. Both Bonny and Lafont were executed after the war as well.

what he had answered, and what he had inferred from their inquiries. He needed to know how much they knew, so he assumed the role of the cowardly prisoner, eager to tell all. It must have proved nearly impossible to trip him up. Thirty-eight times—and who could remember that number better than "the blind guy"?—he made the trip to Gestapo headquarters in Paris. Relentlessly questioned, he never revealed a real name. At one point, Jacques recounts, his interrogators decided to use physical methods to get his attention.* An officer threw him against a wall, then picked him up and threw him again. "I lost my temper and shouted, 'You are a coward! Even if I wanted to I couldn't defend myself.' The brute laughed, but they didn't touch me again." [36]

During his six months of incarceration in France, both his friends and strangers assured him that he would be freed. Certainly, the authorities would not transport him hundreds of miles only to watch him die in the separated camp hut where they placed handicapped and feeble-minded prisoners. One of his fellow prisoners, a road worker, said, "What in the hell could they do with a blind man?" [37] He was young, another reason that he might be spared. But, they added, should he be sent to a camp, knowing German would allow him to gather news and learn of their plans. In an emergency, this knowledge might even save lives. Jacques took hope from these assurances; still, as other prisoners disappeared into the Nazi gulag, he could only wait patiently, and often alone, for his eventual release.

Then, after six months, and without explanation, he was sent with others to a transit camp near Compiègne, outside of Paris, where he was loaded onto one of the infamous cattle cars that moved victims

---

* When we read such passages, we must ask: Is this Jacques Lusseyran in the 1960s refurbishing his memories so that his readers will recognize the value of his blindness? Or is this an accurate memory that shows that the Germans were intimidated about dealing with such an important source, though blind? The consistency of his written memoirs leads even the most suspicious reader to lean strongly to the second interpretation.

relentlessly eastward. At first, Lusseyran was unsettled, bewildered to be surrounded by all these men whom he did not know. But soon enough, a few of his former team members, who had been arrested while he was incarcerated, found him and began again to take care of him. "My friends made a chain, and never let me go for a minute. I seemed to be a lucky piece for them, a kind of fetish. Perhaps it was because I couldn't possibly do anybody any harm."[38] Beyond this circle, as he always did when surrounded by the unknown, he sensed humanity and patiently found solidarity with new comrades. After all, they too had challenged the Germans and the Vichy government; they too had held secrets and had passed information; they too had been separated from their friends, their families, and their homes. Lusseyran found himself admitted to a brotherhood of the captured, a fraternity of the courageous, despite the anxiety that haunted all of them about their futures. "There were lawyers there, peasants, doctors, radio operators, people in trade, teachers, hawkers, former ministers, fishermen, railroad engineers, conspirators, [soccer] champions, professors at the Collège de France, newsboys. All of Resistance France, big and little, all mixed up together."[39] Their clandestine and subversive activities had both built muscle and created an affection, even love, among strangers. This phenomenon would be tested in a new environment: Buchenwald.

CHAPTER FIVE

Life as a J3 During the Dark Years

Adults easily forget, even often pardon, the harm they have experienced, but children never!

—RAYMOND RUFFIN[1]

In its last months of existence, the Third Republic had established a system of food distribution in response to the threat of blockades and in preparation for war. After several adjustments and an armistice, the Vichy État Français produced a finely categorized plan for the food coupons that would be used during the remainder of the war. Initially, there were categories for infants and children, then further categorization of children (such as ages three to six and six to twelve), adults, rural workers, the elderly, and so forth. Beginning in July 1941, the category "J3" was announced, designating "adolescents of both sexes 13 to 21 years of age."[2] It was the first time the state had officially defined an age group as "adolescent," an almost-adult stage in need of a different level of nourishment. This designation would have reminded the youngsters of their special status in the pecking order of this new demographic matrix. The J3 categorization also came to denote a cohort whose ticket holders could be easily identified, and one that would draw more attention from the government.

CATEGORIES OF FOOD DISTRIBUTION IN 1940 AND 1941

CATEGORIES	CRITERIA AS OF MARCH 9, 1940	CRITERIA AS OF OCTOBER 23, 1940	CRITERIA AS OF JULY 1, 1941
E	Children of both sexes younger than three years old	Children of both sexes younger than three years old	Children of both sexes younger than three years old
J	Children of both sexes from three to twenty		
J1		Children of both sexes from three to six	Children of both sexes less than three years old
J2		Children of both sexes from six to twelve	Children of both sexes from six to thirteen
J3			Adolescents from ages thirteen to twenty-one
A	Consumers of both sexes from twelve to seventy not working	Consumers of both sexes from twelve to seventy not working	Consumers of both sexes from twelve to seventy not working
C	Consumers of both sexes from twelve and up in agricultural work	Consumers of both sexes from twelve and up in agricultural work	Consumers of both sexes, from twenty and up in agricultural work
T	Consumers of both sexes from twelve to seventy, working with a need for a large share of muscular labor	Consumers of both sexes from twelve to seventy, working with a need for a large share of muscular labor	Consumers of both sexes from twelve to seventy, working with a need for a large share of muscular labor
V	Consumers of both sexes age seventy and up, and who do not qualify for categories C or T	Consumers of both sexes age seventy and up, and who do not qualify for categories C or T	Consumers of both sexes age seventy and up, and who do not qualify for categories C or T

Sociologists and psychologists generally agree that adolescence is a stage of maturation where one's identity is, at least temporarily, formed by one's social class, school friends, and group memberships. Affiliations, from religion to scouting, from sports teams to political involvement, contribute to a youngster's self-image, and when all these relationships, including one's family, are disrupted by something as violent as a war close at hand, the traditional means of self-identification become, simultaneously, both more important and less clear. The bureaucratic assignment of age groups for purposes of nutrition provided little certainty for adolescents as to where they "belonged" in life.

Raymond Ruffin was born in 1929, in the Calvados region of Normandy. Writing in 1979, he reflected on those who were barely adolescent at that time:

> *The children who lived through these painful events as innocent spectators, necessarily passive and powerless victims, how did they see this era of violence, of constraints, and of suffering? What do they retain of those four years of servitude, deprivation, and grief? What were their reactions to the mutual massacre of "grown-ups"? How did they judge the conduct of parents, educators, teachers, magistrates, of power itself, and of the Occupiers? . . . Too young to have fought, but not to have deeply suffered, this generation remains smothered between a massive defeat [of the French army] and the joy of a victory [the Liberation]. . . . They feel hollow.*[3]

His book, then, is an effort to explain how those "in between" confronted the Occupation as they faced simultaneously their own growing-up.

Ruffin remembers when he saw his first Germans in France in 1940, at the age of ten:

> *Since yesterday afternoon, we are an occupied village. I had just come from some errands, when, turning into the new highway, I saw with my stunned eyes that an impressive motorized column had entered our little town. Ammunition trucks, feed vans, all on*

wheels pulled by magnificent horses with shortened manes, paraded
through, accompanied by proud, helmeted horsemen.[*4]

Soon posters began to appear on the walls of Ruffin's village explaining the new food rationing system, which would deeply affect the health of adolescents over the next almost five years. Even
though the new regulations recognized that growing boys and girls
needed more protein and calories than others, they would still suffer from tuberculosis, rickets, and a general malnutrition that would
mark them long after the Germans had been chased from France.
Stunningly, the average German was consuming over 3,000 calories
per day—2,000 to 2,400 daily calories are recommended for developing adolescents—while the average Frenchman would soon receive
barely 1,200. Finding food became a full-time activity, and children
and adolescents were often on the front lines of this ceaseless struggle.[†] In fact, the Vichy government had instructed all schoolteachers
to include in their physical education curriculum the collection of
acorns, chestnuts, and other foraged vegetation for the general wel-
fare of the growing youngsters. Unless their parents were wealthy
or well connected enough to use the black market at will, or were
deeply bound to the Vichy and German establishments, no young
people could escape the never-ending search for nourishment.

Not only was food itself an obsessive concern; obtaining the proper
tickets, ID cards, coupons, and permissions was essential—as was
summoning the patience for exhausting waits in long lines for various
commodities, frequently in inclement weather or on cold or scorch-

---

* Despite the received image of a heavily mechanized force, the German army, like
other armies, still relied heavily on horses, especially in transporting supplies and
large armament.

† After the war, veterans of the Resistance would admit that they had failed to
notice how hard their mothers worked to keep growing boys fed, because of the
legal rationing that had been suddenly and drastically applied.

ing days. All of this stress brought many a mother to a breaking point when she would find a sign, after finally reaching the door, that read CLOSED. NO MORE X, Y, OR Z. Children were often used as place-holders in lines as their parents ran from one almost-empty store to another in the hope of finding sustenance. The excessive expenditures of time and energy, and the anxiety that weakened the will, lasted for four years as women and adolescents of both genders became a generation of hoarders and "savers" whose attitudes toward waste are still evident among their descendants in France. The French never suffered starvation, but one could argue that sixty months of continuous malnutrition was famine in slow motion.

Of course, the presence of the Occupiers was felt much less in the Unoccupied ("Free") Zone, the third of the country under Vichy governance. After the war, some peasants swore that they had never laid eyes on a German soldier, and it is incontrovertible that the Occupation had much harsher effects in urban and geographically sensitive areas than in the villages of the countryside. Yet even there, young Ruffin remembers, Germans began a census of animals on all the farms in northern France soon after the armistice; they also checked out the number of vehicles available and warned farmers and agricultural workers that hiding English pilots, soldiers, or civilians was a serious offense. Hoarding the thousands of rifles and other munitions left behind by the retreating French army was considered another major crime, often resulting in long prison sentences. Nevertheless, such caches were to be found all over northern France and later would contribute substantially when the Resistance became more present and increasingly violent.

The signs of a new French regime, even a truncated one, had promptly become visible throughout the nation, not only in the southern "Free" Zone. Portraits of Maréchal Pétain appeared on walls, in schoolrooms, in government offices, and on stamps; small busts of the chief of state were available in the smallest knickknack shops. The message was clear: France, no matter its divisions and the presence of Germans, would be under the paternal protection of the Victor of Verdun. French Jews, especially those thousands whose relatives, or who themselves, had served in the Great War, were naively confident that being French trumped nativist antisemitism. However, with growing awareness of vicious pogroms and roundups in eastern Europe, conducted by Russians and Germans, as well as deportations to mysterious work camps in Poland and Germany, few Jews felt completely relaxed.

Ruffin and his friends would ask their elders endless questions about war, death, and the Germans. Old resentments from the devastations of World War I cropped up in the answers they received—about the cruelty of German soldiers, the difficulty of finding something to eat, the destruction of villages and towns by artillery, the disappearance of relatives, the desperate loneliness of bereft wives and mothers. Nevertheless, a mild confidence could still be felt that France would pull itself out of this mess, as it had so guilefully done in 1917–1918. They were ready to take a stand against anyone foolish enough to permanently occupy France, loudly declared the impressionable and almost adolescent Ruffin and his companions. Yet when the Germans did arrive, there was no one to lead them, and the tight surveillance of their parents kept the youngsters as close as possible to the family home.

Daily life was fractured and unpredictable in surprising ways for this "in-between" generation. In the summer of 1941, after the invasion of the Soviet Union by Hitler, a German corporal who had been billeted with his family came into the kitchen where Ruffin and his godmother were eating. The "invader" apologized for the noise from his room the night before. "We are leaving in two days, Madame. It's a shame; we were enjoying ourselves here." An uncomfortable silence followed this announcement.

*I watch him; all his haughtiness, all his pride seems to have aban-
doned him. He stares absent-mindedly at the frame and medals
[that held the portrait of Ruffin's dead godfather, killed in the
Great War]. . . . His thoughts are far from here. Despite ourselves,
we respect his meditation; I remain with fork lifted, while Godmother twists her napkin.*

    — . . . We are entering a new war, the most difficult possible.

    —A new war? I blurt out.

    *—Yes, against Russia; it's bad luck . . . a major mistake. The last
three words are said in a low voice. He continues:*

    —Russia, it's too much . . . too big, too . . . populous.

    A brief pause, and then:

    *—Well, a soldier doesn't think about these decisions, he obeys.
Excuse me, Madame, for having interrupted your meal.*[5]

How was a twelve-year-old like Ruffin supposed to react to such
ambivalence on the part of his enemy? Hope that the Germans would
be defeated? Fear that Russia would become the new enemy?

||||||||||||||||||||||||

Another young boy, André Kirschen, was barely fourteen when Hitler's
army invaded Poland. He had been born in Budapest in 1926, and his
family had immigrated to Paris in the early thirties. They spoke French,
as many bourgeois Rumanians did, and they assimilated rather quickly,
but they were always made aware that they were strangers, that Parisians saw them as foreigners first, even before they were recognized as
Jews. From his early teens, André was fascinated with politics, and he
was an enthusiastic member of the Amis du Front populaire, a large
club of leftist supporters of the Blum government. His parents were not
thrilled that he had joined such an organization; they, like most immigrant parents, argued that foreigners should keep below the horizon of

French politics. Nonetheless, they did not forbid him to get involved. In fact, after André and his brother became active in the underground, "our parents were very worried, but they never tried to stop us. In other families such activity would have provoked arguments, pleas, even family trauma."[6]

As a teenager, André stood out from his fellow students at the intellectually prestigious and unmistakably upper-class Lycée Janson-de-Sailly as he drew closer and closer to the French Communist Party. He proudly and openly read *L'Humanité*, the Communist Party newspaper, attended mass communist rallies, and listened obsessively to the radio as the news of impending war became increasingly frantic. Understandably, it did not take much for the young boy to find the courage to join resistance groups early in the Occupation, even with his hands tied by the August 1939 non-aggression treaty.[*] The pact lasted only ten months, until Germany invaded the Soviet Union in June 1941, but during that period, despite the Party's official admonition to remain neutral, youngsters like André (and Guy Môquet) continued to publish and distribute their own pamphlets, as well as Party newspapers. They had spirited debates among themselves about whether they should support Stalin, who had partnered with Hitler, the devil himself, rather than his fellow Bolshevik and archenemy Leon Trotsky, exiled by Stalin for his apostasy. Most other noncommunist groups engaged in similar activities. They were not combatants but rather gadflies, waiting for someone to tell them how to resist other than by printing tracts and distributing them.

But with the onset of Operation Barbarossa (Hitler's code name for his invasion in June 1941), the young communists, not satisfied with

---

[*] We have seen that this pact was one of Hitler's most successful diplomatic coups. He convinced Stalin, still reeling from a massive political elimination of most of his army officer class, that their nations' best interests would be served in acting as pincers to control eastern Europe and its massive oil, agricultural, and ore reserves.

only increasing their nonviolent resistance, were ready for combat. The announcement was met with a combination of relief, for now there was clarity, and apprehension, since the gloves could finally be taken off:

> *Everything was returning to a natural order after the malaise created by a German-Soviet pact which had for the most part been accepted [only] by command, and with the conviction that this unnatural order of things could only be temporary. No sweeping gaiety however; each [of the youngsters] anticipated that the future would be tough.*[7]

André Kirschen was occasionally asked if he was worried about the racist Nazis in Paris. His answer was cautious, for he rarely thought of himself as Jewish. His family were casual practitioners; they had not immigrated because their religion had endangered them, but because André's uncle lived in Paris and had offered a job to his father. Indeed, until 1940, being Jewish was the least of his concerns. His father had been drafted into the French army, and the family business had run into financial difficulty. How his family would get enough to eat was his preoccupation.

Yet, despite his initially casual attitude about being Jewish in an increasingly racist state, André began to recognize how insidiously antisemitism revealed itself in Occupied Paris. The German soldiers were flooding into the shops and stores of France's capital, buying what they could not afford or obtain in rationed Germany, to the delight of the French merchants.* At one shop, André remembered, he

---

* My favorite anecdote touches on the subtlety of the French response to this increase in business. A German soldier is happy to find so much more to buy in Paris than was available back home. And the owner of the shop is quite polite to him. "I just love Paris," he tells her. "You should've seen it before you came," she coyly replies.

overheard a conversation between two women, the owner and a client: "They all told us that they were barbarians; look how correct they are!" And the shop-owner said, "Yes, it'll only be bad for the Jews. They'll hang them all." The customer calmly answered: "I'm not Jewish."[8] Still, the youngster could not have imagined the fate that awaited his fellow Jews. It was still early days, but in Vichy and German offices across Occupied France plans were already being drawn up to discriminate officially against Jews—both domestic and foreign, and the *rafles* (roundups of the latter) would begin soon.

||||||||||||||||||

Maroussia Naïtchenko, born in 1923, was the daughter of a Ukrainian father and a French mother. Her father does not figure significantly in her story, for he was rarely part of the family. Her mother, Annette, on the other hand, belonged to an aristocratic French lineage whose members had been shocked when she married a communist from the Ukraine. Maroussia's maternal grandmother blamed all Russians for the Revolution of 1917 and for the creation of what she considered the nadir of political ideology, communism. Though she loved her daughter Annette dearly, she could not hide her aversion to communist values; Annette's older relatives spoke of her lifestyle and her commitment to the values of the French Communist Party as one would discuss a gravely ill or demented person. Maroussia and her sister grew up in a house filled with both love and tension. They absorbed with equanimity the heated arguments between their mother and the rest of the family, learning how they too might navigate the prejudices against young women.

In the mid-1930s, when Maroussia was twelve, her mother took her to the local communist club, near where they lived in the upper-class seventh arrondissement of Paris. It was reached via a narrow passage, not even a street, and was recognizable to the initiated only by its large green door. Her mother peremptorily announced to the older teenagers gathered there that she wanted to enroll her daughter in the Jeunesse communiste. Amused, a young leader asked Maroussia how old she was; she fibbed, saying she was thirteen and a half, even though she was more than a year younger. Thrilled by the attention, by the lies she had to tell (in front of her mother no less), and by the sense of mystery surrounding the group of young communists, she enrolled. She had not suddenly become a leftist, but joined in order to choose sides between her reactionary grandmother and her pro-communist, progressive mother. This was an adventure for a girl who was bored with school and reaching the cusp of adulthood. Like other young resisters, Maroussia was initially acting not strictly from political or ideological motivations, but for social and personal reasons. A sense of adventure, the chance to belong to a group dedicated to a cause, and being treated with the respect most adults did not give young girls allowed Maroussia to begin a life of clandestinity that would endure for a decade.

When the Spanish Civil War broke out in 1936, Maroussia, now almost fourteen, became active in organizing satellite organizations, composed mostly of girls and young women, to raise money for the Republicans. As a resident of one of the most aristocratic and conservative parts of Paris, she discovered young women who sympathized with her, but who often complained of having too much to do—too many parties to go to, too many boyfriends—to dedicate their social lives to a foreign cause. She complained to her leaders, but no one provided her with the funds to build a dedicated cohort. Still, Maroussia had less of a social life than other teenagers and thus could spend uninterrupted time working for this good cause. In addition, her mother's somewhat naive trust permitted the young teen to walk the streets of their neighborhood seeking support for the Republicans, a demanding and scary job: "The collections that I made alone in the apartment buildings terrified me. I was continuously afraid of being thrown out by a furious tenant or owner. This little fourteen-year-old revolutionary feared everyone, from the policemen to the concierge!"[9] It soon became obvious that the efforts of those supporting the Spanish Republic were having little effect: "At home, the map of Spain, tacked up in the dining room, broke our hearts. The Republican front was becoming smaller and smaller, and the heroic fighters were defending, step by step, smaller parts of the government's territory."[10]

We have seen how the defeat of the Spanish government by the Franco mutiny marked a major turn in the psychological growth of many French girls and boys. The good side lost, and those who could have helped had been either reluctant to lend aid or even totally against the Republican cause. For the first time, realpolitik, even though they may not have known the term, confronted their simpler ideas of justice versus injustice. For those in large cities and in smaller ones near the Pyrenees, the sight of thousands of refugees, fleeing a new terror, had its effect. Hitler had come to power in 1933, and by 1936 he had become confident enough to help destabilize another European nation. This was remarkable. And Blum's government, increasingly burdened by international events, had lost its earlier élan. The militancy of its earlier supporters had waned, and eventually the young communist cohorts seemed to be the only French men and women ready to fight in some way against the spreading, noxious cloud of fascism. Wrote Maroussia:

> The political events that were happening one after the other upset me. Nothing had prepared me for these failures of political will. All European nations seem to be sinking more and more into totalitarianism where repression became more and more savage; and, in France, the situation seemed to be getting worse day by day. How had we come to this?[11]

The August 1939 non-aggression pact signed by the Soviet Union with Germany had also been a shock to Maroussia. She searched for answers, trying to balance an understanding that Stalin might want to put off a conflict for as long as he could with the criticism that he was associating with a leader who had murdered communists in Germany. Again, politics appeared to be about compromising rather than moving toward justice; clarity was dimming. Yet, gradually, loyalty to the principles of the Great Revolution overcame these political and diplomatic missteps. Then, of course, the PCF was outlawed, and communist deputies and other figures in the government were dismissed, arrested, and imprisoned. Many fled to other countries.* Solidarity among supporters of the Soviet Union strengthened. Still, Naïtchenko and her friends, including Guy Môquet, did not stop their anti-establishment resistance. Without funds, without leadership, and with the French police on their heels, they continued their activism against this new blow to their sense of social and political justice. Though France had agreed, with Great Britain, to support Poland in case of invasion, neither did much as that nation was steamrollered by combined Nazi and Russian armies. Urban youth wanted to let the French government know how they felt: "Once night fell," Maroussia observed, "we found the streets blacker than an oven. But that was quite good for us to write on walls, for the darkness would hide us from the very few passersby. I liked to draw the hammer and sickle, symbol of the Communist Party, to show that it, though outlawed, still was not dead."[12]

Maroussia had to be cautious, for not only the police but most Parisians were anticommunist. She and her friends could be betrayed by anyone from a friend's mother to a cleaning lady who discovered some inked stencils in a wastebasket. But the youngsters were

---

* After the Franco-German armistice in 1940, while the Soviet Union was an ally of Germany, the French Communist Party tried to convince the German authorities to reverse sanctions against it and to allow it to resume printing its newspaper, *L'Humanité*, in Paris, but to no avail. *L'Humanité* remained underground until 1944.

becoming astute in their surreptitious actions; what they learned during the year when the PCF was outlawed would serve them immeasurably when France and the Soviet Union found themselves on the same side after June 1941. For instance, Maroussia and her comrades began noticing and imaginatively utilizing their built environment. They learned how to enter apartment houses stealthily, and they befriended concierges, identifying which ones paid close attention to comings and goings. They even went so far as to discover which buildings in their neighborhoods had two entrances, ideally onto separate streets.[*]

                              |||||||||||||||||||||

From early on, the German authorities knew that they had a huge job on their hands. The Wehrmacht, which was at first the only executive body in charge of the Occupation, had to ensure not only stability and security among the civilian population but the military effectiveness of an army facing England (whose adamancy had made them a worrisome adversary). How to do this? The first response was to be lenient toward those early malefactors who were only aggravating, buzzing around in a spontaneous, but usually nonviolent, effort to remind the Germans that France was not totally subservient. There were few arrests of those who quickly passed around printed tracts or wrote "V" (for victory) on the walls of the city. As long as the German soldiers felt relatively safe and the resistance to the Occupation remained "modest," the MBF was content to let the French police take care of these minor infractions.

Most often the miscreants were youngsters who were either blindly impatient or cynically being used by warier adults as guinea

---

[*] In my *When Paris Went Dark* (2014), I mention that the Germans made a point of occupying as many of these buildings with multiple exits as they could find, not only for their own needs but to prevent them from being used by possible antagonists.

pigs to see how the Occupier would react. The trials of those who were caught, either by surveillance or even especially by good police work, were often show trials, meant to send a stark message that resisting the Occupation was an activity that would not be treated lightly by the authorities. Seconded by the French police services (who were much more knowledgeable about the population they "protected"), the Germans were masterful at directing this drama of French versus French.

However, the youth of urban France especially were not willing to be so complacent, and to the surprise of the Germans, they challenged the Occupation massively only four months after the armistice. The imprisonment of increasing numbers of young men would grow. Parents were informed when their children had been jailed, and that they had seriously violated the understanding that the presence of the German Reich in France was to be unquestionably supported. Their release was sometimes obtained, but erratically. The Germans' hostage policy added a horrific dimension to their stress. A student arrested for a peccadillo could suddenly be treated as though he had shot a German officer in the back.

Even though it varied from year to year, the Occupation Authority's responses to the Resistance grew relentlessly more vigorous. Four key events during the twenty months between November 1940 and June 1942 had a demonstrably disruptive effect on the Wehrmacht's carefully planned attempts at keeping the French population calm and quiescent. The first, we shall see, was a major student demonstration in November 1940, when the Germans had to admit that occupying France would not be smooth sailing. Then came the June 1941 invasion of the Soviet Union by the Germans. This upset carefully regulated plans to contain the French communists and raised the intensity of their activities, especially among the Jeunesse communiste. Then, in August 1941, a German naval intern, Alfred Moser, was assassinated by a group of young gunmen in a metro stop in the middle of Paris; two months later, in October, Guy Môquet and dozens of other hostages were executed by Germans. Finally, the transfer of all police powers from the MBF, by Hitler's order, to the SS and the Gestapo in June 1942 certainly weakened any attempt to keep reprisals under military, and thus ostensibly more clement, authority.

What added so much uncertainty to these events is that none of the policies initiated by the Germans were ever made clear to the French. At first, it was only after an attack, a public trial, and executions that relatives learned of the dangers of resistance. Even then, the news was censored or glossed over with benign language: collaborationist newspapers and large posters in German and French on prominent walls and in metro stations announced the executions, often with the names of those who had died but only the barest details of why they were executed; usually "terrorism" was cited. These and other bits of information only allowed the French to infer what the rules were at any one time. And they changed often: curfews shifted unpredictably, new laws forbidding some activity or another sprang up, or suddenly foodstuffs were allocated differently.

For years after the war, historians—and apologists—of the Wehrmacht attempted to whitewash the army's activities in the repression of Jews and members of the Resistance. But newly opened archives have shown that, if the Wehrmacht was more reticent than Berlin or the SS and the Gestapo, it was for reasons of policy—the belief that there was no need to anger the population, for resistance might grow—rather than for moral or legal reasons. Successful resistance actions had also become clearer to the civilian population—often via those darkly printed or red announcements plastered on the walls of metro stops and kiosks. A few hours after the shooting of Moser, the following *avis* from the commander of Paris began appearing on the walls of the metropolis and other large cities, as well as in national and local newspapers:

On the morning of August 21 [1941], a member of the German armed forces was the victim of an assassination. As a consequence, I hereby order:

> 1. *All French citizens held in detention, for whatever reason, in France by German authorities or on behalf of German authorities will be considered hostages as of August 23.*
> 2. *For any new incident, a number of hostages, depending on the gravity of the attack, will be executed.*[13]

The trepidation that such announcements must have caused in hundreds of families with younger members in jail, mostly for minor offenses, would have been overwhelming. Panicked parents and siblings rushed to prisons and local jails, demanding to see their relatives, bringing food packages and promises of help from their connections, before the worst happened.

|||||||||||||||||||||||

Not all adolescents paid close attention to what was going on during the early Occupation, even though their daily lives were affected. They were, of course, aware of the changes, even curious about them, but not enough to put their lives or their families in any real danger. Micheline Bood was the typical bobby-soxer. Like the boys, she and her girlfriends were fascinated with the decorum, the appearance, and the confident masculinity of the young German soldiers, some only a half-decade older than she. Thanks to Micheline, we have an invaluable document that reveals how complex it was to grow up in a city filled with foreign soldiers who were trying to keep the population respectful. A combination of almost erotic fascination and fear informed the actions of numerous young women in their first encounters with the German Occupier.

Micheline was fourteen years old when she started keeping a journal, about a month before the Germans began their Blitzkrieg against
France.*[14] She was not a member of a network or official movement;
she had no ideological certainty other than a superficial patriotism
and a love for Great Britain. (Her brother had escaped from Dunkirk
and was now flying for the Royal Air Force, which he would do for
the rest of the war.) She could have stayed passively interested and
avoided making decisions that would cause ethical friction, but her
diary repeatedly veers into the effects of the war: *How should I react
to the foreign soldiers in my city? Can't I just lead a "normal" life? Why
should I not express my sentiments openly? Why should I totally ignore
the presence of these flirtatious Germans?*

Like other girls of her age group, Micheline did "resist," if only modestly. She tells a story that any teenage girl would love to tell, about dis-
covering, as a lover of prunes, that if she left the pit moist, she could
spit it out at the backs of young German soldiers, who would look up
to see if a bird had left them a gift. Micheline and her friends found
this hilarious, none of them recognizing that such pranks would later
lead to prison or worse. Even when her friends all joined the large student march on November 11, 1940, she still saw it as a bit of a parade
or student jaunt. It would not be until the French police and Germans
started firing shots and chasing students carrying signs and armfuls of
tracts that she realized that such confrontations would not go unpun-
ished. When one of her girlfriends was arrested after tearing down a
pro-German sign and sent to prison for three months, it was fully clear

---

* For years the diary went unpublished and lay in her mother's home, forgotten.
But in 1972 it was discovered by chance and published, with Bood's permission, in
1974, almost in toto. Again, it would rest on library shelves for almost four decades
before some of her reminiscences began appearing in accounts of young women who
had lived, and come of age, during the dark years. Though Bood's teenage musings at
times verge on the insipidity typical of the early writing of most teens, this valuable
document brings us quite close to understanding how the Occupation affected noncommitted youth.

to Bood that there were no innocent acts of confrontation with the Germans, and that age and gender were no barriers against military judgment; being a girl would give her some protection, but not for long.

Still, the sociability of challenging the stuffy Germans enhanced the excitement, so why not write Vs—for *Victoire*—on walls, especially where there were signs and posters calling on the French to serve the Vichy government? Or at the same time, why not hold out a welcoming hand to the Germans, who were doing their duty, and thereby assuage their anxiety about serving as police in an unfamiliar environment?

Micheline's journal reveals four years of such indecisiveness and confusion as she struggled to understand, while her body was changing, what was appropriate action, given the extraordinary circumstances. This is what makes her diary so readable despite its incessant detail: she mixes the mundane with the exceptional, the pleasant with the frightening, the physical with the psychological.

For instance, she and her friends—the same ones who drew on the city's walls—frequented the city's municipal pools, where they would play water polo and flirt enthusiastically with the young German soldiers, always maintaining enough decorum to avoid being called "whore" or "slut" by the older women who were watching. Micheline filled pages with her concern that she should not be consorting with Germans, that she should be a loyal French woman. On the other hand, she was determined to be free to do what she had the right to do, or at least had the right to do before the Germans arrived, and that was attracting boys—German or not.

Her dilemma was not resolved when a close friend began dating a German soldier:

December 1941. . . . It was I who introduced her to Ludwig, and that keeps me up at night. . . . They saw each other again yesterday, and it seems that they kissed a dozen times! I just have to resign myself to the situation.

> *In the end, this whole affair has caused me to reflect [on my flirt-*
> *ing with the Germans]. As far as I am concerned, I've vowed never to*
> *allow a Boch [sic] to kiss me. You can flirt with a Boch, but at our age*
> *it's never very serious (especially in my case); he's still a Boch. And*
> *I would have too many regrets afterward if I gave my first kiss to a*
> *man I did not know, and who was an enemy. . . . When a girl wants*
> *truly to be "well-raised," she does not act like a girl from the streets,*
> *and she never throws herself at a soldier who is occupying her coun-*
> *try. What must they think of French women, the Germans?*
> *That's a question every one of us should consider.*[15]

As this list of contradictory reactions reveals, Micheline cannot help herself. Children, adolescents, husbands and wives, merchants, teachers, priests, and retired folks—all had to interact regularly with the Germans, and with their Vichy supporters, but without a cultural road map to warn them about which paths led to humiliation or loss of status. The same was true for teenage girls who were vibrant and sociable but who were also intelligent enough to know that somehow they were transgressing.[*]

While her journal reveals no identifiable ideological penchant, there is barely a single page that does not mention some deprivation or event dealing with the war. Bood was intelligent, persistently worried about her grades, and eager to grow into a young woman. Fortunately, her mother's strong character kept her in tow. There were parties and brief escapades with other teens, including boys, but nothing too dramatic; Micheline's mother ensured that she was safely home every night. She remained torn between hating the German army and liking its young soldiers, between despising the troops of her own country

---

[*] Micheline assures us, by the way, that she was still a virgin at the end of the four years of the Occupation. She was kissed only once, sloppily she insists, by an older, fat German officer who had helped her out of a scrape.

for not having persevered and praying that the British would prevail. She counterfeited a German *Ausweis* (pass) so that she could ride the metro free and avoid lines and random searches. It did occasionally cross her mind that she was leading a somewhat edgy life.

Micheline was certainly not a joiner; she never attached herself to any group except for study or going out together. She knew that some of her teenage friends were passing out clandestine leaflets, gathering information, helping hide downed pilots, even transferring armaments, but she refrained from such obvious subversive activity. As the underground became better organized and began to use weapons against the Occupiers, Micheline, over the course of two years, persistently commented on how ineffectual such actions were:

September 1941: The murder of Germans has increased lately. I find this really disgusting, because there are terrible reprisals, and many hostages are shot. Beginning tomorrow evening and until the 23rd, everyone must be home by 9 PM, and those who are arrested in the streets after that will be considered hostages.[16]

One evening in September 1942, a year later, she awoke to the sound of a loud explosion not too far from her family's apartment. Immediately, she knew that the target was the German Navy Club. Her reaction again revealed how hesitant she was to justify forceful resistance:

September 1942: The result of this attack is a curfew at 8:30 PM. What a band of idiots, those who did that! They aren't even capable of defending our country when we ask them, and now they attack shops because German is written on them. I'm beginning to have enough of this filthy city. I am in a state of indescribable anger.[17]

The passage of time is more intense for young people than for adults: their bodies change, their relations with their families evolve;

their moods are often febrile; and, though they become more independent, they remain reliant on the protection of their home life. The Occupation began as a game with some of them, an excuse to make fun of the Germans—for their stiffness, their language, their impassivity—but slowly these soldiers became part of the community. It was not unusual for Micheline and her friends to paste pro–de Gaulle posters on top of German propaganda signs in the morning and play with German soldiers in the city's public swimming pools in the afternoon. Micheline came, quite naturally, to hate the "Bochs," while liking individual Germans.

In late 1943, as she begins her last *cahier*, the then-sixteen-year-old reflects on what she has written. Events had been so sudden, so brutal, and so frightening that taking the time to reflect on them as they occurred had seemed an unimaginable luxury. Now Micheline tells us, while rereading her journals (they would take up several thick school notebooks), that writing has given some solidity to her disrupted life.

||||||||||||||||||||

Philippe Pétain famously said, more than once, that France's defeat in 1940 had been attributable to its lack of children. Germany, with Austria, had a population of 80 million, while France was barely at 40 million. The average French soldier of the World War I trenches, known by everyone as the *poilus* (hard-bitten guys), had fought bravely, standing face-to-face with a brutal enemy and keeping Paris from being occupied.

By contrast, thought former leaders, the feckless recruits of May and June 1940 had spent their youth enjoying the amazing changes in daily life and the counterculture of the 1920s and 1930s, and had lost any sense of patriotism, honor, or pride. They had run at the first sign of a German panzer. This was indeed a fiction, for the French recruits, though poorly led, fought often like lions; they were nonetheless overwhelmed by a technologically sophisticated and masterfully led army acting with such unpredictable rapidity that it had thrown the French general staff flat on their backs. Still, a public excuse for such a massive defeat had to be provided, and a remedy found. The result was a massive amount of attention paid by the early ministers of the new État Français to the organization, preparation, and rehabilitation of France's confused and misled youth.

Beginning in the 1920s, regimes and political organizations in Europe—fascist, conservative, communist, socialist, religious—had begun showing demonstrably more political interest in the education (read: indoctrination), control, and motivation of their younger citizens. Middling population growth, the Great Depression, and political partisanship to the point of civil war—all seemed to demand a virile, athletic, better-educated youth corps. As the historian Susan B. Whitney succinctly claims:

> By [the late 1930s], youth occupied a place in French public life very different from that . . . [of] two decades earlier. Political and religious leaders competed for their allegiance and featured young supporters in mass demonstrations, rallies, and pageants. At this time of ideological tension and fear of war, the ability to rally large numbers of young people demonstrated strength, and was assigned symbolic significance. The young themselves engaged more fully, joining youth groups in unprecedented numbers. These activists were now female as well as male, for youth had become a mixed-sex political category and constituency.[18]

Youth organizations reinforced a sense of patriotic duty, but the motives of the organizers of these groups and camps were not always consistent or clear. A disparate jumble of initiatives appeared, including the massive adoption of outdoor camping, and increased attention to gymnastics and physical activity, characterized by new scouting organizations, showed that the development of youthful bodies had

become as important as intellectual growth. The organizations sought
to keep their charges under draft age physically occupied, especially
during the summer months. Religious service to the needy and to the
multitudes of refugees reinvigorated the Catholic Church's social role
among youngsters, and the incorporation of immigrant youth into
these groups introduced young French citizens to their contemporaries who had fled political oppression. Government-initiated ministries
of youth were now de rigueur for politicians; equally visible was the
addition of organizations for the young by all major adult membership
groups, ranging from the Freemasons to the Brownshirts of fascism.

One of the Vichy government's first massive actions was to try to
create a nation of "collaborators" by organizing France's young. The
main obstacle to building hero-worship of the old *Maréchal* among
the youth, as the Germans had done with Hitler, was that, for those
between ten and twenty, Pétain was a nonentity, a figurehead more or
less admired by their parents, but with no connection to them. Back in
early August 1940, when the Occupation was barely six weeks old, the
Vichy minister of education had sent out a directive memorandum to
all elementary and high school administrators, as well as to university deans and presidents. At the first class of the academic year, in all
educational institutions, the following program was to be followed:

—A minute of silence will be observed in memory of those who
died during the recent war [just finished];
—A reading of portions of the calls to action [*appels*] to the French
nation of last June 16, 20, 23 and 25, by Maréchal Pétain, head of
the État Français;
—A short speech [by the professor] inspired by these calls to action. These remarks will address the important conditions of our
national recovery, the new duties that it imposes on all Frenchmen, most particularly on our youth, who carry the promise of
the future.[19]

The youngsters to whom this bit of theater was addressed were already involved in minor disobedience, such as passing notes in class that derided the French collaborators, and especially Hitler. They mumbled when they were supposed to sing the quickly adopted hymn of the Vichy government, "Maréchal, nous voilà!" (Marshal, here we are!). The refrain of this song was a would-be national anthem, competing, barely, with the forbidden "La Marseillaise," which was still sung overtly on any possible occasion. The paean to Pétain was derided by many as an anti–Republic anthem.

Maréchal, nous voilà!
Devant toi, le sauveur de la France
Nous jurons, nous, tes gars
De servir et de suivre tes pas
Maréchal nous voilà!
Tu nous as redonné l'espérance
La Patrie renaîtra!
Maréchal, Maréchal, nous voilà!
[Marshal, here we are!
Before you, the savior of France,
We swear, we, your guys,
To serve and to follow your lead.
Marshal, here we are!
You have given us hope!
The fatherland will be reborn!
Marshal, Marshal, here we are!]

The song, pastiched from better-known lyrics and music, was a rather sad attempt to inculcate loyalty in the young. Of course, younger children would have joined in eagerly, but older ones, as they heard their parents, teachers, and even priests begin to question the *Maréchal*'s politics, were increasingly prompted to question rather than conform.

Though obsessed with reeducating France's youth, the Vichy bu-
reaucracies remained oblivious to how Pétain and his government
were being seen by young French boys and girls, men and women.
Nevertheless, the new government was convinced that its future lay
in paying attention to thousands of youngsters who were still reeling
from the defeat, the exodus, and the Occupation. Two recent historians of French collaboration during the war write:

> Founded on a desire to weaken or suppress traditional counter-
> weights to their power (local councils, department and urban gov-
> ernments, professional organizations, and labor groups), the Vichy
> regime began by creating an archipelago of youth organizations.
> Focused on national moral and physical regeneration, the National
> Revolution was logically led to pay important notice to youth.[20]

Two large youth organizations were founded almost immediately,
one state-supported, the other voluntary, both with state permission.
The first was the Chantiers de la jeunesse française, which immediately recruited young men of twenty (but again, no young women, who
were supposed to stay at home, learning how to be wives and mothers).
They were put to work clearing forests and toiling very hard to build
the mental and physical muscle that the government thought had been
wasted away. Almost ninety thousand youngsters—including former
soldiers, those not yet in the army, and students—were recruited. (By
mid-summer 1942, Jews had been excluded from participation in the
Chantiers de la jeunesse.) For many participants, their service and ded-
ication were to the person of the *Maréchal* first, to the new state second.
As time passed, their ideological commitments began to evolve, and
many would leave these organizations, but most served their time, remaining pro-government, if anti-German.

There were pockets of young men in the Chantiers de la jeunesse
who, believing that they should be preparing some sort of revenge

against the Germans, requested permission to build secret caches of arms for future use. The officials in charge refused and chastised them strongly, explaining that the Chantiers was an organization in service to the new National Revolution first and foremost. Policy was up to the leadership of the State, not to them. Still, small groups remained recalcitrant and would later slip away to join an increasingly restive resistance.

Another Vichy-approved, if not supported, group was the Compagnons de France. Aimed at fourteen- to nineteen-year-olds, it was essentially, with some minor exceptions, the same sort of organization as the Chantiers. In this case, the government was worried that so many unattached, uncommitted, and anxious teenagers were wandering around the still-traumatized country. Thousands upon thousands of foreign immigrants, most of whom had no permanent ID papers, were confused about whom they could trust. There was a whole subpopulation of young people who were resistant to inconsistent orders yet desirous of leadership. And their choices seemed to be commitment to either the National Revolution or the rigorous order offered by the Occupying Authority. The Compagnons de France would help focus and compartmentalize these teens.

Setting up camps and hostels, with regularly promoted activities for physical exercise, was one thing; educating these young cadres about the values of a new type of government was another. The Germans were of no help, for they suspected any French organization that had ten or more members. But the Vichy government confidently believed that the example of the Victor of Verdun could keep youngsters in line. Pétain's reputation, though he was considered weak and too politically cautious after the war, remained strong among many French citizens until the very end of the war, and his example was used as a means of keeping the more politically sensitive of the youngsters in line. They were reminded that no other such prominent French leader had stayed in France and given himself to his people. *Why not support*

him? Many teenagers and young adults who were more deferential
would easily make the transition from the Compagnons to the Chantiers, and finally to the Milice. And not a few would be bewildered at
the end of the war when their revered leader, Maréchal Pétain, was
arrested, tried, and sentenced to death.

|||||||||||||||||||||

One of the earliest embarrassments for the new Pétain-Laval government was its tepid response to the vigorous annexation by the Reich of
Alsace and the Moselle portion of Lorraine. The events surrounding
this illegal appropriation would have consequences that lasted until the end of the war, and afterward. French citizens began reading
in their newspapers and hearing on their radios about the disloca-
tion of families who lived in the Alsace and Moselle regions of eastern France. The sudden and forceful evacuation of over twenty-two
thousand French citizens shattered any notion that the Germans
planned a "friendly" Occupation. More than one hundred thousand
French citizens from this region who had temporarily left during the
brief war were not permitted to return and had to remain where they
had taken refuge.* The Vichy government was taken by surprise, and
despite official, though weak and ultimately fruitless, requests of the
Germans to desist, it was shown, once again, to be the weaker "part-
ner" in the post-armistice agreement. The Wehrmacht, and later the
SS, aggressively assumed complete political and cultural authority
over this area.[21] By December 1940, most Francophones, Jews, Roma,
foreigners, and French who had immigrated there in the recent past,
as well as anyone considered a troublemaker, had been expelled to

---

* I recently learned of a large family named Muller who left Alsace to find security
in France. But they soon realized that the French did not trust Alsatians, considering them more loyal to Germany. The family changed its name to Carré so that they
would be considered more French than German, though their accent may still have
betrayed them.

France proper. This was the first large population that had to be assimilated by the French in the newly restructured France. Most of these Alsatian-Mosellans were Protestants and were settled in southwestern France, a traditional Protestant area.

The Germans wasted no time in asserting their control of this territory bordering on the Rhine. The new ordinances of the Reich's *Gauleiter* (governor of a district) were especially directed toward the youth of the region. Almost immediately after Germany annexed this area, young Alsatians and Mosellans were encouraged to join the Hitlerjugend or the Bund Deutscher Mädel (for girls). These organizations had goals similar to those of the Vichy groups, though there was a much stronger military emphasis for boys:

> *Sport will be especially important, as well as a spirit of camaraderie, discipline and obedience, and devotion to the National-Socialist cause. For it is necessary to form at the same time a future soldier and a future party supporter. "Each one must learn early to obey, in order later to command. Thus German youth will become the root of the political unity of our nation."* [22]

A subtler, and thus less advertised, mission of such organizations was to reduce the family's dominant role in indoctrinating their own children.

School curricula in the annexed areas were immediately changed, more so than in France, and soon all young Alsatians were in a German school system. Ominously, a program called the Reichsarbeitsdienst (National Work Service) was introduced, and in February 1941 the first draft notices went out, requiring all Alsatians and Mosellans, at twenty years of age, to register, take a physical, and wait to be called up for six months of service. The work comprised helping with harvests, clearing forests, draining swamps, and constructing highways. Much of the labor was an aid to the German war effort; some prescient youngsters realized that the next step would most likely be a draft into the Wehrmacht itself. As a consequence, young Alsatians began to hide at home or in the countryside, slip across the border into nearby Switzerland, or go to France proper to escape the call-up. Some were found and brought to court; one group of youngsters who had passed around tracts asking their friends not to sign up were tried by a military tribunal, sentenced, and then shot. The German authorities thus hoped to discourage any further attacks on their plans for young people.

As predicted, the inevitable did happen, and one of the saddest, and most misunderstood, events in France's war history occurred. On August 25, 1942, a new ordinance announced that Alsatian and Mosellan youth would be eligible for service in the German armed forces. The Germans had first asked for volunteers, but the response had been feeble, so forced enrollment became necessary.* This was an internationally illegal act: the citizens of France, or any occupied country, were not to be drafted by a victor. (Needless to say, international agreements never impeded the Germans from doing what was best for the Reich.) Soon, similar edicts were promulgated in the rest of Lorraine (Moselle was a large province within Lorraine) and in occupied Luxembourg. This call-up took place as the Reich was entering into its second invasion of the Soviet Union in the spring and summer of 1942, after having failed to defeat the Russians in 1941–1942. More soldiers were needed all over Europe, for the best were being pulled out of their Occupation duties to confront the increasingly successful Soviet forces. The edict increased by thousands the number of *réfractaires* (those who refused) among the male youth of the annexed provinces. One hundred and thirty thousand were eligible for the draft, so thousands found ways to avoid it. This began a long, mostly futile, but nonetheless passionate resistance against the Germans in Alsace and

---

* This "draft" model would later be used in Vichy France to send French men and women to work in Germany, though for civilian, not military, duties.

Lorraine. Needless to say, some of those who escaped, or never signed up, took what skills and passion they had and either joined the Free French or served in a variety of guerrilla groups throughout France.

Those who did eventually put on the gray-green uniform of the German army would call themselves, and be called, *les malgré-nous* (reluctantly, against our will), though a good number willingly joined and fought against the Russians. The response of the families of these reluctant young people was almost universally condemnatory. The Germans had by this action lost most of its claim to being a benign protector of this region. And the Vichy government's reputation for protecting the French against an arbitrary Occupier, revealed once again as impotent, was diminished even further.

More than 130,000 Alsatians and Mosellans served in German uniforms—some willingly, but most of them very reluctantly—often on the Russian front, and about a third of those were killed, maimed, or listed as missing. Most of the *malgré-nous* were quite young, some still in their teens. Some communities lost as many as 50 percent of their young citizens to service in the German forces. Never trusted by the officers in the German army, nor by the Russians who captured them, these young soldiers of French nationality were also suspected of treason by the French when they did return after the war. No subsequent government has recognized the international crime committed against these young men dragooned into service by the Wehrmacht. After the war, the *malgré-nous* would loudly claim that they had been forced to join, no matter the crimes that they might have committed.[*]

---

[*] The most famous case was that of the destruction in June 1944, only four days after the Allied invasion, of the French village of Oradour-sur-Glane in west-central France and the murder of its 642 inhabitants—men, women, and children—by an SS unit, Das Reich. More than a dozen members of that unit were *malgré-nous*. After the war, they were tried and found guilty. One who had volunteered for service was shot; the others, draftees, were sent to forced labor camps. In 1953, all *malgré-nous* draftees were pardoned, as victims of an illegal German policy. Not everyone was pleased with this attempt to bind wounds still bleeding from those awful events.

Their fate for having been born in those eastern provinces, right across the river from Germany, was to be considered pariahs for years.

The Germans did not gain a substantial number of converts to the Third Reich with these disruptions of daily life. In her contemporaneous memoir of her life endured under the Occupation, Pauline Corday wrote as early as 1942 that "the story of the resistance of the Alsatians and the Lorrainians will be a long one that will be known in depth only after the Liberation. A German is supposed to have said: 'It's here where we expected to be the most welcome, but it's here where they were the most hostile to us!'"[23] The example of those French who lived on the border with Germany would impress many in the rest of the country and set a standard of action that would reverberate with the legions of youth desperately seeking both to hide from and respond to Germany's arrogance.

<hr/>

The socially and politically conservative L'État Français restored the traditional position of the French Catholic Church, which was relieved, for the most part, to see the return of its influence as a moral arbiter. Yet many Catholics, especially the young, had an attitude of "Yes, but. . . ." They had enthusiasm—indeed, love—for their country, but they were not interested in being led indiscriminately to affection for a government that claimed to be traditionalist but had quasi-fascist qualities, especially regarding Jewish and other refugees. Thus, despite the insistence of German propaganda that de Gaulle and the Free French were godless, that his way would reproduce the chaos of the socialist Front populaire, Catholic youth reserved judgment at first, even while continuously pressured to wholeheartedly commit to L'État Français.

Average Catholic citizens, however, paid little attention to the Church's hierarchy, being much closer to the priests and nuns who participated in their day-to-day lives. Many effective resistance actions during the Occupation were supported and performed by some of the most courageous of French patriots—the clergy on the ground. The liberal wing of the Catholic Church was best exemplified by a group formed in Belgium in the 1920s: the Jeunesse ouvrière chrétienne (JOC). This religious organization was essentially leftist (though of course it could never say this openly), insofar as it sought to lift up the poor, both materially and politically. By 1943, the Vichy government and the Nazis had outlawed the organization in France—a sign of its influence—but more than a few Catholic nuns and priests had already inculcated in the minds of young members the premises of fair play, antiracism, and social action. Still, most French youngsters—no matter their social milieu—anxiously waited, like their parents, for the next shoe to drop, as did youngsters in other social and religious groups.

In his memoir of those years as a fresh recruit to Vichy's Chantiers de la jeunesse, Paul Huot writes that the camp he was sent to was not too bad at first. Forestry, a useful trade, was taught there; the boys planted trees and maintained trails. It was 1943, and he remembers that none of the boys spoke openly about any "resistance," barely even about the war. Soon, however, just as in the prisons, word began to leak in via new recruits or from family letters. It appeared that the Germans were being set back on their heels in Russia and that increasingly effective groups of *résistants* were forming, both in urban areas and, more important for those in the forestry camp, in the Maquis. Soon campers began to notice that some of their comrades were not present at roll calls; they had been forced into brigades that were being sent to work in Germany. Their empty barracks were filling up with German soldiers, and the young campers found themselves bunking with their Occupiers. Tensions rose, and expectations became increasingly confused. Word went out that there were Maquis groups in the forests that would welcome campers—young ones especially. Still, it was not easy to leave, and none of these adolescents understood for sure what the events they were hearing about foreshadowed. As Huot recalls:

"Resistance": this word was in our minds, though rarely uttered in conversations. Prudence was our most important concern; so, we were ignorant of the thoughts of most of our comrades. For my part, I only spoke to two or three of the leaders. . . . And it was clear from them that it was important to wait for the "right moment" to seek out the Maquis. The term "right moment" was an important code word, for the Chantiers had been directed to never [change location], except for an emergency.[24]

Waiting for the "right moment" to do something none of them really understood how to do proved to be almost intolerable for the lads. Who would give the signal that the moment had arrived? Were there secret leaders among the camp counselors? No one was ready with answers. As time passed, they began to hear of reprisals against families of young campers who had left their *chantiers*, which only increased anxieties. Still, little by little, after lights-out, more and more of the young campers began serving a local Maquis group by doing light surveillance and foraging, sneaking away from their lightly guarded camp, while maintaining their regular jobs during the day. That was not their only encounter with the greater struggle. As the Allies increased their bombing of sites all over France, the campers were called on to clean up bomb debris, and many for the first time saw destroyed civilian bodies lying in the rubble. The war was becoming more and more palpable, less a hazy nightmare than a frightening and unavoidable reality.*

As the war interfered with daily life, membership in most official and religious organizations fell off; many youngsters avoided being drafted into any of them, and slowly most of the projects disintegrated. Those who stayed and participated eagerly were, of course,

---

* In September 1944, well after the Normandy invasion, Huot's brigade left the *chantier* and joined a Maquis unit nearby, where he became an official *résistant*.

strong supporters of L'État Français and would become members of the state militia (Milice) established in 1943. But other young people had slipped away to return home to hide, or else joined one of the increasing number of Maquis encampments hidden in the forests and mountains of France. For these and other reasons, the German Occupation Authority did not trust Vichy's youth groups. They felt—and they were astute about this—that such organizations in a febrile occupied country, without the powerful tools used by the Third Reich in creating the Hitlerjugend movements, would result in only casual support at best, or dissatisfied antagonism at worst, among the increasingly frustrated citizenry of an Occupied nation.

The Scouts de France tried, with some success, to remain separate from government control, but they were too prevalent and too well organized to be totally ignored. And while the Vichy organizations, the Compagnons de France and Chantiers de la jeunesse, tried mightily to encourage younger citizens, if they were jobless, to channel their relentless energies into unquestioning support, both physical and patriotic, of the regime and to form leaders for the next generation of the "new order," these efforts were anemic compared to the activities of the other groups that were less attached to L'État Français. The Scouts de France were quite successful in attracting young recruits (though the organization had separated itself from the Éclaireurs israélites de France [EIF]—the Jewish Scouts—in 1930, at the beginning of the resurgent antisemitism that had been dormant since the Dreyfus Affair of the late nineteenth century).

Immigrant, Jewish, and communist youth were especially preoccupied with changes in Vichy government policies. After all, there was no doubt what Hitler thought of Jews and communists. Even non-leftist French Jews had learned to be wary of France's—or Vichy's—support. Many Jewish immigrants were socialist or communist, and French Jews who were not wondered how the government would distinguish between "good, patriotic" Jews and those who had recently immigrated or who had been critics of the Third Republic. Gentile youth would look to their scout leaders, often only a few years older than they were; to their priests, especially those who worked with the workers and the poor; or to their teachers, a good number of whom remained pacifist or leftist. Unconcerned about the racist policies of the Nazis, their decisions to resist could take more time, be a bit more deliberate.

As often happens in times of crisis, small differences among groups or friends or within families exploded into matters of emotional significance. Among communists, the questions were: Did you support Stalin or Trotsky? Germany or the Revolution? Catholics asked each other: Were you pro-Vichy, a very Catholic but quasi-fascist state? Or were you pro-France, a secular country? Among Jews: Were you a French Jew, here for generations, or a recent immigrant, poor and barely speaking French? Only the Protestants seemed to be of one mind: they remembered their own pogroms, now two hundred years past, and welcomed many—including Jews and Catholics—who had sought havens in southwestern France.

On the moral and educational issues of the Vichy government, the French Catholic Church stood somewhere between neutral and vocally supportive. It felt that this new state was restoring the Church to its earlier influence as the moral arbiter of the nation. Indeed, the Catholic Church hierarchy had played a rather duplicitous role, supporting the Vichy government while ostensibly bemoaning the straits of an Occupied France. The cardinal of Paris, and the de facto head of the French church, Emmanuel Suhard, was a well-known *Pétainiste*. Even though Suhard generally supported Vichy's moral priorities, he never publicly exculpated the Nazis, though he did write a bishopric letter condemning the roundup of Jews in July 1942. But he had ordered his bishops to keep a low profile on other political issues.[*]

---

[*] De Gaulle thought Suhard unsupportive of the Free French, and of the Resistance in general; many even stuck the term "collaborator" onto his reputation. To

⁞⁞⁞⁞⁞⁞⁞⁞⁞⁞⁞⁞⁞⁞⁞⁞⁞⁞⁞⁞⁞⁞⁞⁞

Roger Fichtenberg was nineteen years old when Germany unleashed its surprise attack on France. His family had been French for generations and lived comfortably in Paris's eleventh arrondissement on the Avenue de la République. Like other French Jews, they felt secure in that they were French first, and also they believed that France could easily withstand the motorized land and airborne mayhem that Germany had visited on Poland nine months before. But to be safe from aerial bombardments (which proved not to be a major factor in the capitulation of Paris), Roger's father decided to move the family to the town of Lapalisse, just twenty miles north of Vichy. There they planned to sit out the war, which they hoped would be over in a few weeks or months.

On June 19, 1940, after Generals Pétain and de Gaulle had made their opposing calls to service and to resistance, young Roger saw his first German soldiers:

> *The Germans arrive in motorcycles with side-cars, on their way to Roanne [farther south]. One contingent stays in Lapalisse. They are superb in their impeccable uniforms; more important, they are disciplined, friendly, almost considerate with the citizens. The officers sleep in requisitioned schools with their men. . . . The Germans seem to be in maneuvers rather than at war.*[25]

Doubtlessly like other witnesses, Roger hoped that this military invasion would end soon, and that the German occupation would be brief.

But the Fichtenbergs soon learned that they still had to stay alert.

---

dot the "i," de Gaulle forbade him to attend the celebratory mass held at Notre-Dame Cathedral at the liberation of Paris in August 1944.

On July 22, 1940, the État Français established a commission to review all naturalizations since the 1927 law that had permitted them to be French citizens. Many were revoked. On September 27, in the Occupied Zone, the German officials promulgated the order that all Jews who left that area for the Unoccupied Zone (where the Vichy government was located) could not return to their homes in the German zone. That would have included the Fichtenbergs at Lapalisse. The ordinance also stated that there would be a census of all Jews living in the Occupied Zone, and that all Jewish-owned businesses were to post a sign on the premises stating that fact. A week later the Vichy government passed a further law excluding Jews from certain professions and from serving in civil positions. A day later a more chilling announcement came: Jewish immigrants, depending on the whim of the prefects of *départements* in the Unoccupied Zone, might be sent to French refugee camps. Though less brutal than German and Polish camps, they were still areas surrounded with barbed wire and guarded by the French police. And no one knew how long a "sentence" would last, or whether the Germans might replace the French administration. Ordinances followed over the next several months in both zones, ranging from forbidding the hiring of Jews by "Aryan" businesses to the assignment of Jewish-owned businesses to "Aryan" owners.

It was still much easier to be Jewish in the Unoccupied Zone than in the German-controlled one. Nevertheless, the interruption of their commercial, educational, and social lives meant that most young Jewish boys and girls had to quickly adjust to the new order. In April 1941, Roger tried to join the vestigial armed forces (only 100,000 men permitted) of the new French state but was refused because he was a Jew. Soon after that, he was asked by a scout leader to lead a troop in the Éclaireurs israélites de France, which, amazingly, was still allowed to function. (This would only last until November.) Roger explained to the recruiter that:

I had never been a scout, but knew the Baden-Powell method well, having practiced it as a young middle-schooler in the mid-thirties. I let [the recruiter] know that I was ready to serve. It turns out that there were more than a few Jewish kids [in Lapalisse] who had been cubs or scouts, and whose parents would love to see their children in a Jewish troop. . . . Little did I know how important that decision would be for the rest of my life.[26]

He recruited about twenty young Jews and began building a doubly clandestine organization: first, because the Jewish Scouts had been outlawed, and second, because their search for "merit badges" would now be focused on undermining the antisemitism of the German and Vichy states.

In March 1942, Roger was suddenly drafted into the Chantiers de la jeunesse, the Vichy equivalent of the Hitlerjugend, only to be thrown out a few months later, forbidden membership again because he was a Jew. In late November 1942, the Germans occupied the whole country, and the leaders of the still-disorganized Resistance, which he wanted so desperately to join, told Roger that he could be of more use than just being a scout leader. He was instructed "immediately to take our bikes, and spread the alert in Vichy and its suburbs. All foreign Jews must go into hiding. . . . You are all mobilized."[27] Thus began a vigorous undercover network among Jews and their sympathizers to ensure the safety of hundreds of children, and occasionally their parents as well. This was not an easy time; the Germans were omnipresent now and less tolerant of resistance. The news from the Russian front was making the Reich's leaders apprehensive about their ability to maintain both a massive army fighting the Russians and an Occupation force strong and agile enough to plug all of the trouble spots that dotted France. As a result, the Gestapo and other German police forces assumed responsibility from the Wehrmacht for maintaining order. The repression was fiercer, and danger to young scouts a more fearsome possibility.

Fortunately, the Jewish Scouts found, especially in the south-western parts of France, that they had courageous young allies in the Protestant scout groups, such as the Éclaireurs Unionistes, who "furnished us with maps and insignia from their uniforms which allowed us to 'Aryanize' young Jewish refugees."[28] Fichtenberg learned that, since the age of majority was twenty-one, he and his younger scouts did not need official ID cards. They could get by with only student IDs or scout IDs, which were much easier to forge, borrow, or steal. Indeed, confusion over age requirements—officially and unofficially—created a large gray area where clandestine workers could operate. Wearing a scout uniform, which Fichtenberg did regularly, served as a *laissez-passer*, allowing him to wander the byways of the countryside. When stopped, he would explain that he was either leading a group or looking for good places to camp. Many of the boys and girls looked younger than they were (especially as malnourishment advanced in France), so they could pass for not yet being adults and thereby avoid arrest or, with the right documents, escape the calls to register for the "draft." This "natural" camouflage became a useful tool, as useful as the bicycle, for those youngsters willing to play the dangerous game of resistance in an increasingly nervous France.

⫶⫶⫶⫶⫶⫶⫶⫶⫶⫶⫶

Bicycles were so commonplace in resistance movements, especially for the youth, that their importance can easily be overlooked. Without them, there might well have been a quite anemic confrontation with the Occupying forces. The *bicyclette*, the essential mode of travel besides human feet, was used by resisters both young and old for five years. (In French, they were often referred to as *vélos*, an abbreviation of their earliest name, the velocipede.) They were not only a convenience but a necessity. Making personal contact when directly passing information and documents had become de rigueur. Forwarding messages through a third party or using telephones too frequently (especially public ones found in places such as bars and post offices) were considered sure ways to be betrayed. Riding bicycles through the countryside, from village to village, was the most expedient means for resisters to exchange the intelligence and goods necessary to warn and protect those most vulnerable to roundup by the Germans and the Vichy police.

Automobiles and trucks were essentially unavailable to anyone without a hard-to-obtain pass; farmers were permitted to have tractors, but their consumption of gas and oil was closely monitored by the authorities. (There were few mechanized farms in France at this time; horses were the primary source of agricultural power.) Only the rare doctor had an automobile, though house calls were still expected, even during the war years. In 1939, there had been three hundred thousand privately owned automobiles in Paris; by late 1940, there were only seven thousand. Trains, intercity buses, and the subway were efficient but also easily swept by the police, with unexpected security checks a constant concern. Bikes were ubiquitous, so much so that the authorities insisted that they be registered and carry a license plate (first tin, then cardboard). Yet their very numbers allowed many juvenile cyclists to disappear into crowds. The young Frenchwoman Pauline Corday explains in her memoir how nervous bicycles made the German authorities:

> They made certain streets one-way just for bikes. Thus, from the Opéra to the Boulevard Montmartre, traffic was forbidden to cyclists. As well as from Rue du Cherche-Midi to the Croix-Rouge intersection. . . . At first, this permitted cops to check IDs, and later, to threaten [scofflaws] with fines if they did not adhere to the new rules.[29]

They also, to the amusement of younger cyclists, forbade them to ride side by side; this would supposedly prevent resistance codes and information from being exchanged. So the riders would pass one another, repeatedly, which made more work for the patrol officers.

Bike merchants and warehouses were often raided by resistance groups, almost as frequently as arms depots. And when the police or an informant discovered undocumented bikes near a warehouse or a military establishment, they often recognized it as the first sign of clandestine surveillance (or at least some sort of mischief). German soldiers would stop youngsters on their bikes and search their saddlebags, if they did not simply requisition them for their own use. Rubber tires and the materials needed to repair them—patches, glue, pumps—all became as important to resistance groups as arms themselves.

One woman remembers how every ruse was used to befuddle the Germans as they learned to search all bikes with a saddlebag. Three youngsters were asked to quickly ferry hand grenades and other small arms from one part of eastern France to another. The two boys loaded their sacks with food and other mundane contents, while the young girl was to carry the contraband. Sure enough, they were stopped. The Germans flirted with the girl, who flirted back. (She remembers that they kept saying *"Schöne, schöne"* [pretty, pretty].) They opened the boys' bags and threw out all of the contents, but when they got to hers, they took out a bunch of greens, left another bunch for her, and sent the teenagers on their way. The arms of course were under the second bunch of greens. Thankfully, their thumping hearts had not betrayed their innocent smiles.[30]

Paul, a fifteen-year-old Jewish boy, had fled Paris, at his parents' urging, to hide in the southwest of France. He began to look for a Resistance group to join, but soon realized that membership could be wished for much easier than found. Since no one knew him, his chances of penetrating even a disorganized group of *résistants* were almost nil. Finally, he made the right connection and joined a group of the communist Franc-tireurs et partisans français (FTP, French ir-regulars and partisans).* For his first mission, he was ordered to steal a bike. "Steal a bike?!" he challenged querulously. "I didn't join the Resistance to steal bikes from kids like me!" But his leader riposted: "How do you think we get around, kid? In a car, perhaps?" Seeing the confusion in his young recruit's eyes, the group leader explained in a friendlier tone:

> *Listen, my little fellow, the* vélo *is our crew's train. Not only can we get hold of one easily, but for a partisan who operates in a city, this is the perfect vehicle: not cumbersome, easily handled, and anonymous. Especially anonymous. Who pays attention to a guy on a bike in the middle of the street, huh? Attacks, we make them on the* vélo. . . . *One day, one will have to put them in the Invalides, like the Marne taxis.*[†][31]

Still, the teenager hesitated. Finally, lacking a good counterargu-ment, except that he did not want to be seen as a thief, he answered, "OK, OK. I'll steal a bike for you."

Such illicit commandeering was a good test for these young as-pirants to clandestinity. Not as difficult or as dangerous as stealing weapons, stealing a bicycle still demanded a spot of courage and inspi-ration. It also enabled the recruiter to test the willingness of a young person to go against all of his or her religious and parental training and break a law, even commit a crime. "Stealing a stranger's bike was an essential test for those initiates wishing to enter the clandestine world."[32] So Paul stole a bike.

---

* This consolidated group of communist networks, created in early 1942, would be-come perhaps the most effective movement of the Resistance.

† Even taxis were commandeered in 1914 to rush troops to the Marne River to meet the Germans closing in on Paris.

IIIIIIIIIIIIIIIIIIIIII

On their bikes, Fichtenberg and his scout troop transported dozens of young Jews from town to town, farm to farm, often double- or even triple-riding on weakened tires. Despite the notion that France was rife with antisemitism in those days, "more and more, we received help from charitable organizations, religious institutions and priests. The youngest [Jewish refugees] were welcomed by families. Older ones were placed in elementary, technical, and artisanal boarding schools, or in seminaries. Older adolescents were placed on farms."[33]

So many French farmers were still in POW camps in Germany that the lack of agricultural workers had become a national economic concern. Accepting a strapping adolescent rarely occasioned a request for an ID, and after all, people reasoned, what difference did it make if one were Jewish if the cows got milked and the fields plowed? "As well, there was a certain solidarity amongst 'Gaullists.' If they were told that it was a question of saving a Jew, they would happily agree. As a consequence, we found a good deal of places for our refugees."[34]

Of course, though he does not mention it, Fichtenberg must have been aware of the danger of exposing his troop to a wide public of potential helpers, some of whom could have other motives in mind. Non-Jews gladly accepted young refugees because they needed unpaid servants and helpers. Knowing that the youngsters could not object, they often treated them with disdain, if not cruelty. Some refused to even take a Jewish kid unless he or she agreed to convert. For personal gain or out of jealous intent, there were always neighbors or other employees who might report the presence of a refugee. And of course children, no matter how much they were welcomed, could never be completely counted on to hide their identity. Jewish boys had been circumcised, and for that reason some French would take only girls. Yet Fichtenberg and his companions were not ignorant of these potential traps; as thoroughly as they could, they vetted the hiding places they chose, and for the most part stories of child protection ended happily.* Groups like Fichtenberg's provided Jewish girls and boys with access to a quasi-military organization that emphasized solidarity, clean living, and, most appropriately, lessons in living and operating innocently in the country and the city, without too much adult supervision.† The first two years of the Occupation were turbulent for young Jews and others, who tried mightily to outfox the Germans and the Vichy authorities as ordinances and laws were passed closing off Jews' opportunities for any civil or military service. Roger returned to his scout troop and began, again under the cover of a scout leader, the important work of hiding young Jewish refugees, spiriting them over the Pyrenees into Spain and over the Alps into Switzerland. His group discovered ways to forge documents and to "clean up" documents that could not be forged, and they devised strategies to lead children to safety.

Roger became increasingly involved with the clandestine world as the war progressed. He was soon an important link in the relay that hid young gentile Frenchmen trying to escape the Service du travail obligatoire (STO) among the Maquis irregulars. Many of these youngsters were not fighters and had never broken a law in their lives, except to refuse to enlist or to be forced to sign up for labor duty. They needed hiding places, false papers, and other forms of support. The pressure on these networks was intense. As for the scouts themselves, the number who wound up in the Resistance has never been determined,

---

* Two first-rate French films offer touching stories about the complications of hiding young Jews: Claude Berri's *Le Vieil homme et l'enfant* (1967) and Louis Malle's *Au revoir, les enfants* (1997).

† Though outlawed, the Éclaireurs israélites de France (the Jewish Scouts) still operated clandestinely; often the boys would wear the scout uniforms from secular scout organizations to confuse the inquisitive Vichy police. A clandestine branch of these scouts was instituted and referred to as "the Sixth." It would become a major source of information about the movements of Germans in Vichy France, especially after the German invasion of that region in November 1942.

but the movement was so popular that scout packs were established in German POW camps, where there were plenty of young men under the age of twenty.*

|||||||||||||||||||||||

One of the most powerful motivators of sudden courage on the part of French youngsters was Vichy government policies. Yes, there was disgust, if not hatred, at seeing uniformed Germans in major population centers, at having to step aside when they passed on the sidewalk, at having to show ID, at reading posters that listed resisters and hostages who had been shot, at having to work daily to find enough for their families to eat. But the German curfews and identity checks and even the imprisonments and executions were not nearly as persistently disrupting to adolescent lives as the policies of the Vichy government. Writes Olivier Wieviorka, a major historian of resistance to the German Occupation:

> *The French State [Vichy] had established a resolutely devitalizing politics for its youth. Deprived of public dances, urged to sacrifice themselves for the common good, invited to obey without demur, placed in morose youth organizations, then given up to the Occupier as possible workers in Germany, adolescents were in effect not protected by [their] government, [one] that promised an unattractive future.*[35]

The cultural, political, and social transition from the tense, but relatively carefree 1930s to the suddenly restrictive 1940s could not

---

* Roger Fichtenberg ended the war as a member of the Forces françaises de l'intérieur (FFI), and afterward became involved with both public and private organizations that worked with returning POWs, refugees, and displaced persons. Eventually he became active in Parisian city government; in 2014 Fichtenberg was made Officer in the Légion d'honneur, the highest civilian designation.

be better explained. The two most counterproductive regulations imposed during the Occupation, one by the Germans and the other by the Vichy government, were the mandate on Jews to wear the yellow star and the Vichy government's 1942 agreement with Berlin to provide thousands of French workers for Germany's war machine. The first will be discussed later; here, in discussing the growth of the Resistance, it was the second that demonstrably was most important. This was la Relève (the voluntary "replacement" of POWs by French working in Germany), eight months later transformed into the much more coercive *Service du travail obligatoire* (the STO), which had such importance for decisions that growing teenagers were having to make about living in an Occupied nation.

Back in late 1940, Pierre Laval, the president of the Ministerial Council (and thus second in line to Pétain), had been fired by the old general, whose aides and advisers had thought Laval was too eager to acquiesce to German demands, thereby threatening the quasi-independence of L'État Français. Nevertheless, by April 1942 (and sixteen months seemed like a century during the war), under pressure from the Germans, Laval had returned as prime minister, with more power than before. At his return, he remarked that the mood in France had changed considerably since his dismissal. The increasingly visible roundup of Jews by French police, especially of Jewish families (both French and immigrant), had finally caught the attention of the Catholic Church, whose bishops were beginning to speak less timorously from their pulpits about such antisemitism. More violent acts of resistance were occurring, with a consequent increase in executions of malefactors, as well as those unfortunate enough to be counted as hostages. The Wehrmacht's Russian campaign had bogged down, and more and more Frenchmen thought that they could sense an end to the war that would bring at least an armistice between Germany and the Allies. Nonviolent opposition became less timid. To rely on an ersatz patriotism, based on admiration for Pétain and his "new order," was becoming very delicate, and more difficult, for Laval and his government. The Pétain regime was weakening, and those who had previously thought Laval an impediment to the "new order" now saw him as the best insurance against total German control of France. Unfortunately for them, however, his reappointment also drew greater German scrutiny of the inefficacy of a government still marking time in the spa town of Vichy.

By this moment in the war (mid-1942), the Germans were worrying about their industrial production. Albert Speer had been put in charge of the defense industries, and he was doing a near-miraculous job of meeting the military's needs (for which he would be tried and found guilty at the postwar Nuremberg trials). Now he needed more laborers, especially since all available German males were fighting a two-front war. He looked naturally to the most populous and the most productive occupied country, France. We saw how the Relève was Laval's answer to this German demand. Fritz Sauckel, Speer's special envoy who was known as the "slaver of the Reich," suddenly appeared in France with the specific charge to find as many French "volunteers" or "recruits" as possible to send to Germany for work in its war economy. In families with eligible recruits, his name soon became a code word for the devil incarnate.

Before Sauckel's arrival, about one hundred thousand French workers had already gone voluntarily to Germany, most for the pay. Laval and his newly reacquired propaganda machine used an even more clever subterfuge to encourage French men—and women—to cross the Rhine to help the Germans. They first played on patriotic sympathies by promising that for every three Frenchmen who went to Germany, one POW would be released. (At the end of the war, between one and a half and two million French POWs remained in German captivity.) The radio, newspapers, and recruitment posters even announced that "every comfort will be provided: showers, bathrooms, central heating, abundant food prepared by French chefs." In other words, volunteers would find in Germany what they could not even dream of having now in France. Insidiously, Laval, prepared and seconded by Sauckel, argued that volunteers would not only alleviate the hunger that now had spread across France but provide better and more food for those French soldiers who remained in the German POW camps.

Youth, freshly out of school and often unemployed, were promised generous salaries. One should not judge them for grabbing a branch that might pull them out of the whirlpool of destitution and despair. But the German war machine needed more "volunteers" than those few who lined up to free their compatriots from camps, or who sought to help their families. Though the Germans did release some prisoners, that plan essentially failed: instead of the two hundred and fifty thousand volunteers requested and expected, only thirty-one thousand were on the trains to Germany by the late summer of 1942. Since the call to arms, a total of only ninety-one thousand "volunteers" had arrived in Deutschland. The Nazis, desperate for manual labor, were frustrated and furious.

As a result, Laval was forced to announce in February 1943 that all Frenchmen between the ages of eighteen and fifty, and single women ages twenty-one to thirty-five, would have to register for a work draft. This was the infamous, despised STO, which forced thousands of youth to go into hiding, to leave school, or to join in resistance, if for no other reason than to have a place of safety.* It has been estimated that two hundred thousand young men and women became *réfractaires* (defiantly unwilling) and hid throughout France, and that another thirty-five thousand went over the Pyrenees to Spain. Many, if not most, of those on the run had previously avoided active

---

* For a week it was called the *Service obligatoire du travail*, with the unfortunate acronym SOT, which means "idiot" or "fool" in French. The draft's name was immediately changed to *Service du travail obligatoire*.

involvement in resistance activities, but this draconian ordinance gave them little choice. Hundreds tried to find means to join the Free French in Africa and in London. And thousands went into hiding in the mountains and forests of south-central France, creating their own groups or joining an established Maquis camp.

The draft did provide hundreds of thousands of French workers to the voracious German war machine. As a result, Germany could release large numbers of its own workers to join its armies at war in the east. Some historians put the total number of Frenchmen who worked for the Third Reich—and who were still in Germany at the end of the war—at about two million, comprising volunteers, those drafted under the STO, and those held in POW camps, who were increasingly made to labor on farms, in mines, and in factories.

ıııııııııııııııııı

It was the third Christmas of the Occupation, and there was no longer any avoiding the fact: food, even for celebrations, was increasingly scarce and dearly expensive on the black market (now being run in the main by the Germans themselves or their acolytes in the French police). Raymond Ruffin's mother had managed to scrounge up one piece of meat for the whole family and had cooked a broth with vegetables that almost reminded them of past Christmas dinners. As soon as he was finished, young Raymond ran downstairs to share his holiday news with his best friend. On the floor separating their apartments, a door suddenly opened, and the excited boy bumped into a large German in uniform who was carrying trash, mostly empty champagne bottles. He was drunk, and as Raymond tried to move around him, he felt his shoulder grabbed, and a brusque voice said: *"Frohe Weihnachten!"* (Happy Christmas!) Frightened, the boy froze, then allowed himself to be led into the requisitioned apartment. There several Germans, apparently officers, were sitting around the dinner table with several German women, most likely *souris grises*—gray mice, as the French called the women who had accompanied the Occupying forces as secretaries, nurses, assistants, and so forth. They had been drinking for hours and kept speaking in German to the young boy, for whom apparently they had taken a sentimental liking. After all, it was *Weihnachtszeit*.

Raymond could not take his eyes off the table, laden with half-eaten terrines of foie gras and vegetables that were neither rutabagas nor Jerusalem artichokes, the humble ones that the average French citizen could most easily find. There were several desserts, and the fruit was bright with color, even at that time of year. Half-eaten steaks and turkey mesmerized him; he could feel his mouth watering. Finally, one of the women picked up a piece of white cake and offered it to the visibly hungry boy. "Take," she said. "It's Christmas." Raymond shook his head: "No." They all laughed, for they could see that he was dying to take a bite, his eyes and lips betraying his efforts at self-control. She pushed the dessert closer to him so he could smell, if not quite taste, it. He still said no. Why? Years later, he wrote that he did not know. Was it because he knew his family was upstairs and that they would have nothing, while he indulged himself? Or was it because he felt it was his patriotic duty to resist German blandishments? Finally, they tired of this docile young man and showed him out of the apartment, as puzzled as he as to why he had refused what he wanted more than anything at that moment: good food.

Any day could bring another potentially perilous moment of engagement. Running like feral animals down a crowded Parisian street, totally oblivious to who or what was in their way, Raymond and his friends saw one of their buddies suddenly trip beside a café table. In trying to catch himself, he grabbed the table, which overturned; coffee and liqueur spilled onto the tablecloth and onto a German officer. The soldier, whose foot had been too far out on the sidewalk, did not apologize; rather, he jumped up, cursed, grabbed Ruffin's friend, and slapped him a couple of times. Another friend, Sylvain, immediately

slapped the officer, and a brawl began among the three or four teenage boys and uniformed members of the Wehrmacht. The boys were
in serious danger, as those around them knew, of being thrown into
prison and perhaps winding up as hostages to be shot, should there be
a "terrorist" attack in the next few weeks.

Suddenly, two French police officers arrived and respectfully asked
the officers what had caused this fight. When told, they assured the
Occupiers that they would resolve this matter immediately; the officers gruffly took the boys off to the nearest police station. There the
officer in charge immediately lined them up. Rather than throwing
them into cells, he said, "Do you know how stupid you are to attack
German officers in full daylight? Are you ready to go to Fresnes or the
Cherche-Midi prisons? You've put me in a real situation here."

They looked abashed, and aside from a few "buts," no one said anything. The officer, obviously one of those Parisian policemen who
were appalled at how youngsters were being treated by the Germans,
then asked a cunning question: "OK, Sylvain, you slapped the German
officer because he had slapped your friend. Would you have done the
same thing if it had been a French businessman who had insulted your
buddy?" Thankfully, Sylvain saw his way out: "Of course, M. le commissaire. I was only responding emotionally to what I thought was an
injustice." "Good. I'll call your parents, while you boys are put into
cells until they come release you, and learn of your shenanigans."[36]

Such events happened daily, and the potential for trouble went well
beyond an overturned café table. Fun was still had with friends, but
at the same time the teenagers had to talk about provisions, clothing
(after all, they were all growing), and schoolwork. If they had Jewish
friends as well as Vichyist friends, there was rarely peace. There was
always something to worry about, even when one innocently went
out for a walk. Some would keep their eyes focused on the pavement
and try to avoid even casual encounters. Others would push the lim-
its, occasionally too far. And still others would realize that their loss

of freedom was a sign of a bigger issue—namely, the country's humiliation by the Germans—and react assertively, if not violently.

One day, again roaming the streets on their way to the hospital to visit a friend, Raymond and his buddies saw a scene that, thirty years later, was still bright in his memory. As they suddenly turned a corner, three large trucks came screeching to a halt in front of a large apartment house. Soon, men, women, and children—whole families—were being herded out of the building by the Groupe mobile de réserve, a French paramilitary group assigned to keep civilian order. As Raymond's small band stood quietly in place to watch, the officers began to separate the males from the females; defiant men were beaten as they climbed into one truck. Then the horror multiplied as the French policemen began separating children from their mothers, forcing the women into a second truck and the children into a third. The boys were quick to realize that these were Jews—the bright yellow stars on their chests told them that—and they stood transfixed, unable to turn away from the children screaming, clinging to their mothers' clothing and to each other. Mothers tried unsuccessfully to hide toddlers under their coats and dresses, begging the police to leave their babies with them. Finally, after the sad separations had been effected, the trucks drove off. No one explained to Ruffin and his gang what was going on, but they knew that the events they had witnessed transcended their own modest worries about getting a piece of Christmas cake or being dropped into a cell for a few hours. Being Jewish was a prison sentence at best, and something terrifying, they could only imagine, at worst.

||||||||||||||||||||

Certainly, imposing the work draft on young people to go to Germany had been a huge error by the Vichy government. The Germans made a similar error, one of the most significant proscriptions of the Occupation. About a year before, in May 1942, any Jew above the age of six

had been ordered to wear a yellow star over his or her left breast. This
cruel injunction brought visually, forcefully, to the attention of gentiles that the Nazis were racists; the yellow star ordinance provided
clear and unsubtle evidence of their aim to dehumanize a vulnerable ethno-religious group. Friends, colleagues, doctors, merchants,
nurses, caregivers, nannies, waiters—all suddenly had this mark on
them. The stars not only humiliated and angered the Jews themselves
(who had to pay for them with tickets from their clothing allotments)
but embarrassed their gentile neighbors. To its credit, no matter how
antisemitic it was in law, L'État Français refused to adopt the ordinance, which for a time pertained only in Occupied France.

When the yellow star ordinance was implemented in mid-1942,
the Church's hierarchy had continued its ostensible political neutrality and remained mute, though it did not rush to endorse the edict. In
fact, archbishops in major cities like Toulouse and Lyon purposely
and specifically called attention to the inhumanity of making this
distinction between Christians and Jews. Catholic families consulted their priests and had discussions about this new order: Should
they continue to invite Jewish friends or neighbors to their apartment for kids' birthday parties? Should they go out of their way to
befriend Jews? Memoirists remember, with still-lingering pain and
embarrassment, that wearing the star to school for the first time
taught them to recognize apprehension, even fear, on the part of
their gentile classmates. But often too the stars provoked small but
powerful acts of courage by gentile children, who reached out to hold
a hand, still played games with Jewish children, or walked home with
their newly marked friends. And not all of the priests and nuns of the
Church were enthralled with the Vichy government; some, as is now
well documented, went to their deaths defending Jews, communists,
and others who stood against the evil of the Third Reich.

For Ruffin and his band of friends, the effects of the yellow star ordinance became horribly intimate when their close friend Jackie, an

attractive teenager who had won the hearts of the boys in the group, turned up one afternoon with a yellow star on her dress. "Why are you wearing that?" they cried. "Because I'm a Jew," she calmly answered. They had never known, for they had never talked about their religious beliefs; they were more interested in what parties were being held and who was flirting with whom. Besides, Jackie's family was deeply assimilated and did not practice their religion except on rare holidays. *Still*, they thought, *she was their buddy; she would be all right. What's a silly star after all?*

But on Friday, July 17, 1942, the terror of what was happening around them finally hit the small clan. Raymond noticed that groups of his neighbors were gathering around concierges' posts, muttering. On his return, one of his friends told him the news: They had taken Jackie. Who had? asked Raymond. The cops, the French cops. But why? His exasperated friend asked: Haven't you been paying attention? They're rounding up Jews, taking them off to camp, and then sending them somewhere far away. The Jews and the communists, they're eliminating them! But she's only a kid, like us, answered Raymond. They're taking mothers and babies too, his friend almost yelled. And the old folks—everyone!

The friends heard that the rounded-up Jews had been taken to a gymnasium, where trucks would arrive to take them elsewhere. They ran to the site, clambered up to the third floor of a building across the street, and peered out at the drama on the street below. Soon, the trucks turned into the street, and gendarmes began loading women holding on to their babies, old men, girls, and boys. There was an eerie silence as the prisoners stepped up into the vehicles.

And suddenly there she was! I recognized her brown head of hair; yes, it was Jackie walking slowly beside her mother. . . . Her handicapped father limped behind her, a backpack on his shoulder. My buddies saw her . . . as we pressed our faces against the dirty window.

Sylvain tried desperately to open it, but it was rusted shut. He then started to run down the stairs; Claude and Robert grabbed and held him: "Stay here! You'll only get into trouble, and there aren't enough of us to fight the cops." Defeated, he sat on the steps, and sobbed piteously.

My eyes had not left Jackie; I saw her lifted into the truck by two gendarmes, and step inside. For the last time, I glimpsed the white oval of her face, and the mass of brown hair that rolled down her shoulders, and then ... nothing.[37]

Such a scene changed the boys' previously rather cavalier attitude toward the Occupier: "This sudden awareness of [the danger our friends were in] showed to what point our youthful consciences had been awakened, in spite of the massive dose of 'tranquilizers' that official propaganda was daily pouring over us."[38]

These memories of Ruffin's reveal how many adolescents, though not directly engaged in clandestine activities, were touched, inconvenienced, threatened, and infuriated by the actions of both the German Occupiers and their Vichy supporters. Once again, resistance is not always easily identified as such. Repeated small acts of courage, of friendship, or of basic humanity can often "resist" the status quo, slowly eating away at the already tenuous architecture of a dictatorial state. These impulses would push many youngsters into activities significantly more deleterious for those who would control them and their society. Indecisive J3s would suddenly find the courage to take on Europe's most powerful army.

———

CHAPTER SIX

Sudden Courage

———

Then there was the war, and I married it because there was nothing
else when I reached the age of falling in love.

—GUY SAJER, YOUNG GERMAN SOLDIER,
ON HIS WAY TO RUSSIAN FRONT

Just as many more Americans "remember" being at Woodstock or
at Martin Luther King's "I Have a Dream" speech than were actu-
ally there, so have many French adults "remembered" being routed
on the Champs-Élysées by Germans and French police at the aforementioned demonstration on November 11, 1940. That event remains one of the key dates of adolescent resistance to the German
Occupation and the new French state.

The fall of 1940 had been as beautiful as the summer; no one was
expecting the vicious winter of 1940–1941, which the Occupation
would exacerbate. School had been in session about a month. For
the first time since the armistice the previous June, students were
gathering up and down the Boulevard Saint-Michel in the Latin
Quarter to debate what had happened and either to devise options
for resisting the Occupier or to shout in resistance to the resisters
of the new French state. In general, most university students were
from upper-class families, and except in the humanities and the social sciences, most faculties, unlike those from the more egalitarian
lycées, were politically center or center-right. This student district

had not yet been identified with open rebellion, though the number of high schools with hundreds of restless students did concern the authorities. Still, the country had been relatively passive over the past four months, with only a few attacks against German telecommunication centers and no serious attacks against German personnel. Especially after *la Rentrée* (the return—both the beginning of the school year and the beginning of the professional year), youngsters would ride their bikes wildly in the streets, hooting and whistling at Germans in their fancy cars or sitting languidly in sidewalk cafés, but that was to be expected by the authorities, who held their breath that nothing more serious would disrupt the order and security they were commissioned to maintain.

In his detailed book about the events on and around November 11, 1940, the historian Maxime Tandonnet states plainly that "the French Resistance was born in the autumn and beginning of winter 1940"; the first major street demonstrations occurred in the Latin Quarter at that very moment.[1] The spark was the arrest on October 30 of Professor Paul Langevin, an eminent physics professor, a supporter of Dreyfus (the Dreyfus Affair had been "resolved" barely three decades before), and a strong believer in pacifist diplomacy. Langevin's public stands against fascism made him a target of the early Occupation, a period when such prominent "troublemakers" (not yet "terrorists") were quietly silenced.[*] The arrest and dismissal of Langevin brought the arguments and debates about the Occupation to a head. Left- and right-wing students began harassing each other, and signs and posters appeared on the walls of the universities and the *lycées*.

Word spread that there would be a gathering outside the Collège de France, where Langevin had held a prestigious professorship, on the

---

[*] Langevin was first imprisoned and then sent to the provinces to teach in a women's school of education. He would return to Paris a Resistance hero in 1944.

Rue des Écoles, in the center of the Latin Quarter. That demonstration, though small, was loud and at times violent as students supporting Langevin tried to gain entry into the Sorbonne and surrounding buildings. Soon bigger plans were concocted, and rumors grew that there would be a major student march on the Champs-Élysées on November 11, the anniversary of the French victory over the Germans in the Great War. Of course, these plans also reached the ears of the university authorities, who immediately published an announcement to all academic rectors, deans, and heads of faculty:

You know that the government has decided that this year, because of our nation's mourning [over the defeat], academic work will continue on November 11. . . . There will be no ceremony. The government counts on you to make sure that our students abstain from any demonstration, either on campus or off, which could harm the gravity of our mourning, but as well the respect we all have for our work.[2]

Imagine the response of professors who received this admonition from higher up. Most of them were not in any way engaged in actions against the Occupier or Vichy; they wanted to keep their jobs and continue to educate their students in the bubble of the Latin Quarter. Yet they knew, better than their leaders, that their students were increasingly concerned about the future of the nation—on both sides—and that to ignore what was happening would only bring this anxiety to the surface.

Not unexpectedly, student-produced tracts appeared that called for public demonstrations to protest the dismissals of Langevin and other professors and to warn the university leaders that such arbitrary acts by the Germans would be met with loud objection, if not something more serious. On the student-filled streets of the quarter, one poster read:

STUDENT OF FRANCE!

November 11 is still your national holiday!
Despite orders from the oppressors, it will remain a

DAY OF REMEMBRANCE!

Attend no classes.
Join in honoring the Unknown Soldier at 5:30 PM.
November 11, 1918, was the date of a great victory!
November 11, 1940, will mark an even greater one!

VIVE LA FRANCE!

(Recopy these lines, and distribute them!)

By noon on November 11, students—and others—began arriving at
the Rond-Point des Champs-Élysées, less than halfway up the long
avenue from the Place de la Concorde, where they would start a slow
march westward to the Arc de Triomphe. At this rotary stood a statue
of a vigorous Georges Clemenceau that had been placed there in 1932,
two years after the square was named for "the Tiger." The crowd grew
larger as young people and their elders poured out of the side streets,
which led primarily from the direction of the Left Bank to this special
spot on the Right. Protest signs were raised, and kids carried two fishing poles, called *gaules*—that is, *deux gaules = de Gaulle*. The V sign was
raised by hundreds of hands. Flower wreaths were respectfully laid at
the foot of Clemenceau's statue, and the students sang the outlawed "La
Marseillaise" (and the young communists sang the "Internationale,"
the anthem sung all over Europe by communist and socialist students).
The mood was celebratory; almost every *lycée* in central Paris had representatives, and professors mingled with students. As they passed
by the numerous cafés that lined the avenue, they would notice and
wave at the dumbfounded German soldiers who were lounging there,
most on leave from less glamorous assignments, stunned to silence

as they watched such a casual yet large opposition to their presence. (Estimates range between three thousand and five thousand marchers; there are no records or photographs that allow a firmer figure.)

There could no longer be any doubt: a major file of Parisian citizens was marching in opposition to Pétain's unfortunate armistice and to the presence of German soldiers in the capital city. Quickly, the French police began forming into groups of baton-carrying thugs, trying to disperse what was becoming a much larger crowd than had been predicted. Finally, whether called by the French or on their own initiative, German troops arrived. Much less patient with the crowd, they used their trucks and motorcycles to break it into groups; then machine guns began firing, first into the air. The crowd panicked and began running down the same streets that had brought them to the grand avenue, rushing to get back to the neighborhoods they knew better. But by then the French police had been reinvigorated; they followed, beat, and arrested dozens of young people.

The writer and professor Jean Guéhenno left an invaluable journal that he kept during the Occupation. He describes what happened next:

> Around 5:30 on November 11, Armistice Day, I went to the Champs-Élysées. I saw French policemen following German orders and taking away the flowers that passersby had thrown at the foot of the statue of Clemenceau. I saw German soldiers charge young people from the schools on the sidewalks of the avenue with their bayonets, and [French police] officers throw them to the ground. Three times I heard machine guns firing.[3]

Besides dozens of arrests, the Germans also closed down the Latin Quarter the next day. Guéhenno describes what that day felt like:

> Today the Sorbonne is closed. The students have been sent back to their provinces. Students from Paris are required to show up at their

local police stations every day. I feel such disgust that I cannot even
write in detail what I saw. Submerged by idiocy. At a moment like this
I don't even know what I think anymore. I no longer have any desire
to think anything. I need to start over from zero, and rebuild a mind
and a soul once again.[4]

Miraculously, and despite contrary charges from both sides, it appears that no one was killed or even seriously wounded. A few hundred young people were rounded up and sent, not to the local jails of the French police, but to the most notorious prisons in Paris. And as Guéhenno noted, the German military authorities came down on the students like a load of well-stacked bricks:

1.   *Classes are forbidden in all the universities and graduate schools*
of Paris until further notice. (Individual research of professors may
continue.)
2.   *All students who live with their parents in Paris must return*
home, and remain there until further notice. All French students
living in Paris must report daily to their local [meaning their home]
police station.
3.   *All police commissioners must daily report which students*
showed up for this requirement.

Since only a small number of *lycée* and university students had been involved in the march up the grand avenue, and only a handful arrested, the rest, who thought they were minding their own business, were stunned by the austerity of the punishment. Of course, this insult to their good behavior would only serve in the long run to bring more of them into the ranks of clandestinity, either benign or violent.

The significance of this march and the subsequent clash was underestimated at the time; the demonstration was seen as a useless provocation by a disorganized group of students. But there are several reasons why this was a misinterpretation. First, de Gaulle had recently complained that the French seemed to be passively accepting the consequences of the *Débâcle*. Yet here was the first major, and peaceful, show of resistance to both the Germans and the palliating propaganda of the Vichy regime. Second, through their chants and songs, the students boldly brought the name of Charles de Gaulle, along with his symbol, the Cross of Lorraine, to a larger public. (One of his closest aides has written that when he heard the story of the *deux gaules*, tears suddenly appeared in his notoriously emotionless eyes.) Third, the demonstration revealed the perturbation that was spreading through the *lycées*, even more than through the universities, as high school students became increasingly serious about confronting a pitiless government. The youth of France could no longer be ignored in their attempts to awaken the nation to the nefarious presence of the Germans. The very impudence of the youngsters as they poured into the Champs-Élysées was palpable evidence that the pleas, threats, and propaganda of the Vichy regime had so far had little effect on them, but in fact had been diluted by the experience of resisting and by the persistent mentoring of some of their most revered teachers.

Fourth, the parade had shown that the French Communist Party, even though outlawed, was still the best organized opposition, and the most successful at recruiting youngsters of both genders to its ranks. Though the parade was not a communist affair, the presence of communists would be used later as evidence of their passion and commitment to a cause larger than the rescue of France itself. And fifth, for the first time it was obvious to those who watched what happened, and to those who experienced it, that the French police were allies of the German Occupation Authority. For the most part, arrests were made by the French, and frequently the captured were sent into the hands of the Germans for questioning.

This event would leave an indelible memory for those who were there or who learned of it, for they were poised to resist the abolition

of the Third Republic and the humiliations of the German Occupation of their nation. Many citizens, and many youth, had tested the
authorities, measured their reactions, and their appetite for resistance had taken on a new edge.

In August 1941, a bit less than a year later, Germany was approaching Moscow at unheard-of speeds for a massive army. Stalin had released all communist parties throughout Europe from the shackles of
the August 1939 treaty with the Third Reich. At first, early resistance
by youngsters was disorganized, haphazard, and generally ineffective,
but the Occupying Authority was sensitive to it, for they knew that, if
supported by the populace, it could grow. In particular, they feared
that a steadily strengthening resistance would require more troops
in France, thereby affecting Germany's pressing military needs elsewhere. The war in the east took precedence over chasing young boys
and girls around the streets of large French cities. So the Occupying
Authority called on the French police and gendarmes to do their work
for them and monitor young "terrorists." Not until 1941 did reprisals
against partisan activities become severe, but by that time the earlier
groups had also become bolder, better organized, and more efficient at
clandestine communication.

|||||||||||||||||||||

The boy was handed a pistol compact enough to fit comfortably in his
small hand. It was probably a Beretta 6.35, about six and a half inches
long, with a barrel of less than four inches. Some called it a "lady's pistol," for it was accurate for only a few yards, but it was easy to con-
ceal. He was only fifteen (born in 1926) but looked twelve, yet he had
about him an air of seriousness that had impressed the older members
of a resistance team. Having had some training in grenade-throwing
(with rocks) but probably none in the use of firearms, he answered his
adult supervisor, who had queried his preparedness, "In order to kill

someone, you just fire, and that's it."[5] His friends laughed nervously and suggested that two of the band go with him in search of a German soldier whom young André Kirschen was to shoot. No, he would be less conspicuous alone, he countered. Not chary of killing an army or SS officer, the young communist did not want to shoot an enlisted soldier or a communist one like himself. No matter, his comrades answered, "just shoot a German." Putting the small arm in his pocket, he accepted the challenge.

Kirschen attended school the next morning (with the pistol in his pocket), and when classes finished, he set out in search of a target. (If the way violent resistance was integrated into mundane daily activities shocks us, then we should recall that such was life for many during the Occupation.) The previous week one of his comrades had fired three times at an officer, but none of the bullets had reached their mark. In fact, it was this failed assassin who had lent André the pistol he was now carrying. Walking up and down the streets of Paris, the young teenager at first had no luck; the only Germans he saw were walking in pairs. Perhaps his predecessors had been right: killing a German was not as easy as it sounded. Then, suddenly, he noticed

a magnificent German soldier descending the stairs to the Porte-Dauphine metro [on the western edge of the city in a posh neighborhood]. Doubtlessly an officer, with a very good-looking uniform, wearing a dagger. I follow him. No one in the corridor [leading to the tracks]. No more excuses not to complete the act.

I took out my arm, placed it on my hip, and shot him in the back. I was two meters from him. He fell into a heap. It took me a bit to realize what had happened. I looked left and right: no one. I ran toward the exit, scrambled up the stairway, and took the first street to my left, then the next on the right, and so forth. In a few minutes, I was

far from the metro stop. . . . I rendezvoused with my pals, and said
something stupid, as I handed over the pistol: "One bullet's missing." [6]

How had a fifteen-year-old boy, in 1941, become a would-be killer?[*]
Direct, credible, and moving, Kirschen's oral autobiography, *La Mort
à quinze ans* (Death at fifteen), composed when he was almost eighty
years old, is one of the most intimate accounts of how a young teenager found himself drawn to those who would violently confront the
Germans during the Occupation.[†] The communist youth groups that
André frequented were relatively homogeneous politically, but their
members were of different nationalities and spoke several languages,
with Yiddish tending to be the lingua franca. Again, not unlike young
Ruffin, André found himself moving from the margins to the center;
he was one of those who wanted to take more effective action than
pasting notices on Parisian walls. The French Communist Party had
spent the decade of the 1930s building a community of young, eager
adherents—male and female—who forged tight friendships. Maroussia
Naïtchenko, Thomas Elek, André Kirschen, his brother Bob, and Guy
Môquet had all known each other. In June 1941, when the Party ban
against resisting the Germans in France was lifted, these small, cohesive groups were ready and primed to move directly to action.

||||||||||||||||||||

Back in the summer of 1940, young André (called Hank by his family)
had been surprised when his older brother, Bob, a diligent, intelli-

---

[*] Did the soldier die? No. Kirschen would learn years later that he was a quarter-
master in the German navy and was probably only slightly wounded. He does not
tell us of the reactions to this attempt by the Germans, who at this time would have
certainly threatened to execute some hostages. His lack of success in this attack did
not lessen Kirschen's will to do something meaningful, which suffuses his memoir.

[†] Touchingly, the book was dedicated to "My brother Bob, and Maroussia [Naïtch-
enko]," who both played major roles in his clandestine life.

gent student, confessed to him that he was a member of a clandestine communist group and was considering becoming more active
in the Resistance, despite the admonitions from Moscow to avoid
any antagonistic actions against the German army. Then came the
question: would André like to be a member of the group? André's acceptance of this invitation was most likely not politically motivated;
he was elated to hang out with the "big boys," alongside his revered
older brother. Bob showed him that he had a cache of hidden tracts
in his room, and André suggested that they use a toy printing press
to publish more of the leaflets. (These little printing presses soon
disappeared from toy shops across Paris as other teenagers had the
same idea.) Such modest acts of resistance were still a lark for many
of the adolescents involved, but the next steps taken would have
heavy consequences for André and his family.

A tight group of fervently communist youngsters began meeting
regularly in Bob's room, among them Maroussia Naïtchenko. The
Kirschen apartment was in the upper-class sixteenth arrondissement, between Avenue de la Grande Armée and Avenue Foch, where
many of the luxurious apartments had been confiscated by senior
German officers and diplomats. The neighborhood was not far from
the Hôtel Majestic, Wehrmacht headquarters for all of Occupied
France. To say that these youngsters were operating under the noses
of the Gestapo, the SS, and the Wehrmacht is not to exaggerate. At
first, there were games of hide-and-seek with the French police as the
youngsters shouted out at public meetings or mingled in crowds of
supportive students after professors at the Sorbonne had been fired,
or they brought flowers to the Père-Lachaise graves of those who had
established Europe's first communist government in 1871. At the movies, when the newsreels of German propaganda came on, they would
boo and stomp their feet until the lights went up, and the projectionist
stopped. André Kirschen recounts that they were not afraid, for the
arrests and executions that would mark most of the Occupation had

not yet begun. And as Kirschen later reflected: "We were not aware of the gravity of what was waiting for us."[7]

It was fun with frissons. The youngsters also enjoyed the solidarity of their peers and the umbrella of adult approbation that came from the leaders of the French Communist Party. At the same time, they couldn't have cared less whether a comrade was a Stalinist or a Trotskyist, or whether Engels or Marx was the most important theorist. Like the Catholic, Jewish, and Protestant members of the group, they were interested in hanging out while devising uniformly naive schemes to harass the new French state and the Germans. As the historian Gilles Perrault observes in his interview with Kirschen: "The young Communists in the working-class neighborhoods of Paris lived in a bubble created for them by the Party. They saw it as living in a people's commune."[8]

But reality interrupted this adolescent idyll. One day in November 1940, returning from school, André saw a band of police in his apartment house's stairway. He followed them up to his parents' apartment, where his brother was being interrogated. Compromising tracts and pamphlets had been found in his room. Bob could not deny his participation in an underground group. He had not been betrayed, but the arrest of a group leader had revealed the organizational chart of the team, and Bob's name was prominent. It was only his age that kept the younger Kirschen from being dragged down to the police station as well. Bob was found guilty and sentenced to ten months in prison for "illegal" actions against the state—mostly, in his case, for passing out clandestinely printed leaflets.[*]

At the time, it was not yet generally known that to be arrested and convicted to a relatively minor sentence was often a path to death.

---

[*] In August 1942, Bob, with his father, would be executed at Mont-Valérien as hostages in reprisal for attacks on German soldiers, and also as relatives of a known "terrorist," André, himself arrested in March 1942.

The front page of *Avant Garde*, 1944. The communists used Môquet (notice misspelling) for propaganda purposes throughout the Occupation. *Bridgeman Images*

The Môquet Metro station in Paris's seventeenth arrondissement.

The Guy Môquet stamp, printed early in Sarkozy's presidency, 2008. *Author photo*

Léon Blum, the first socialist and Jewish prime minister of France. *Agence Meurisse*

A fort in the extensive Maginot Line of fortifications. © *IWM (O 227)*

General Charles de Gaulle at a BBC microphone in 1940. *Bridgeman Images*

The flag of Free France with the Cross of Lorraine.

MARECHAL PETAIN

Maréchal Philippe Pétain, the head of L'État Français (Vichy) government.

Pierre Laval, twice prime minister of the Vichy government during Occupation. *Agence Meurisse*

The infamous handshake between Pétain and Hitler, October 1940. *Bridgeman Images*

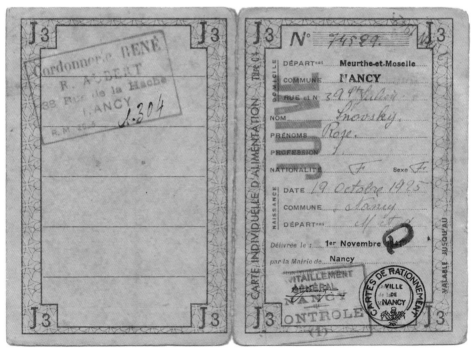

A J3 ration card for a Jewish adolescent. *With thanks to Laurent Nesly.*

A Vichy poster showing ancient Gaul protecting a young supporter of Pétain. *Mémorial de la Shoah*

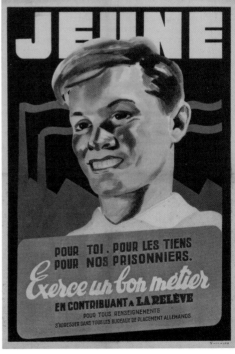

A Vichy poster urging youth to volunteer to work in Germany. *Mémorial de la Shoah*

A Vichy poster asking youth to join the Jeunes du Maréchal. *Mémorial de la Shoah*

A Vichy stamp in honor of POWs still held by Germans. *Author photo: from collection of Philippe Rochefort*

Jacques Lusseyran, who became a professor after the war. *Bridgeman Images*

The front page of the clandestine paper *Défense de la France*, July 14, 1943.

The front page of the clandestine paper *Défense de la France*, December 15, 1943.

A *Ronéotype* (mimeograph) machine used for clandestine printing. *Author photo*

André Kirschen, at fifteen years old. *Mémorial de la Shoah*

A sculpture of Jean Moulin, the coordinator of the Resistance for de Gaulle, in Aix-en-Provence. *Marcel Mayer*

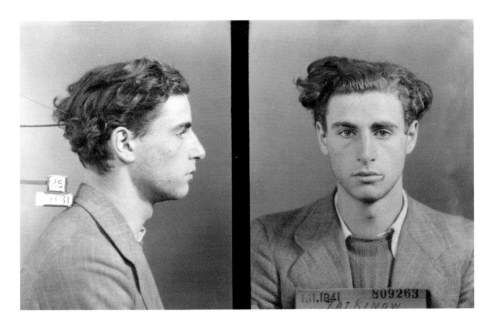

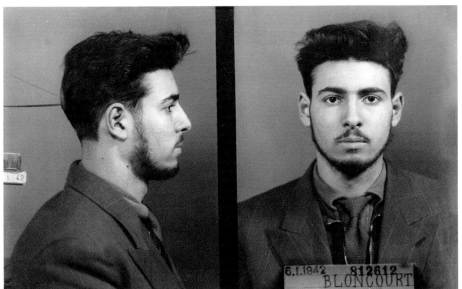

Top: Fernand Zalkinow, nineteen, was tried in the Palais-Bourbon trial and later executed. *Préfecture de la Police*

Tony Bloncourt, twenty, was tried in the Palais-Bourbon trial and later executed. *Préfecture de la Police*

Geneviève de Gaulle, niece of Charles de Gaulle, following her return from Buchenwald. *Bridgeman Images*

Robert Lynen, as a young actor in *Poil de carotte. Bridgeman Images*

Thomas Elek holding a wrench used to sabotage rail lines, as posed by the Germans. *Mémorial de la Shoah*

Executions at Mont-Valérien of the so-called Manouchian group, of which Elek was a member.
Mémorial de la Shoah

Training young scouts to use arms.
Bridgeman Images

Explaining weapons to young *màquisards. Bridgeman Images*

Hidden Jewish children, working in the fields. *Mémorial de la Shoah*

Jewish *màquisards* in Tarn. *Mémorial de la Shoah*

Young *màquisards* in the Haute-Loire. *Mémorial de la Shoah*

Màquisards of Camp #15 in the Vercors Maquis. *Mémorial de la Shoah*

A monument to the thirty-five young men shot by the Germans on August 16, 1944—only nine days before the liberation of Paris—in the Bois de Boulogne. *Author photo*

Close-up of above. *Author photo*

One of many plaques throughout Paris memorializing youth who died during the liberation of the city. *Author photo, thanks to Richard Beban*

A wall of the Mémorial de la Shoah in Paris covered with the names of gentiles who helped save Jews during the Occupation. *Author photo*

The boys justified to themselves that the posters the Germans put up naming those executed as "terrorists" did not apply to them. They seemed oblivious to the ad hoc "hostage code," promulgated in the tense year of 1941–1942, that had doomed other youngsters, such as Guy Môquet. The code called for the arrest of miscreants and their possible execution as hostages whenever a German soldier was shot or attacked. For Bob, branded as a communist, Jew, and "terrorist," this meant being transferred, after serving his ten-month sentence in the harsh environment of La Santé prison, to Les Tourelles, a better prison camp, and finally to the notorious transit camp outside of Paris, Drancy, where hundreds of Jews waited unknowingly for transport to the death camps in the east, especially Auschwitz.

Even when arrests became more frequent and friends of his disappeared for a while—or forever—André, taking advantage of his very youthful appearance, continued his resistance work. Several friends would later cease their clandestine activities, afraid of what might happen to them or to their families, but he persevered. Decades later, Kirschen wondered why his parents had not insisted that he stop his own underground activities after the arrest of his brother. They worried, he knew, but his passion was strong enough to counter parental dissuasion. At any rate, they did not prevent him from leaving and returning at odd times during the day and night. He also intuited that his parents were secretly proud of him for his efforts.

As his bold exploits continued, André became well known among young communist high schoolers. He would speak to groups and encourage them to stand firm. Again, he did not see the promulgation of Party propaganda as his mission, but rather the encouragement of young people to resist, to stand against the increasingly violent representatives—both German and Vichy—of evil. There were few communist families in the sixteenth arrondissement, but they were an influential group who came from wealthy bourgeois families, lived in large apartments, and were well educated. These would be the leaders, he thought, of a powerful new force of resistance. But it was a small number, and until June 1941, the accursed Soviet Union–Third Reich treaty remained a strong brake on anti-German activity.

|||||||||||||||||||||

Violent actions increased in number in 1941–1942 and were not limited to the young communist cadres. Paul Collette had joined the French navy in 1938, at age eighteen, because he sensed that war was imminent. During the Norwegian campaign of the spring of 1940, he found himself in the North Sea, fighting the German navy. At one point his ship was torpedoed and went down fast. Many of the well-trained sailors managed to cling to lifeboats and lifesavers as they waited for rescue by the British navy. Suddenly, German aircraft came roaring over the horizon and pitilessly shot at the survivors. Collette survived, but as he wrote shortly after the war, "it was at that moment that hatred for Germans entered my heart. . . . I decided that I would avenge my murdered buddies."[9]

After the armistice, Collette was demobbed and suddenly found himself without a job, or a clear future. He tried to find a link to some resistance group, but without much success beyond volunteering to distribute leaflets, which he did, though with little enthusiasm. Yet his analysis of the situation was evolving—as it was with increasing numbers of the population—into a subtle awareness of who the real and most hateful enemy was: not the Germans now in his country, but the right-wing government that had enabled their rather smooth Occupation.

The traitors were not the Germans. They had vanquished the French, but as soldiers, face-to-face. . . . The real traitors are those despicable Frenchmen who, not content to see our nation founder, were now selling it, without scruples. Those traitors needed to be

*harmed; a Frenchman should make them realize that the whole
nation hated them, wanted them thrown out. A few needed to be removed as an example so that others will continue what I began.*[10]

Having seen the light, Paul decided to assassinate a Vichy bigwig as an
unmistakable act of resistance by an independent Frenchman, under
no one's orders but his own.

In June 1941, after Hitler's invasion of the Soviet Union, the
more radical fringe of the Vichy contingent, with the concurrence
of the SS, formed the Légion des volontaires français contre le Bolchévisme (LVF). These French volunteers wore German uniforms,
marched under the swastika flag, and fought on the eastern front
against the Russians. The official launching of the group was to be
held at Versailles, with all of the major figures of the government
present. Pierre Laval had been invited, though this was in August
1941, while he was still out of office; at the last moment, he decided
to attend. Collette, who had falsely indicated that he might join the
LVF, had been given a ticket to the event, and when he saw Laval
suddenly appear with the other dignitaries, he could not believe his
good fortune. Pulling from under his jacket a small-caliber pistol,
he shot five times, wounding Laval seriously. "I had succeeded. An
immense joy filled me within the space of a few seconds, and I realized what a perfect happiness comes from the satisfaction of a job
well done."[11]

Both the Vichy and German guards had scattered at the shots, but
when they returned fire, Laval purportedly yelled, "Don't harm him."
Laval was sent to the hospital, where he almost died; one bullet, lodged
close to his heart, was left inside, too delicately positioned to remove.
Collette was immediately interrogated by the police. At first they
thought he had been a member of some established resistance group,
or perhaps this was another part of the plot that had recently killed a

young German cadet in Paris just a few days before.* But Collette was direct and honest in his rationale for having shot at Laval and others. It was patriotic to blow up ammunition dumps or a convoy, he argued, but it was unethical to aim at individual soldiers who were only doing their job and following orders. Besides, killing a German officer would bring the execution of fifty hostages in reprisal. But assassinating a traitor was another thing. Any German patriot would have done the same in his own country. "That's why I shot Laval."[12]

Collette was tried by the Vichy judiciary and sentenced to death. For reasons still unclear, that sentence was commuted to life in prison. Who approved this decision? Pétain? The government? The Germans? He never learned. Collette spent the rest of the war being moved among prisons in France and was finally sent to a camp in Germany, but he survived the war. He learned from other prisoners and from sympathetic guards that his act had resonated throughout Europe. Free French radio and other broadcasters "from Boston to Moscow" had "kept millions breathless by showing that the Vichy government was not the people of France. To the contrary, the latter, conscious of its duty, was in rebellion against those who pretended to impose a reign of national-socialism."[13]

The story of this young man is gripping in and of itself, but it also serves to illustrate how independent and idiosyncratic many acts of resistance were. Nevertheless, "lone-wolf" actions—that is, individual, noncoordinated, but serious actions—were rare. For greater and sustained resistance, a team was necessary, and eager would-be resisters would generally first turn, as we saw in the case of Jacques Lusseyran, to their network of friends. These closed circles were plentiful and not always overlapping. Much official and academic history since the war

---

* In the first public assassination of a German officer, young resisters had shot and killed a German naval cadet in the Paris Barbès-Rochechouart metro station a week earlier.

has argued that the Resistance was a monolithic but well-organized, well-led organization. The variety of motives and actions befuddles even the most objective of those efforts—as it did the leader of the Free French.* As de Gaulle gained prestige and support, he began to worry more and more about the state of resistance activities within France, which he watched with a jaundiced eye. There was no unity, and very little communication, among the various groups, which included communists, immigrants, rightists, and Gaullists. They often acted independently, even competing with each other. Their clandestine publications carried a bewildering variety of messages and instruction that often confused those who were desperate for information and who might have wanted to participate, even peacefully, in some sort of resistance. Because the groups were poorly armed, they often put themselves in danger in order to rectify this lack of matériel. They all wanted some sort of recognition or support from London, which hesitated to deliver arms to any group without a coordinated leadership.

Early on, de Gaulle had established an intelligence office, known as the Bureau central de renseignements et d'action (BCRA), as a means to coordinate and control clandestine operations under the Free French flag. He sent his most accomplished masterful bureaucrat, Jean Moulin, to France several times to effect a difficult coordination of all major resistance groups, which would later be stereotyped as *the* Resistance. The first meeting of its leaders was held in Paris near Saint-Germain des Prés, in the sixth arrondissement, on May 27, 1943. There have been many debates about the effectiveness of this organization, especially since so many independent operators—for example, the volatile Maquis

---

* At the Musée de l'Ordre de la Libération at the Musée de l'Armée of the Invalides in Paris, there is a description of the Resistance: "From 1940 to 1944, progressively, showing inventiveness, in the midst of immense difficulties, the interior Resistance [notice capital R] organized itself into networks, movements, and Maquis, then coordinated and unified until the battles for the Liberation." This is an idealized, and misleading, description of a chronically disorganized group of networks and individual operators.

groups and immigrant groups—were minimally involved. But there is general agreement that this first attempt at coordinating strategy was quite helpful immediately before and after the D-Day invasion a year later. Still, as it became clearer that France would be free of the Germans and that L'État Français would sink into ignominy, resistance networks began to joust for postwar political position. From the Normandy invasion until the liberation of France and after, blood would be shed as competing cadres attempted to assert political dominance over one another.

||||||||||||||||||||||||

There is, and always will be, debate among historians of the Resistance, as there was among its veterans in the 1950s, 1960s, and 1970s, about how influential the French communist youth were at the outset of the Occupation. Robert Gildea, the respected student of France during the Occupation, is quite blunt in his appraisal: "Communists were perhaps the most radically inclined to resistance, although the path from [French Communist] Party . . . was a complicated one and not all took the same route."[14] There is no gainsaying that the youth leagues of the French Communist Party during the 1930s were instrumental in educating their adherents—girls as well as boys—who signed up in their early teens. They met regularly, not only for indoctrination but also for social reasons. In some ways, these groups, led by older adults, were the counterpart to the scouts, who were doing the same thing but who were not as fundamentally ideological. The communist youth groups went camping, had parties, organized dances, and cycled in groups in the countryside. Several members as young as sixteen even joined the International Brigades to fight for the Spanish Republic during that nation's brutal civil war (1936–1939). The police estimated in the late 1930s that there were thousands of members of the French Communist Party ready to take up the fight to preserve the French Republic against the quasi-fascist right. This was the eager cohort itching to continue the fight against fascism in Occupied France as early as June 1940.

Consequently, when the Soviet Union had directed these cadres not to fight the Germans between August 1940 and June 1941, the only way these youngsters could relieve their frustrations was to take on the Vichy government itself. There was little violence during this first year of the Occupation; most of the communist youngsters' efforts lay in printing and distributing tracts, putting up posters, writing on walls, and keeping the embarrassment of the *grande débâcle* before the attention of the French.

||||||||||||||||||||

A few years ago, Pamela Druckerman wrote an article in the *New York Times* about one of the most interesting personalities to come out of the knotted story of the French resistance. His name was Adolpho (he had been born in Argentina) Kaminsky (he was of eastern European Jewish stock).[15] He was only thirteen when his parents, who had emigrated from Poland, had to leave Paris, not because they were Jewish, but because his father had been involved with a communist journal and the French government was increasingly suspicious of the French communists who had supported Russia during its ill-fated invasion of Finland (1939–1940). The events in Nazi Germany, especially *Kristallnacht* in 1938, had caused them to feel uncomfortable in a large metropolitan area, and the Kaminskys, more prescient than most Jews, fled the capital city for Vire, in Normandy's Calvados region.* Their arrival in the small town (made possible by his father's brother, who lived in Vire) doubled the Jewish population of the town. But they were well received, and the children soon finished their schooling. (Fourteen was the terminal age for public schooling in France.)

---

* *Kristallnacht* (so named for all the broken windows) was an organized action throughout Germany in November 1938 led by brown-shirted thugs who damaged

In his last year in high school, Adolpho and a friend began printing a school newspaper, an experience that provided him with an
education in presses and inks and paper, knowledge that he would
exploit later as the most important forger in the Resistance. Soon
both Adolpho and his older brother, Paul, were working, first for their
irascible uncle, who sold millinery in the town market, and then for a
small factory that manufactured airplane instrument panels. There
Adolpho came into contact with politically sensitive members of the
working classes, and the fate of one especially, Jean Bayer, would
mark a major step in his rapid advance toward adulthood.

"Then, one day, they arrived. It was June 1940." Adolpho had been
biking along a road when he was suddenly confronted with a column
of German tanks:

> Brand new, as if they had just rolled off the production line. And the
> soldiers all in gleaming boots and impeccable uniforms. Then I un-
> derstood what my father meant when, on seeing the French draftees
> in their uniforms that didn't match, some without helmets, he said
> "This time it's certain. We've had it. We're not going to win the war
> with an army like that." [16]

Immediately life changed for the village and its Jewish citizens
as the Germans billeted themselves in Vire, anticipating an invasion
of England. The aircraft factory closed briefly, only to reopen under
German management to produce matériel for the German air force.
Immediately, all Jews were fired, and Adolpho and his brother were
rudely marched past their friends to the exit; their coworkers showed
their solidarity by hooting at the German police. Some had probably

---

the shop windows of Jewish-owned businesses and burned down synagogues. International outrage over this early harbinger of Hitler's "final solution" was unanimous, but had little effect.

not known until then that the boys were Jewish. Now unemployed, they still had to earn some meager living to help their parents. As it would turn out, racist policies had just freed a young man to pursue another profession, one that would make him one of Germany's most wanted men in Occupied France.

Adolpho answered an ad for an apprenticeship with a dyer (a *tein-turier*), who specialized in cleaning clothing marked by difficult stains. Rather than remove them, he would often re-dye the garments. But his new apprentice soon discovered ways to remove the original stain— blood, wine, ink—and return the original item to its owner as if it had never been damaged. His study of the chemical reactions that could change colors, and the chemical principles in general, would inform his future resistance work against the Germans. "I'd found my vocation."[17]

Soon the young man became a local celebrity, for he had also figured out how to make soap (then very rationed) and candles (increasingly necessary), and how to "clean" salt that had been discarded because of contamination from other metals. The latter process was especially useful, as the Germans had severely rationed salt, fearing that local farmers would use it to cure pork and then hide the meat from the Occupiers, who continued to send three-quarters of French livestock to Germany. Adolpho "cleaned" so much salt that he became a hero to the wily Norman farmers (and also provided his family with enough food to live somewhat more comfortably).

By 1942, now sixteen, Kaminsky had befriended the local pharmacist, who helped him continue his education in chemistry. In late 1940, when Adolpho heard that Jean Bayer had been executed for subversive activities, he learned the brutal truth: the Occupiers treated opposition seriously, and mercilessly. He itched to do something effective against these foreign soldiers and often expressed his wish to neighbors and friends he could trust. It turned out that the pharmacist for whom he worked was a Gaullist agent using his shop as a cover for clandestine acts. Sensing the youngster's anti-German sentiments, he asked Adolpho if he was interested in making items more important than soap or candles. The hint was obvious, and the boy affirmed enthusiastically that he indeed was.

> *From that day on [late 1942], as well as bars of soap, candles, and salt, I made more harmful products that corroded the transmission lines, and made little railroad parts rust, and detonators as well. Being involved in the sabotage meant for the first time I didn't feel entirely impotent following the death of my mother [most likely pushed from a train by Germans on her way to Paris] and my friend Jean. At least I had the feeling that I was avenging them. And I was proud; I was in the Resistance.*[18]

Then terror: in the summer of 1943, Adolpho and his whole family were arrested and sent to Drancy. Through his brother Paul's clever persistence, the Argentine consul was warned, and after three months in detention, the whole Kaminsky family was released, as Argentine citizens, even though they were Jewish.* Lost in Paris, without ration tickets or housing, they eventually found succor from others and began to take up their lives again, only to be rearrested soon afterward and returned to Drancy. Bureaucratic confusion again allowed their release and return to Paris. The destitution and fear that he witnessed in that transit concentration camp marked Adolpho for the rest of his life, and to have survived two imprisonments there most likely added to the lifelong guilt he carried as a survivor.

Back in Paris again, he soon joined a resistance network in the capital, and quite by happenstance his superiors found out that he

---

* They at least did not have to wear yellow stars. Jews from neutral or German allied nations were exempt from this requirement, another example of the idiosyncrasies of racial politics. Argentina, a nonbelligerent during the war, had large pockets of influential German immigrants. The Reich wanted to keep that South American nation as "neutral" as possible.

was a specialist in inks and ink removal, paper preparation, photography, and other skills that made up the artisanal armory of a forger. Setting up two laboratories in separate locations in the Latin Quarter, Adolpho became the master forger of northern France, known not only for his exquisite precision in imitating official documents—ID cards, ration tickets, passports, birth certificates, baptism and wedding certificates—but for getting the job done immediately, always a requisite of such clandestine work. As the tide began turning against the Germans in 1943, they began vigorously rounding up Jews rather than concentrating on protecting the Reich from the increasingly aggressive and well-trained armies of the Soviet Union. By his almost continuous forgeries of official documents, Adolpho put sand in the gears of that nefarious bureaucracy. His work, and that of two or three close comrades, saved hundreds of lives—especially of Jewish children—during the rest of the war.

As the armed resistance became more active, easier travel within France by agents was essential; no one could move even just a few blocks or kilometers from home without having to show an ID card. London was parachuting agents into France, all of whom needed new identities. Adolpho became the key to a door that opened France to groups of bold agents, spies, and warriors smelling the defeat of Germany and wishing to advance it. In enabling the resistance activities to run smoothly, Adolpho never complained, nor did he ever consider quitting his work as a forger. As he said after a long pause when asked why he worked so hard, so courageously even after the Liberation, he remembered the liberated death camps he had visited and their dying inmates. And those who had died during the Occupation. How could he not offer his skill as a forger when so many had perished?

||||||||||||||||||

Obviously, Jews had a major reason for joining the Resistance: their lives, and those of their families, were at stake. In France, unlike in

Russia, there were no squads of German soldiers—the infamous SS Einsatzgruppen (deployed task forces)—especially trained to line Jews up in front of their own graves, then shoot them. (It is estimated that more Jews, Roma, and communist partisans were killed by these forces than by gas in the concentration camps spread across eastern Europe.) But the diligence of the French police and their German minders did lead to Jews in larger numbers being taken in roundups, sent to transit camps, such as Drancy outside of Paris, and then put in cattle cars to end up in labor and death camps.

As a consequence, Jewish youth, banded together in secret groups at school or, while it lasted, their own aforementioned scouting organization, began resisting by printing and publishing two-page newspapers that tried to run down the rumors coming out of the east, forging papers, finding hiding places for the most vulnerable, and, especially, taking care of the hundreds of children who had lost their parents or whose parents wanted them sent to safety. They were proud of their work and diligent in organizing, but they carried an extra burden should they be caught: being Jewish, they would themselves be sent immediately to Drancy or another holding camp in France and eventually transported eastward. No trial would take place, unless it was for show; no special dispensations would be possible, not even for the well connected; and no bribes would be sufficient to challenge the authorities. Unlike many other *résistants*, Jewish resisters would have no escape.

Those Jews who resisted by hiding abandoned children had even more to worry about, for not only were they in danger of being discovered, but so were those they were hiding. Jean-Raphaël Hirsch, an eminent physician in Paris, has written a chilling biography of his father, Sigismond—and thus an autobiography as well. Hirsch's book *Réveille-toi papa, c'est fini!* (Wake up papa, it's over!) also introduces the youngest *résistant* in our book, Jean-Raphaël himself, who, at the age of ten, was suddenly a liaison for the groups taking care of the children hiding throughout the region.

Sigismond and Berthe Hirsch had taken every precaution, even as the local Vichy agents and their Gestapo colleagues began to close in on those who were hiding Jewish children. After arriving in France as immigrants from Romania, they had immediately volunteered in 1940 to run a network that was keeping track of over four hundred Jewish orphans sent to southwestern France for safety. They found an isolated house, with a gated entrance, and kept a low profile as just another refugee couple from Paris.

And then there was Dick, a watchful, protective dog who barked at every stranger who came near the house. But that morning Dick had trotted off to visit the village, after chewing through the cloth "chain" that had attached him to the gate. With the warning system gone astray, the Gestapo's vehicle was able to unobtrusively slide past the gate and park next to the house. Quietly, agents moved toward the front door; rushing in, guns drawn, they asked the young housekeeper where the Hirsches were. Easily found, they were just rising from their bed, still in their nightclothes. Thinking quickly, Sigismond rushed toward a large window, jumped out, and ran toward the woods. This distraction allowed Berthe to take the lists of hidden children, kept in her baby's bassinet, and throw them into the room's stove. That act alone probably saved the lives of dozens of Jewish children. Soon, Sigismond was recaptured, and he and Berthe were taken to Toulouse, put in jail, and interrogated and tortured for weeks. Their ten-year-old son, Jean-Raphaël, known as Nano, was off on an overnight mission to deliver news to locally hidden children. When he headed home on his bike later that morning, a friend stopped him so that he would not return to the now-ransacked house. Reluctantly, he turned around to pedal to his aunt's house, where he would hide. Nano would never see his mother again.*

Despite the dangers involved, Hirsch *père* had needed efficient and

---

* They would eventually be deported to Auschwitz, where Berthe died; Sigismond survived, and after the war returned to Paris to live a long, though bereft, life. The

faithful help to keep track of the dozens of hiding places where Jewish children were lodged. So, as Nano recounts in his memoir, his father decided to recruit his own son to be a liaison between him and the various scout and Maquis groups for which he was responsible.

> *It was [in 1943] that—we are never better served than by our family— my father had the notion to give me a bike, and to include me in his clandestine work. Ten years old, and doubtlessly one of the youngest résistants in France. I was expected to carry messages to all of the children for whom my father had responsibility, and to do so on almost impassable paths leading to isolated farms, difficult to reach.*[19]

Nano was what was called an *agent de liaison*, a messenger between and among groups of resisters, and to those who were hiding children. On the one hand, it was not a very dangerous job—unless one was caught, of course. Children, for quite a long while, were generally ignored by the security police; if out after curfew, they were picked up and quickly returned to their parents after a frightening night in jail. On the other hand, the danger for the networks was that they had a good deal of information in their heads about hiding places, Maquis camps, and group leaders.

Nano was exceptional, but he was not the only child engaged in such work. Though rare, there were a few whole families engaged in clandestine activities. They were mostly Jewish, of course, but some non-Jewish families were quite sensitive to the plight of their fellows; it seemed to them that, from both a moral and functional perspective, it was inappropriate to exclude any son or daughter, or brother or sister,

---

younger Hirsch became a successful surgeon; Sigismond's rich and detailed memoir, written seventy years after the events, offers a deeply moving history of Jewish resistance in southern France. (The title of Jean-Raphaël's book refers to the nightmares his father had for the rest of his life.)

from having the opportunity to stand for something larger than the family itself. At first, before the Germans took over the Unoccupied Zone in November 1942, it had been relatively easy to house the children in what amounted to orphanages, run by either Protestants or Catholic sisters with the help often of young Jewish men and women. Boys and girls cohabitated, and the local communities, especially in southern and southwestern France, paid little attention to their presence. Hundreds of Jewish children were hidden and saved during this period through the good graces of French men and women who found hunting for children a repulsive trait in the Germans, but especially in their fellow citizens who were loyal to Vichy's laws. We have seen how the best-organized and most reliable organization was the network of young members of the Éclaireurs israélites de la France, the Jewish boy (and girl) scouts. These youngsters had been scouts since before the war began, and their leaders had been scouts before them, so as of May 1940, this was the most cohesive and best-trained group of youngsters ready to confront the Germans. The EIF scouts would prove invaluable in moving the hidden children from one sanctuary to another.

With the German army's occupation of southern France in November 1942 came the imposition of stricter laws regarding Jewish citizens and noncitizens. Suddenly, the orphanages, usually in large abandoned schoolhouses or chateaus, became too dangerous—a single raid could capture dozens of the children, who would then be sent off to camps in France and eventually put on trains to eastern Europe. The scouts' efforts to disperse the children and place them, one by one, throughout the district was made even more difficult, and dangerous, by the fact that many of the children who had sought refuge in France spoke only German. When Roger Fichtenberg was asked at a 1994 conference whether these efforts could have succeeded without the training that the Jewish Scouts had received, he answered, "No, it would have been impossible."

As the Occupation continued, local bureaucrats were increasingly pressured by the Reich to produce Jews for Germany's intensifying efforts at racial cleansing. Word spread about which farms and which convents might be hiding these children. Simultaneously, the work of constantly transferring them from place to place, usually by foot or on bicycles, was taking its toll on the young scouts, many of them scarcely older than the children they were protecting. As the Maquis began to grow in 1943, especially after the imposition of the draft for forced labor in Germany, some of the children, as they approached or entered their teens, began to slide quietly into the forests, where they were reluctantly admitted into underground groups. Some could serve as messengers, and others could help maintain the camps, but the ever-vigilant guerrilla forces could not handle a large number of children.

Sigismond Hirsch had begun his work almost immediately after the armistice was signed, and his leadership and amazing success at hiding young Jews would last until his arrest in 1943. His son remembers:

> So many years after the events, it remains difficult to imagine the extraordinary work [of these] benevolent young people between the ages of 20 and 30, having their own problems to deal with. They did the impossible: to hide in the wink of an eye children and teenagers, or to re-hide them. . . . Each case was different, for each hidden child demanded urgent and specific action. They had to be taken from schools to parsonages, from high schools to convents, from an isolated farm to another farm. Some were kept in place, others moved, and all kept dispersed [throughout the region]. To hide someone meant, more often than not, re-hiding them later, often several times. . . . Each time, a new host had to be convinced, a child had to be reassured that this new move was necessary.[20]

And more than a new host had to be found: new false papers had to be created, new names invented, and new liaisons established with local citizens, both in the Resistance and not.

Girls were quite successful in this sort of clandestine work. As we have seen elsewhere, they were even more ignored by the police than young boys, and if they were older, they were urged to pretend to flirt, to dispel the idea that they were on any but the most innocent of errands. Jean-Raphaël Hirsch has an especially poignant view of the young women and girls who were as committed as the boys to saving children: "One cannot but admire them, [for] these female children too had the sad feeling that they were skirting their youth."[21]

This idea of a lost childhood, not only for those being hidden but for those who were instrumental in hiding them, is recurrent in Hirsch's memoir. The psychological and moral effects on these youngsters were profound. Their childhood—and Hirsch's—had been lost, never to be remembered as a time of security, freedom, and days of mostly trivial threats when "torture" was nothing more than the pain of an unrequited crush, not the relentless pounding of a Nazi cudgel, and high stress was taking a school exam, not watching in horror as friends were led away, never to return.

In 1942, while still living with his family in Paris, nine-year-old Hirsch had been forced to don a yellow star. His mother, while sewing it onto his school uniform, admonished him to wear it without shame, to be proud of his Jewish heritage. But that attitude lasted only until he was first taunted on the school playground:

That star soiled the world of Jews as well as that of the goyim; it soiled the entire world. And a child perceives this quite clearly. Indeed, having to wear the star meant that he was no longer a child. He had suddenly become an adult, prematurely an adult whose childhood, whose purity had been stolen. In effect, I was no longer

a child; I was no longer pure; I was no longer kind; I was ill—I was
smoldering with rage.[22]

Later, as he rode fearlessly through the hills of Languedoc, searching
for places to hide more vulnerable Jewish children, this "rage" would
serve to give him the confidence to do what children in wartime must
often accomplish.

In a provocative passage of his memoir, Hirsch offers an explanation as to why so many young people were able to fight confidently a
well-armed enemy and manage to, if not win all the time, at least apply persistent pressure that kept the Occupier continuously on alert.
First, Jewish Scouts in the south (they were banned in the northern
Occupied Zone) had successfully hidden caches of arms and other
matériel discarded by retreating French troops. The content of these
caches would prove indispensable later, from 1943 on, for the Allies
were reluctant to drop arms into a heavily occupied section of the
country. (They were also hesitant to arm the communist groups who
made up a significant portion of the *résistants*.)

Moreover, Hirsch suggests, the arms used in this war were not
nearly as heavy as those used in the last one, and they were less complicated to operate.

Because of the evolution of modern arms, of their "miniaturization"
and their formidable and murderous capacity to kill, a child was able
to shoot a small Sten machine gun, or another make, could carry a re-
volver, or a small package of plastic explosive. None of this required
the muscular capacity of an adult, for a child's finger was more than
able to pull a trigger.[23]

And many of the other "weaknesses" of the *résistants* were in fact
strengths. Qualities that would not have been assets in other con-
texts were quite useful to the clandestine groups' needs. Younger

resisters were "immature, without reflection, without experience of life or death." They did not have an overweening empathy for those whom they did not know. Given an order, these young soldiers would execute it as faithfully as possible, often without pity, for like all child soldiers, they were guileless. On the other hand, it is difficult for most adults to see a child being so independent and so potentially dangerous. This worked to the advantage of the child *résistants*, of course, and their short pants, their freewheeling bike games, and their cheerfulness often protected them as much as a camouflage uniform. They were intuitive, canny, very fast in making decisions— and always fearless.

The adventurous life secretly dreamed of by most boys, a father who trusted him completely, his own natural resilience, a pride in his Jewish heritage—all of these characteristics gave Nano the courage that he was suddenly called on to assume when threatened with the specter of two pitiless and racist regimes, one foreign and one homegrown.

||||||||||||||||||||

Claude Weill's father, who had served in the French army during World War I, owned and ran a successful printing business in Paris. After the Germans set up their bureaucracy, they began to appropriate Jewish businesses by assigning "Aryan" Frenchmen as their managers. They did not have to look far for avaricious Parisians who would, in effect, take over all aspects of the business, including, of course, its profits. For a while the Weills felt safe, but with the imposition of the yellow star (Claude himself wore one for about a month, he recalls), their luck ran out. When the authorities arrived at Mr. Weill's office in the summer of 1942, they told him that he had to leave immediately, refusing even his request for permission to say good-bye to his employees, most of whom had worked with him for years.

Weill described his father to me as morally conservative, obsessed with assimilation, and proud of his French heritage. He often told young Claude that he preferred that he bring home gentile rather than Jewish boys. When German Jewish refugees would knock on his door, asking for help, he referred to them as "Boches" and rarely gave them alms, a memory that still haunts Claude. Weill *père* could not believe that Pétain would forget his soldiers, no matter their religion. After the theft of his little factory, his father died later that year, of cancer, though Claude still believes that his father died of a broken heart.

Thanks to forged documents obtained from Catholic friends, the Weill family had been able to flee into the Unoccupied Zone and eventually settled in Terrasson, a small town with three thousand to four thousand residents in the Dordogne region. Claude was about fourteen years old at the time. The Weills found safety there, and fortunately Mr. Weill's gentile secretary, still working in the newly managed printing firm, regularly sent them funds that she skimmed, under the eyes of the Aryan manager, from the business's profits.

Claude remembers that there must have been other Jewish families in or around Terrasson. (The area was known for its sympathy toward refugees, given its long tradition of protest against Catholic hegemony, dating to the Reformation; exiled Alsatians and Mossellans had been resettled in the area as well.) The local Catholic priest agreed to provide the family with false birth certificates, but on the condition that the children take lessons in the catechism and be baptized as Catholics. They did, reluctantly; Claude found it amusing that he had already had his bar mitzvah in Paris, and here he was passing another adolescent rite. He knew to be careful, not to speak of Paris or of Jews he might have known, and to hide the fact that he was circumcised. Still, his mother must have been concerned about her son, for when she was approached about his joining the local Maquis, she quickly encouraged him to do so, to leave home from time to time and live in the wild with a resistance group. He thinks that she was proud of him for wanting to fight the Nazis, and the head of the region's underground group was a respected village doctor, so she believed that Claude would be watched over carefully. He would return home weekly, but for over two years he was a courier, like Nano Hirsch, between different guerrilla groups operating on either side of Terrasson. He told me that, though it was dangerous at times, it was also exhilarating. "It was like the scouts, though more dangerous."[*]

Weill's group was constantly in search of food and supplies and found most farmers in the area to be helpful. They had use of the doctor's car and would arrive at a farm, weapons at hand, with strong appetites. I asked if they ever stole food, and Claude smiled. "Well, we were in the doctor's automobile; yes, perhaps one could say we 'stole' sometimes." I failed to ask him why the farmers they "stole" from never reported their actions to the local authorities. But research has shown that frustration with the activities of a guerrilla group, even anger, often did not overwhelm the animosity that the locals felt toward the French government and the Germans. Also, such groups were armed and known to exercise their own penalties.

Occasionally, there would be brief skirmishes with the Germans on patrol, but Weill never fired a shot, nor was he ever in danger from a firefight. He always carried a pistol when they were laying out flares for parachute drops or standing guard, but never when he was performing his main work as a courier, one of the most common jobs given to youngsters in the Maquis and in cities. Youthfulness was often a useful camouflage for clandestine activities, as was being female. Adults also traveled on bicycles, but a youngster on one usually received only passing glances. Not that they were always safe: passing messages sometimes required carrying maps and other revealing

---

[*] Weill told me that he had been a member of the Éclaireurs de France, but not of the Jewish scout organization. "I was French, after all, before being Jewish. One of my ancestors had fought in Napoleon's Army of Italy!"

documents, and especially as the war continued checkpoints would be set up suddenly and all riders searched thoroughly. Still, a kid on a bike was so commonplace as to be just part of the scenery.

Nevertheless, Claude's most frightening experiences occurred when he was stopped on his bike by a German or Vichy patrol. Once he almost got caught; he was carrying incriminating papers in his pocket when a member of the Vichy government's Milice peremptorily asked him to get off his bike and started to question him. As he was about to be searched, a German officer interrupted to ask the militiaman a question, and Claude was able to pedal off untouched. Had he been caught with the papers, it would not have been too long before they discovered that he was Jewish, and though he did not realize it at the time, he would have almost certainly ended up being sent to Drancy, then to Auschwitz or another extermination camp.

||||||||||||||||||||

One of France's best-known child and adolescent movie stars in the 1930s and early 1940s was a handsome young heartthrob named Robert Lynen. Lynen had become famous by playing a forlorn little boy in a hugely successful 1932 film called *Poil de carotte* (Carrot top), directed by Julien Duvivier. From that triumph, he continued to act in films until 1942, when he was twenty-two, even though, with no crisis of conscience whatsoever, he had earlier joined a resistance group. When we take a closer look at this remarkable young man, we realize that for someone who was so well known, who still sent out hundreds of his publicity photographs, joining a clandestine organization took the counterintuitive tactic of "hiding in plain sight" to the next level. He regaled his fellow *résistants* with tales of how he would be recognized in restaurants or on the streets and begged for his autograph, even by German soldiers. Arrogantly bolder than his fellows, he often frightened them with his braggadocio in the company of Germans and the French police. Of course, this too was part of his "disguise," for he had realized that his stardom allowed him to tease the police, often in bars, about having machine guns for sale, and hand grenades for only a few francs each. The brazenness of his boasts, plus his celebrity status, protected him for a while, though it made nervous wrecks of those who were working with him. Lynen had a marvelous sense of humor and was always ready with a quip or clownish face to amuse and relax his friends, who were not protected by his veneer of notoriety. This chameleon ability to be both brazen and clandestine at the same time amused Lynen to no end, and it most likely protected him for three years.

Indeed, Lynen was so well known that the Germans themselves tried to recruit him for films made by their French film company, Continental. But he was a patriot; legend has it that when he was offered the unimaginable figure of a million francs to sign a contract with Continental, he took the pen proffered him by the German agent and, using it as a dagger, crushed it in a fancy ashtray, saying to the agent: "If you have this much money, buy the town a drink, and make a toast to Hitler, but don't count on me."[24]

His fame combined with his physical beauty, reinforced by his above-normal height, to make him the most visible of persons in an invisible world. His brother-in-law Pierre Henneguier, himself a major Resistance leader who would survive the war, described him in this way: "He is as handsome as the young prince of a fantastic Nordic tale, with his blond hair, blue eyes, his thin figure, and svelte silhouette. His attitude is empathetic, and he cannot count his friends. Everyone loves his gay, lively, courageous, and, yes, sometimes outrageous, character."[25]

From the beginning, he and Henneguier, as well as a close Irish friend, Robert Vernon, were not only pasting anti-German notices on walls and standing up in cinemas to insult the German newsreels but had managed to become owners of a trucking business, one that allowed them, from 1940, to hide and transport arms throughout southern France. Azur-Transports (as it was named) was also a means of income, for despite his success as an actor, Lynen had little ready cash and had to take care of his mother and, later, his sister May.

Robert learned to drive the large trucks and was happiest when they were filled with hidden rifles, ammunition, and other matériel. Incredibly, these trucks were never stopped or searched. Lynen's role as an agent evolved, and soon he was gathering and passing information rather than arms. He traveled all over France under the code name Aiglon (Eaglet),* but rarely incognito. He also learned to use a shortwave radio, met parachuted agents in the fields of France, and passed back and forth (often with a false ID) over the demarcation line that separated the two major zones of France. One of his friends remarked that he seemed almost to enjoy the danger, for he had confidence in his will to thwart the Occupiers and was amused that he could do so even though, with his famous face known everywhere, he was the antithesis of a clandestine operator.

Lynen had starred in thirteen films, his last being *Cap au large* (Toward the Open Sea) in 1942, filmed while he was still serving as a courier and planner of a resistance group that worked at first in the Unoccupied Zone and then in the whole of Occupied France for the British Intelligence Service. But as often happened, the success of the network was no guarantee that just one traitor would not reveal its complex organization. Lynen and his companion, Assia, were returning from Paris to his friend Vernon's Cassis home in the south of France. Lynen was due to arrive the very day that the Gestapo raided Vernon's home and arrested him. Lynen had sent a telegram

---

* This had been the nickname of Napoleon II, the son of Napoleon I and Marie-Louise, his second wife. It was also the name of a popular nineteenth-century play by Edmond Rostand that featured the beautiful young Napoleon II, dead early of tuberculosis in 1832. It was his remains that Hitler clumsily returned to France in December 1940.

to Vernon announcing his arrival, and the Germans got there just as his friend was reading it. In fact, the telegraph office, knowing of the Resistance network, had read the message first and quickly sent someone to the train station to warn Lynen. As luck would have it, however, Robert had illicitly boarded and could not be found. (He often jumped onto trains without a ticket, leaping off on the other side as the train pulled into a station. Why? As a game, a joke, a way to show his indomitability.) Departing the station by another exit, Lynen missed the man sent to warn him. When he arrived at Vernon's home, he was arrested along with his girlfriend. This was in February 1943, and Robert Lynen would never be free again.

Most likely, the Wehrmacht, to which he was first turned over, would have offered him a deal; if he were to give them a few names, perhaps they would allow him to go to Germany and make films. But he doubtless would have refused—Lynen had already invested himself in the fight against tyranny and could not compromise, given his notoriety and his age (twenty-three). He was then given over to the Gestapo, who were less solicitous of the young movie star. We do not know exactly what happened to him, but one suspects that he was tortured before finally being transported to Germany with other young *résistants*. One cold morning he was led out, holding the hand of another young man, stood before a post, and shot. His body fell into a ditch filled with other victims, well over half of whom were twenty-four years old or younger.

After the war, Robert Lynen's family moved heaven and earth, as did two of France's best-known movie actors, Claude Dauphin and Jean-Pierre Aumont, to recover his remains (which were ultimately found, still recognizable, in that German ditch). They repatriated Robert's remains, first to Strasbourg, and then, in 1947, to Paris for a public ceremony at the Invalides, where the earlier Aiglon had been laid to rest in 1940. Claude Dauphin wrote a widely published article that not only praised his fellow performer but spoke eloquently to the prominence and moral significance of all those adolescents who had fought against the German Occupation, often to their deaths.

> *The destiny of our little Robert Lynen, which ends this morning in the nave of the Invalides, is one that touches you deeply. First, because he was in our craft, one of the happiest of friends, despite his melancholy, and among the most enthusiastic, despite his reticence. And then because he belongs to that very large and sad cohort of boys who died at the age of twenty, for something. It tears at one's soul to die at twenty, but it's honorable to have joined up. And little Robert Lynen, running through the shadowy trails of the Resistance, knew well that such activity was not an act of a play that ended at midnight, but, at every minute, a deadly game.*
>
> *This morning in the Invalides [where heroes are eulogized], we must remember that [story], in front of this coffin, whose contents are more noble and more moving even than that of the [other] Aiglon [the young Napoleon II, Prince de Rome]. We must not forget the moment when twelve black rifles were raised against these children, and when those children did not waver with terror, or from regret, that they had consented to lose all their future Springs, all their pleasures, all their birthdays, and that they died singing the most beautiful song of their country, at the age of twenty. We must remember this—we who have reached double their ages—all those lessons that these school kids have left us, not only of pride, of courage, of greatness, but also of prudent wisdom, and of humility.*[26]

The poignancy of Dauphin's moving eulogy speaks not only to Lynen's courage and that of his friends, but also to the deep guilt of those who had survived the conflict or who had acquiesced, even casually, to the actions of the Occupier and his subservient French supporters. Doubtless many who were "in mourning" had themselves been part of the crowd advocating "just wait," or "better Hitler than Blum," or "never trust a communist"—those who had given Pétain and Laval their support, quietly or loudly, during the dark years. We hope that they were embarrassed by Dauphin's words, that they sought redemption, that they never served in any official position again. But we should remember that hopes are like snowflakes: they melt wherever there is heat.

||||||||||||||||||||||

The estimates of the number of hostages and resisters executed by German firing squads in France from 1940 to 1945 range between four thousand and five thousand.[27] In the early days, most of these were communists, Freemasons, or Jews, executed as hostages when a German soldier was assassinated. These are some of the cruelest stories; those killed were men and boys, like Guy Môquet, who had been arrested for relatively minor infractions and put in jail for several months or a year. Suddenly, they were told only a few hours before it was to happen that they would be executed in reprisal for some violence against Germans. Soldiers as young as they themselves would deliver the announcement to the hostages in their cells, where they had been waiting, sometimes for weeks, sometimes longer. An adjutant would offer them the services of a priest and a chance to write no more than three letters of good-bye. Some German guards even agreed to mail the letters themselves or to pass them on to their addressees. Why were prison guards and officials so "generous"? There is a large gap between an anonymous court's decision to put someone to death, especially a younger person, and a prison's responsibility for ensuring that the prisoners remain calm as they go to their deaths. Assurances were often given that possessions, even clothing, would be passed on to family and friends, or even that their corpses would be given appropriate burial. (The condemned would name where they wanted to be buried, but often they were interred in a common grave, with bodies thrown in pell-mell.) One young man even described in detail in his last letter what he was wearing, so that his parents could recover his body if it was not sent to them. Their relatives would only learn of their deaths when these letters were delivered.

As a more violent resistance began to grow, suspected and actual malefactors were brought to swifter "justice." After the letters had been written and addressed, and after the execution, the authorities would first censor them (with heavy ink, or by cutting sentences and paragraphs from the letters themselves), and then a prison official, priest, or army officer would present them personally to the survivors. The recipients would be admonished not to share the letters with anyone outside the family and not to speak about their contents, under threat of punishment. However, the missives were often read aloud, not only to family members but to close friends; some were copied and passed around; a few were even printed in clandestine newspapers. The anguish and courage and patriotism, especially of the fallen young, became thus boldly manifest and raised the question for all: What am I to do about this Occupation, if this person gave his life at twenty?

These doomed youngsters expressed fear and anxiety not so much for themselves, but for what their death would mean for their survivors—their lovers and wives, their mothers and fathers, and often, their little brothers and sisters. Last thoughts were given as well for the fate of France. Often some reference was made to the afterlife, but almost always as a consolation for the recipients. Some apologies were offered for having gotten into trouble, or not having been an ideal child, but no one expressed regrets for having stood against tyranny. The tone of many of the letters that have come down to us from the condemned is one of self-examination, of wonder at how they wound up where they were at that moment, and hope that they had done well by their beliefs.

|||||||||||||||||||||

It was November 1941; the "easy" Occupation had been over at least since June, when the Germans stormed across western Russia. Tensions were palpable. A young member of the communist Bataillons de la jeunesse had been captured with some comrades after they derailed a train near Lille in northern France.[*] As the hours of his life dwindled away, Félicien Joly, twenty-two, felt that he had two duties when his jailers in a Lille prison gave him writing materials. Of course he wanted to explain to his family how things had wound up like this, but he also wanted to warn his friends that there was a traitor in their midst. Strangely, both missives arrived at his parents' home. There was no doubt as to the urgency:

> *My dear comrades in the struggle ...*
>
> *I hope that this letter will get to you without being seen by others. We are five who have been condemned to death, but I am hoping to be pardoned because I've written to the supreme commander of the German Army. Maurice has betrayed the cause for which we had sworn to give up our lives if it became necessary. He gave the addresses of a bunch of our friends. For instance, he said "Don't arrest Gary now." Not a few buddies will be found out by this action. If they aren't arrested, they should get away immediately. (All network commanders should take every precaution.) All drop-off points have to be changed.*
>
> *You should make sure you aren't being followed.*
>
> *Do your best so that the struggle continues, and soon we will be victorious.*

---

[*] Such actions were more and more common, since they were safer than attacking Germans frontally. A twisted rail could end up killing or wounding many more of the enemy or stop a train loaded with military ordinance.

Bonjour to you all. Have courage. If I am pardoned, I hope to see
you soon.[28]

We can only guess how this letter got past the prison censors. It
was accompanied by another written directly to his parents. One of
the lengthiest I have found, it speaks eloquently to the pride that condemned youth took in their confrontations with a dark fascism. A few
excerpts:

This letter is the last that I write you. You will get it after my death,
and it will waken sad memories for you. It hurts to write it.
    . . . I stayed with my friends until the end. . . . I could have saved my
life by turning in my comrades. . . . I did not do it. I am not a coward. . . .
    . . . Ask for my two notebooks. . . . On the cover of one is a phrase
from Nietzsche: "I want always to climb higher." I leave [that mes-
sage] to all idealistic youth.
    To everyone, remember me as a hardy boy; my name will ring after
my death, not as a funeral bell, but as a sound of soaring hope.[29]

Henri Gautherot, twenty-one, wrote in August 1941 to his father
that "I will know how to die as a Frenchman. . . . I have not had, neither during the judgment, nor afterward, nor at the moment itself, a
single weakness."[30] Other letters sneaked in information crucial to
those families still connected in some way to the Resistance. Twenty-
one-year-old André Sigonney wrote in August 1941 that "I have been
condemned to death by the German authorities as well . . . as others,
because the French police turned us over to them."[31] Again, we wonder why this sentence was not censored; perhaps the Germans wanted
such information to be spread about the active role of French authorities in rounding up youth.

In March 1942, nineteen-year-old Fernand Zalkinow wrote a final
letter to his sister from La Santé prison in Paris. It is another long one,

as if he thought he could postpone the inevitable by keeping his pen from stopping:

> *Since I've been here, I have looked deeply into myself. I have come to realize that, despite all of my faults—and I have more than a few—I wasn't so bad as all that, and that I could've been a pretty good guy. . . . I'm a bit of a blowhard, I know. But to tell you the truth, I still can't explain why I am so calm. Before my sentence, I often cried, but since, I haven't shed one tear. I have the sense of a deep interior tranquility, a deep quietness. It seems I have only one more test to pass, the last, and then everything will be over, nothing more.*[*][32]

A would-be Spanish teacher had he not died, Pierre Grelot wrote to his mother a trenchant narrative of his trial, emphasizing, as others did, that while she might grieve him, she should also know no shame because of his actions:

> *I was tried with my friends on October 15. The trial was a comedy. We knew in advance what the verdict would be, since they gave death for the slightest thing. My crime was "antifascist propaganda against the occupying army, carrying and hiding arms and munitions, etc." . . . Our attitude before the tribunal was dignified and noble. We knew how to garner the respect of those in attendance. The soldiers were moved; I saw one who was crying. Think of it: we were between 17 and 20 years old. When, after the judgment, the judge asked if we had anything to add, . . . I answered: "I am proud to deserve this sentence." If any doubts [of our loyalty] remained, those words removed them.*[33]

---

[*] Zalkinow had been found guilty a few days earlier at the Palais-Bourbon trial, and was executed along with six other young communists at Mont-Valérien. (See pp. 215 ff.)

Bravado in face of the inevitable? Yes. Desire to make his mom proud? Yes. But it was also a message to a wider audience—and to himself—that he had acted as an adult, that he had performed according to the tenets of his group, of his friends, and that he had not faltered. The most poignant letters are written as if the young writer had been in shock: what did I do to wind up here? Most likely they were among those prisoners who had been chosen willy-nilly whenever the Germans had to make a statement about the assassination of a German soldier or officer. We cannot know.

Letters such as Grelot's are so moving because they often have both obvious and not so obvious motives, and they are directed to specific as well as unknown audiences. As these young writers knew, their last written words would be delivered or not at the whim of the authorities; giving them materials to spend their last hours writing letters might have been another cruel trick played on them by their capricious captors. Common sense suggests that such self-aware, often well-educated youngsters had to suspect that these last letters might well wind up in the garbage heaps in the back courtyards of their prison. So again, the main audience, at least subconsciously, was themselves. And then we must think of those letters we shall never see: those half-written, those discarded, or those destroyed by families because they showed anguish, despair, and confusion. These last missives spoke almost certainly too of humanity, and the courage to have faced an enemy of their homeland.

Adolescence is the liminal stage between childhood and adulthood; it is difficult to identify when childhood ends and adulthood begins, especially during times of convulsive social and material change. Yet these letters, besides being palliatives to parents, send a clear message about identity formation that is as much aspirational as confessional: This is who I want to be. This is who I hoped to be. This is how I want to be remembered. This is how I tried to be. I didn't have time to complete my transition to adulthood; remember me as someone who was on the right track, who had absorbed the love and teachings of his parents and mentors, who would have been a person to admire if he could have lived. This is the most poignant aspect of these *lettres de fusillés* (letters from the executed).

Personal memories, published memoirs, unpublished diaries and journals, and letters—not to mention scratched graffiti on the walls of their cells—are full of such tales of modest courage after a confrontation with the enemy. They bring back the question of what constitutes "resistance" in a police state. It is not always firing a pistol at an occupying soldier or policeman; it can be as modest as passing notes, whispering information heard on the radio, or throwing nails under the tires of the Occupier's cars. It can be as fleeting as a teenager jumping up in a crowded movie house and yelling "Vive de Gaulle!" It can be as dangerous as hiding a downed Allied pilot or spiriting someone over the Spanish or Swiss border. Or it can be as quiet as a professor gently reminding his class of the values of the French Revolution, of the motto "Liberté, Egalité, Fraternité."

It takes several generations for a totalitarian regime to inculcate permanent and paralyzing fear in a population, especially when there is almost no outlet for vocal or visible resistance. But even then, someone or some few will find a way to raise a fist or create an artwork or lift a voice that signals, "This will not last." Such was the force of all those who resisted, no matter how meekly, during this deeply complicated period. The brutal tactics used after an arrest—beatings, blackmail, torture—were much less subtle than the means the Occupier devised to recruit spies, track lines of communication, analyze demographic records, patiently surveil families and employers, and seduce when they could not intimidate citizens. These methods are still being used in contemporary totalitarian or police states. And still, streets fill with the young asking why.

CHAPTER SEVEN

Resisting the Resistance

Modern tyranny is terror management.

—TIMOTHY SNYDER

In January 1943, two months after the Germans had invaded the so-called "Free" Zone, thereby occupying all of France, a gutsy professional, the police chief of a district in the southern city of Toulouse, wrote the following statement to the prefect of the *département*:

> *I refuse—and the responsibility is completely mine—to persecute Jews, who, in my opinion, have the same right to life and happiness as M. Laval himself.*
>
> *I refuse to drag French workers by force from their families. I hold firmly to the idea that it is not our duty to deport our compatriots, and that any Frenchman complicit in this infamy, even should his name be Philippe Pétain, acts as a traitor.*
>
> *I stand by each and every word that I have used.*[1]

Our souls stir at such courage. But being moved diminishes the cost that such a letter to his superiors would have incurred. If he were lucky, only Commissaire Philippe's job would be in jeopardy. He would have been immediately relieved of his duties, and probably of his pension. His family would have consequently suffered because of his actions. At worst, he would have been arrested, publicly humiliated, perhaps even jailed. He would not have been sent to Germany or executed, for he doubtless had many supporters among his men and in the community. Still, displays of this sort of public courage were rare among French police officers, who rounded up—and this is no exaggeration—more than 90 percent of the Jews, communists, and other "undesirables" targeted by the Occupational Authority and the Gestapo during the war years.

In his examination of guerrilla (now called asymmetric) warfare or military engagement, the political theorist Michael Walzer makes exquisite distinctions between those who refuse to accept the terms of a treaty or armistice and the expectations of a victorious army. There was a major moral and military conundrum at the various stages of the resistance by French civilians to occupying forces between 1940 and 1945. The distinctions were muddied by the fact that so many different entities were "resisting" a common enemy, but they often also "resisted" the actions of their fellow combatants as well. Early in the Occupation, many French citizens thought that resistance, armed or not, would put them in danger from a nervous German army, one they hoped would soon leave their country. Does post-treaty resistance activity have an obligation to protect citizens who might be held hostage to that activity? Nevertheless, Walzer argues that "after national surrender, if there are still values worth defending, no one can defend them except ordinary men and women, citizens with no political or legal standing. [That] leads us to grant these men and women a kind of moral authority." But he also recognizes that such acts almost always placed the resisters in jeopardy, for, in the rules of war, "resistance is legitimate, and the punishment of resistance is legitimate."[2]

From June 1940 until November 1942, there were two "Frances"—the Occupied and "Free" (Unoccupied) zones. From the beginning, acts of resistance occurred in both, but retribution and punishment were harsher in the German zone. So we come to one of the most persistently unresolved conundrums of that period: if the law was the law, then how did L'État Français deal with French citizens who considered themselves just as patriotic as those who officially pledged loyalty but who disagreed with the state's most egregious policies? Who was more loyal to France: Those who followed blindly the temporizing Pétain and his ill-advised armistice, or those who refused to admit obeisance to any dictatorial state? Those who continued to fight a foreign enemy, after what was effectively a surrender, or those who cooperated and accepted the Occupation?

Even with the exhortations coming out of Vichy that France was on its way to a resurgent, more virile, more productive, and stronger state, the facts on the ground were totally contradictory. And after the Germans invaded Vichy France in late 1942, following the Allied campaign in North Africa, the Germans were omnipresent. The swastika was flying over every official building and monument, a stark reminder of being on the losing side. From the beginning of the Occupation, the French recognized and accepted how organized, predictive, and confident the German bureaucrats were, especially those with whom they had regular interactions. Rules were rules. Follow the rules, and all would be fine. But there remained no clear order of the ever-changing rules and regulations, and disrupted lives could not remain orderly, even for those who strived to do so. Food became scarcer; automobiles were commandeered; daily restrictions on what to read, what to listen to, and what to see in movie houses began to encroach on the French citizen's sense of independence and liberty. Sure, we support order, many French would say, but we support liberty as well.

Almost every historian of the period now agrees that the fact of resistance was as significant as its military performance, if not more so. When we consider only the successful bombings or sabotage, the assassinations or spying, we overlook the slow changes, as the Occupation seemed to go on forever, brought on by the stubborn recalcitrance of a defeated and nervous population. The Germans could not stop the news spreading of the dozens of wasplike attacks all over the Occupied Zone, no matter how small. Local gossip and other means of communication ensured that everyone knew which transformers had been ruined, or how many German soldiers had been injured in a rail attack, or how many pieces of glass had punctured tires at parking lots, or whose children had been arrested. Everyone in an urban neighborhood, or a small town or village, no matter their own political leanings, generally knew who the communists were, who the fervent Pétainistes were, and who the secret Gaullists were. They might even know who the local Maquis leader was. A sense of patriotic solidarity mixed with a fear of reprisal protected the identities of a lot of these folks. Such were the circumstances that faced those in authority as they tried mightily to keep a large, confused nation quiescent. More than a few would be betrayed by their neighbors, but the authorities could not rely only on personal antagonisms or rewards for denouncing malefactors.

The Reich thought they had foreseen this situation. Before the war, the Germans, confident that they would be militarily occupying other countries, some for longer periods than others, had drawn up regulations that they believed could be applied universally, no matter the defeated nation. The official mantra from Berlin was that the German army should provide "order and security"—order in the civilian population and protection for the Germans assigned to occupation duties. However, France would prove to be an especially complex and demanding case. First, it was the most populous nation occupied. It was also a geographically large country, bordered by nonbelligerents (Switzerland and Spain), and thus porous; it had access to four strategic bodies of water: the English Channel, the North Sea, the Mediterranean Sea, and the Atlantic Ocean. Finally, its western coast looked out to the British Isles, which at first had been the target of a planned German invasion; later the French coast became the first defense for an anticipated invasion from the British Isles. The armistice the Reich had signed with the French (Vichy) government had been constructed to address some of these problems, which was why the southern quarter of the nation was given over to French control (except for the far southeast, which was partially occupied by Italian forces), and the French fleet was assigned to protect the Mediterranean border from Spain to Italy. Still, problems of jurisdiction and responsibility confronted the Germans and their Vichy allies from the first days of the Occupation.

As soon as it was clear in the fall of 1940 that Operation Sea Lion (the invasion of the British Isles) was off, Germany began pulling its troops out of France in preparation for the still-secret invasion of the Soviet Union planned for June 1941. Suddenly, the German Military Command found itself severely undermanned for a complete and effective Occupation; it needed support—a great deal of it—from the French, specifically from the Vichy government. Thus began almost four years of three-dimensional checkers, if not chess, because the Occupying authorities found that they were competing with themselves. The German army resented any intervention from the SS and the Gestapo. Pétain's government sought to maintain some judicial sovereignty, even over acts of sabotage against Germans, as well as against its own administration. And bureaucrats in both governments had to be in constant negotiation with their military or police opposites. Clarity of responsibilities was not a hallmark of the Occupation, however, and as a result, resistance members not only had to worry about being discovered or captured, but they had to be concerned too with *who* discovered them; they then had to worry about who would try them and convict them (for they were almost always found guilty). Not a few of the executions or deportations that took place during these dark years were the result of this administrative confusion.

||||||||||||||||||||

Show trials have been centerpieces of totalitarian regimes for centuries. The public presentation of "justice" for acts against the state has at least two motivations: first, to instill caution, if not fear, in any citizen who thinks that the security apparatus is not monolithic; and second, to assure a beleaguered population that the established government will protect them against "bandits," "terrorists," "anarchists," "communists," and so forth. The illusion of process, carefully enunciated, is meant to ensure that citizens know that their leaders are well organized and that rules are well delineated. Consequently, intense preparations were made—through propaganda, the (often state-controlled) medium used to bring the theater of the proceedings and their verdicts (almost always "guilty") into the daily lives of cowed citizens.

The official trials of clandestine actors during the Occupation, some handled by the Vichy state, some in civilian courts, and others within the German military justice infrastructure, tended to group together workers (mostly communist) and foreigners (mostly Jewish immigrants of the last few years). The idea was to continue the existing German propaganda efforts against the Bolsheviks and the Jews and to show that the undereducated lower classes were being duped into fighting for de Gaulle and Stalin. Of course, another reason for the regular interference of the Germans in the trial, sentencing, and execution of troublemakers was to remind L'État Français that they were not doing the job as thoroughly as their masters would like.

Three significant show trials have remained key moments in the memory and history of the Resistance. They were all military trials; though "public" and apparently transparent, friends and relatives of the accused could not attend. Sympathetic journalists were invited, however, with the understanding that they would spread the stories through Parisian and local newspapers, along with unflattering photographs of the accused. The judgments, for the most part, were known before the defendants arrived in the courtroom. The jailers ensured that the perpetrators appeared destitute, unhappy, and foreign (unshaven, mussed hair, careless clothing). Contrary to German expectations, the youthfulness of many defendants would inspire a deeper anger among the French.

A vast roundup of Jews, including French citizens, occurred in July 1942. Gentile French were appalled at the sight of innocent children, mothers, and grandmothers being loaded into trucks and buses to be taken to Drancy; this did not fit into the historical tableau constructed by their forebears depicting France as the guardians of citizens' rights. As direct evidence of cruelty by the Germans and Vichy mounted, their attempts to maintain order and peace by slowing down the robust execution of "hostages" did not mollify an increasingly suspicious public. Finally, by late 1942, more and more French learned, as many Jews had discovered earlier, that there were death camps throughout eastern Europe. No one could comprehend fully the massiveness of this program and the furnaces burning twenty-four hours a day to remove the evidence, but enough rumor had been substantiated to cause suspicion and anxiety among a populace tired of what seemed to be an Occupation without end.*

The trials, then, were another propagandistic antidote to the threat of a more vigorous resistance to the Occupation. Since the point was both to spread the word that the Occupying Authority was serious about attacks against its personnel and to pretend to a judicial objectivity that such retribution was within the international rules of warfare, the trials had to be held in large auditoriums to accommodate the dozens of journalists from across France enjoined to attend. Numerous German officers were ordered to witness the proceedings. Families were not permitted to see the prisoners before or during their trial, nor, for the most part, after their guilty verdicts.

Such a veneer of legality was maintained regarding all of the Occupier's repressive measures. The Germans repeatedly redefined what constituted "terrorism" or "acts against the Occupier," ensuring that each offender had a trial, whether captured by the French and turned

---

* The massive executions that occurred primarily in the Soviet Union, and carried out by special SS squads, were less known at the time.

over to them or discovered by the Germans themselves. Initially, the Wehrmacht had left these trials up to the civil courts of Vichy France, but as it became clearer that their penalties would not be as harsh as the German ones, the military took over the judicial arraignment and trials of French *résistants*. Often families did not learn of the execution or imprisonment of their sons and fathers until they read their names in announcements posted in newspapers and on the walls of cities.

Seven young men—whose mug shots reveal an impassivity that belies the fervor of their "crimes"—were arrested in November 1941, delivered almost immediately to the Germans, and remained in limbo for more than six months as the Occupying Authority twisted and turned bureaucratically in a search for the most efficient and successful means of confronting what they saw as an increasingly well-organized resistance. Fernand Zalkinow, a nineteen-year-old Parisian, worked as a furrier's assistant; his parents were arrested with him and died in Auschwitz. Robert Peltier, age twenty and also from Paris, was a sheet-metal worker. Tony Bloncourt was born in Haiti of French parents; he was a twenty-year-old student. Another student, Christian Rizo, age nineteen, studied at the Sorbonne; he had participated in the November 11, 1940, march up the Champs-Élysées. The youngest detainee, Pierre Milan, was a seventeen-year-old telegraph operator. Roger Hanlet, at nineteen, was a printing mechanic, and Acher Semahya, a Greek Jew born in Salonika, the oldest detainee at twenty-seven, was a mechanic. I mention their biographical data in addition to their names to give some substance to this group of young men: they ranged from the upper and lower socioeconomic classes, and they included intellectuals as well as workers, foreigners as well as Parisians. These seven represented a cross-section of the types of young people who would make up the majority of those executed by the Germans during the Occupation.

To hold such a trial in the halls of the eminent Palais-Bourbon, the last site of the government of the Third Republic, was a striking decision.* (The government of L'État Français remained in Vichy, despite Pétain's repeated requests to the Germans to be allowed to move back to Paris, or at least to Versailles.) The building then, as now, was filled with décor of the eighteenth and nineteenth centuries: walls, ceilings, and accoutrements were gilded, red, and white. The majestic residence of the president of the former Chambre de Députés in the Hôtel de Lassay was attached to the west of the main building; this is where the trial was most likely held, according to the journalists who were present (though some doubt remains about their memories). Why here? We cannot know for certain. Perhaps the idea was to humiliate further the seven ragged young men who were dragged before a formally dressed military court and to remind the public that their great history was on the verge of being smudged by Jews and communists.

Writes the historian Éric Alary:

> *If the German judicial procedure followed in the trial of the seven young communists did not differ from that generally followed in Occupied France, the site of the trial, the Palais-Bourbon, was on the other hand, exceptional, as would be the choice of La Maison de la Chimie, on April 15, 1942. In fact, in order for the trial to have the maximum impact, sites as important and as symbolic were necessary, especially to accommodate the greatest possible number of journalists.*[3]

Found guilty, the seven young men were soon executed at the infamous clearing at Mont-Valérien, where many others had preceded and would follow them. To add to the tragedy of this penalty, only five

---

* It is one of the anomalies of historical memory that the palace that represents democratic government has retained the name of the family that built it—a family whose members were violently executed or exiled in 1793.

firing posts were set up, so two of the young men had to watch their brothers die before themselves being tied to the bloody stakes.

There is another point about this trial that must not be overlooked. The seven young communists or communist sympathizers had been discovered, trailed, and arrested by the French police, the infamous Brigades spéciales, not the German authorities, though they operated under German orders. It was they who turned the youngsters over to the Germans and then washed their hands of the results.

This trial revealed three significant facts about the Resistance against the Occupation. First, it detailed what had only been bruited among the noncommitted French, namely, that there *was* an organized Resistance taking seriously its duty to rid France of the Occupier. Second, even though the Germans thought that the young men's affiliation with the French Communist Party would be good propaganda, instead the trial brought direct attention to that organization's stealthy and important work in resisting. And last, the relationship between the French police and the German authorities was shown to be intimate and firmly entrenched.

The second public trial that drew much attention was held a month later, and at another well-known site: La Maison de la Chimie on Rue Saint-Dominique in Paris. The massive former mansion had been selected after the Great War to be a sort of club where scientists could meet and discuss their research. Not as ostentatiously decorated as the Palais-Bourbon, the building still reflected the grand history of a once-dominant culture and nation. Again, the mixture of the classes and religious origins of the "guilty" was noticeable. When the names were published, some French felt relief that most of the names sounded "foreign." Others may have noted instead the unity of differences among them.

The defendants had been living in Paris when captured, but had come from all over France to join the movements and networks that operated in and around the capital. Of the twenty-seven defendants, seven were younger than twenty; eight were between twenty-one and twenty-five; eight were between twenty-six and thirty-five; and only four were older than thirty-five. Again, for reasons that can only be inferred, youths had been specifically targeted by French and German police, a pattern that runs through the thousands of arrests that took place between 1940 and 1944. All except three of the twenty-seven would be executed: the men were shot, and the women were sent to Germany, where they were beheaded.*

Of course, the judged were not "innocent" under German military law: they had been quite active in the recruitment of other clandestines and were caught with arms, with supplies and machinery for printing tracts, and with notebooks of addresses and meeting places. Some had tried to assassinate German officers, but the "crimes" of most of them had been nonviolent; nevertheless, they had been grouped together because of their friendship or their knowledge of the others. The most casual resister was often defined by his or her acquaintance with the most violent.

Three of the defendants survived the war: the two who were found "innocent" but sentenced to hard labor in Germany for five years, and young André Kirschen, who was barely sixteen and thus, under German military law, could not be executed. He too was sent to Germany.† The rest of the prisoners had already figured out that they were to be executed, but did not know in what manner and when it would take place (though probably right after the trial). Remembers Kirschen,

---

* The Germans shot only two women found guilty by a tribunal during the Occupation. The rest were sent to Germany, where they were either placed in a concentration camp or guillotined. Guillotining was seen as a penalty for civilian crimes, not military ones. At the same time, the Germans often argued that the men condemned and shot were not military but "irregulars." If this sounds contradictory, it is.

† André was surprised that so few of the accused recognized one another—they had known one another only by code names. The strategy of limiting each team to only three persons prevented them from knowing who their fellow clandestines were.

This is how I felt, and I think it was the same for the other accused
[who had been kept separated while awaiting the trial]. Still,
our presence in that great room, with the swastika flag hanging
behind the judges, did represent a momentary distraction. We
thought that at least they would remove our handcuffs, which held
our hands behind our backs, and which we had worn day and night
in the cells; but that was hoping for too much. They only freed us
for the few minutes when we were individually brought before the
tribunal.[4]

Kirschen recounted that, for the most part, the military court's
"trial" was monotonous, held mostly in German, and obviously concerned with justifying its actions as consistent with international
rules of war. Their assigned lawyers barely spoke with each defendant
and were clearly present as window-dressing only. The defendants
could not exchange anything but glances with their fellows. At the
end of each day of the weeklong sham, they were led, incommunicado,
back to their individual cells at La Santé prison.

Before the final sentencing, André was told that, because of his
age, he would be sentenced to only ten years at hard labor. That
sentence, he felt, was a disappointment. While his brothers were
pledging to the judges that they would "die as buddies" (*copains*), he
believed that somehow he was less virtuous for having been spared
execution. He would be judged as not up to their courage.

The newspapers headlined the results of the trial, with varying
emphases, for all of France to read:

Twenty-five communists given the death penalty:
   They were the perpetrators of several terrorist attacks.
The terrorist assassins were paid by Moscow!
Twenty-five Bolsheviks given death penalty!

Two years later, after a long hiatus, the last of these significant show-case trials was held. It would become the best known, or at least the group executed would be, because of a propaganda poster that back-fired on the Germans. The Francs-tireurs et partisans–main d'oeuvre immigrée (FTP-MOI; Irregulars and Partisans–Immigrant Workers) was a group of mostly immigrants who had joined forces with the com-munists in 1942–1943 and raised havoc in the mid- to late fall of 1943. The most active of the armed sections was led by an Armenian poet and refugee named Missak Manouchian, and the names of his group of twenty-four clandestines read like a League of Nations phonebook. For example, the names of those who were twenty-five or younger (half the group) were Coarec, Della Negra, Elek, Fingercwajg, Fontano, Gedulgig, Goldberg, Luccarini, Rayman, Salvadori, Wajsbrot, and Witchitz. They were ideal subjects for a public trial, for they could be made to repre-sent the foreign-Jewish-communist "terrorists" that the Germans and their Vichy allies continued to place at the center of their propaganda.[*]

The group had been followed for months by the Brigades spéciales in one of its most successful *filatures,* or shadowing schemes. Begin-ning in late 1942, the communist-led group, which included French men and boys but was primarily composed of immigrants from east-ern Europe, including young Jews, made several violent attacks on German matériel or on German personnel themselves. They were a tight band with a clandestine hierarchy whereby each member knew only two other members of the wider network. The network was quite

---

[*] Though communist, there was resistance from the Party after the war to giving too much attention to these foreigners, even though a street named after them, Rue du Groupe-Manouchian, had been dedicated in 1954 in Paris's twentieth arrondisse-ment. As a result of the Party's reluctance to acknowledge them, their story has taken longer to enter collective memory. Most historians of the Resistance either briefly mention them or mention them not at all. In 2009, Robert Guédiguian's film *L'Armée du crime* brought the "Red Poster affair" back into popular French history. As a result, in recent years, there has been more recognition for the "Manouchian gang."

successful for about a year, even while being carefully monitored by the police, because sympathizers offered them help: finding temporary *planques*, or bolt-holes, supplying them with cash, allowing them to hide material in innocuous apartments, keeping the neighborhood's eyes on police and Gestapo patrols, and quietly passing messages. These and other activities, more and more frequent as the Occupation continued, allowed the FTP-MOI group to move quietly and effectively through the populace.

But the tenacious French police finally prevailed. The trial, another example of the German preoccupation with "legality," was not as public as the first two, though compliant journalists were invited. Nor did it last long; the verdict was so obvious that the judgment took only a quarter of an hour. The judge was direct in his justification for their condemnation:

> It is clear that the Jews who have dragged France into the war have not renounced their activity, and consider this nation favorable to its propaganda. Bolshevism and its allies are working to increase France's problems under the pretext of striking against the German Army. In the majority of cases, Jews or communists are the leaders of terrorist organizations, working for England and the USSR.[5]

The men were all shot a week after the verdict, again at Mont-Valérien. The only woman among them, Olga Bancic, was sent to Germany, where she was beheaded a few months later.

The best known of this group, besides its leader Manouchian, was a boy of seventeen named Thomas Elek. Like Guy Môquet, Elek was one of the many youngsters to whom many French looked to lead them. His comrades called him *"Bébé cadum,"* after a popular gentle soap formulated for the soft skin of infants. His photographs show a smooth face surrounded by curly blond hair and bright, light eyes. Hungarian-born and Jewish, he had immigrated to Paris with his mother, Hélène, when he was five; she eventually opened a restaurant on Montagne Sainte-Geneviève, just down the road from the Panthéon. Frequented by Germans during the Occupation, for she spoke excellent German and served familiar eastern European dishes, the Fer à Cheval (Horseshoe) was also a meeting place for young members of the underground. Maroussia Naïtchenko, André Kirschen, and others met there frequently, sharing space with German soldiers.

From the beginning of his involvement in clandestine activities at the age of fifteen, Thomas had acted, with increasing violence, against the Occupier. Given his physiognomy, he was never suspected of being Jewish by the prejudiced, nor was his mother, but his horror at what was happening to his fellow Jews gave him the courage to act. For three years, first acting alone, then as a member of Manouchian's group, young Thomas was an indefatigable courier, saboteur, and, eventually, killer. When he was finally captured, the police at first thought he was too young to be jailed, but upon arrest, he hid neither his Jewishness nor his role as a clandestine. Not unlike Guy Môquet two years earlier, he would become a visible example of the pitilessness of a police force that executed baby-faced resisters. In a semibiographical novel about Elek, his nephew Thomas Stern describes his uncle's appearance in the photographs of the German police:

> *In your stare, Thomas, directed outside of the photograph, toward us, dead and alive, there seems to flow a dreamy sadness that comes from the depths of eternity. It's the last glance you offer before leaving us. Soon afterward, there will be the dark circles of the rifles and the fixed stares of those who are aiming at you, without seeing your eyes, in order to kill you. . . . Your stare creates a channel into the impassable swamps of horror. It carries the light of a desperate clarity, one incapable of being extinguished.*[6]

The most important legacy of this specific roundup and semipublic trial was the immense propagandistic benefit the Germans incorrectly claimed they had gained. They produced perhaps the most famous visual of the Occupation, the "Red Poster" (*l'Affiche rouge*), so-called because of its use of red ink in the depiction of the accused and their crimes. A photographic collage of scenes of sabotage and assassinations, overlaid with the images of dark-skinned, bearded men, the poster was sent all over France to be displayed in public spaces and reproduced in newspapers. "Here are your real enemies," the poster screamed, "not the German army, but these foreigners, Jews, and communists who will not let matters rest." But the response, at least as we know it through oral reports and clandestine newspapers, especially this late in the Occupation (February 1944), belied the German premise. By March and April, the clandestine newspaper of the MOI-FTP had concluded that the "campaign of xenophobia" had backfired: "We can say that this spectacle of a trial against the [Manouchian group] has produced results contrary to the ends that the Nazis had hoped for. Many Frenchmen, who might have allowed themselves to be fooled by these xenophobic campaigns, have now understood that the immigrant workers are brothers in the struggle."[7]

The outcome of these trials was the same as with all of the repressive measures established by the Germans and their Vichy allies—the arbitrary selection of hostages, the murder of young men, the imprisonment of girls and young women, the reward incentives, the continuing claim that if the French helped the Germans their loved ones who were POWs could be released, the networks of informants, torture, arbitrary arrests of family members, and so forth. Nevertheless, they never succeeded in crushing—and perhaps could never have crushed—a disorganized resistance, defined often by the youth of the cadres' members, much less an organized one.

|||||||||||||||||||||

A German Catholic priest, Franz Stock (a member of the Wehrmacht), had been commanded to be present at the executions held in the prisons in and around Paris. His *Journal de guerre*, divided into three parts, appeared in French in 2017. The first part is the journal he kept, day by day, while he was in Paris between 1940 and 1944; it describes his duties as chaplain to prisoners, both German and French. The second part deals with his own imprisonment after the war, when he was held by the Allied forces in Cherbourg; the last part describes his work in a seminary for German POWs. Stock was deeply Catholic and had been in Paris since 1934, as the rector of a small German Catholic center. He was fluent in French, loved France, and thought, as did many French and German intellectuals of the period, that Europe would be made safer if France and Germany could live together. When Germany invaded Poland in late 1939, Stock was called back home to Germany, where he remained for a few months before returning as a member of the German Occupation of "the City of Light."

It was November 13, 1940, when Father Stock was first sent to visit prisons, then filled with hundreds of young school kids who had been rounded up two days before, following the first major protest against the Germans. He writes to his superior: "Two weeks ago I received the order to care for a large prison in [Suresnes], and I will receive clearance to care for the Wehrmacht prison in Paris [the Cherche-Midi]. Since all prisoners are French, my knowledge of the language will be very helpful. . . . This new field of work will bring many new opportunities."[8] The naïveté of this observation would be shattered soon after his work began.

At first, he did not keep a journal, but when his duties became much more demanding, he began taking notes in earnest. One of the prisons he visited most often was Fresnes, on the southern outskirts of

Paris. Conceived as a model penitentiary at the end of the nineteenth
century, the massive building was no longer in the best condition by
1940. The Germans had immediately requisitioned it to detain Allied
spies, British airmen, saboteurs, and high-ranking military officers.
Survivors remember it as overcrowded, badly heated in the winter,
and stifling in the summer. Cells often held more prisoners than they
had been sized for; one survivor remembers that, when a new prisoner was brought in, or when a priest came in, the opened door would
spill some inmates into the corridor, who were then beaten back by
truncheon-carrying guards.

All prisons are porous: information can, with some imaginative-
ness, both escape and enter. In these penitentiaries, new prisoners
brought the latest rumors from the outside—about other roundups,
other resistance movements and actions, the progress of the war
against the Germans. And lucky prisoners could sneak messages
out to their friends and relatives through bribed guards or complicit
men of the cloth. Inside, all sorts of methods were found to pass on
information between and among prisoners. Morse code was used on
plumbing pipes, some of which were wide enough to carry voices into
neighboring cells, and with help from complicit guards, written cor-
respondence could help organize groups within the prison. One of the
most disturbing messages that could come from the outside was that a
major attack by the Resistance had taken place. Knowing the protocol
that for each German soldier attacked or killed, twenty-five, fifty, or
even a hundred prisoners might be executed, the inmates remained
silent until further word. Those who had been sentenced to only a
few months or a year were especially anxious, for they were hostages
just as much as those who had already been condemned to die. And
of course Jews and communists knew that they were first on any list
because of who they were or what they believed.

Executions increased after 1941, and they affected almost everyone in the prison. Stock mentions that he witnessed young German

soldiers with tears in their eyes as their brutal brothers beat men on the way to the execution field or who were present when some were allowed to see their wives and children for the last time. Sometimes those younger guards would be punished for showing such emotions. Recalled another survivor of German imprisonment:

> *A firing squad refuses to shoot a priest. The officer in charge approaches the priest, tied to the stake, and shoots him several times in the head. Then the officer orders the squad's arrest. . . . Disobedience to a [German] officer normally merits the offender's beheading. Franz [Stock] somehow gets [the charge of disobedience] dismissed [so that the miscreants might die as soldiers, not criminals]. A [Catholic] soldier . . . assists another priest in giving the condemned their last communion, then picks up his rifle, joins the firing squad, and shoots the Mass celebrants, fellow Germans.*[9]

It is not easy to feel sorry for the German soldiers who did the killing, but certainly one of the most underreported phenomena of these years of brutal punishment is the psychic price paid by those who were carrying out the executions. The élan that had defined soldiers of the Wehrmacht in the first years of the war had weakened, especially with the news of the terrible destruction that British and American bombers were wreaking back home in the fatherland. With this decline, Stock noticed that younger Wehrmacht recruits began to desert; once captured, he had to give these Germans last rites just as he did for young Frenchmen. These few minor rebellions were quietly and quickly suppressed, and we are still left with little information on the personal toll of being an executioner. Some members of the execution squads were more often than not adolescents as young or younger than those they were shooting. We know that some officers felt that the executioners should have received battle pay, and they would often allow a stiff drink afterward, or between executions, but

Stock mentions none of this. Other Germans would be executed for such offenses as falling for a prostitute, passing information to others, and remaining loyal to the German Communist Party even while in Nazi uniform. Stock's most poignant feelings were for those young kinsmen who often refused his offers of consolation and forgiveness.

In his influential history of the Holocaust in the east, Christopher Browning details the psychological effect on members of the SS Einsatzgruppen who killed thousands of Jews in Poland by shooting them point-blank in front of pits where they would fall. He observes that "many of the perpetrators were young men" who had been indoctrinated by Nazi propaganda and had accordingly formed a moral shield for their actions.[10] Yet, Browning argues, it was the social pressure of other recruits and their leaders that was more instrumental in these wanton murders. Despite those who had few problems with the massacres, there was "physical revulsion" and a "broad demoralization" that set in after repeated orders to execute prisoners, even the "guilty" ones. Courage does not always lead to consistent heroic action, but occasionally the horror of events evinces it, even among perpetrators of the horrors.[11] Not unlike the young resisters we have been reading about, young Germans' courage often manifested under such pressure, and their ability to turn away from their heinous duty was a sign of rare fortitude of character.

Stock's personal story is riveting, for he managed both to stay loyal to his country of birth (though he had no admiration for Hitler and Nazism) while doing his best to reduce the terror imposed on French citizens by the Wehrmacht, and later by the Gestapo. He had a pass that protected him from searches as he visited the jailed at Fresnes, and the large Parisian prisons of the Cherche-Midi and La Santé, and even wounded prisoners in the Pitié-Saltpêtrière Hospital. What the guards and prison officials did not know was that Stock was adept at smuggling foodstuffs, writing materials, and books to the inmates; he did the same with messages from the prisoners and messages from their families. Never wearing his major's Wehrmacht uniform when ministering, Stock always dressed in a black cassock (he became known among prison guards as the "black crow") and refused to wear the boots of German officers for fear of intimidating the men he was to console. Considered benign by wardens and guards, he moved freely in the prisons and among the prisoners.

Stock spent final moments with some of the best-known victims of Nazi justice, such as Jacques Bonsergent, the first Frenchman executed in Paris, and Honoré d'Estienne d'Orves, de Gaulle's first spymaster. The work exhausted him; though only in his late thirties, he had a heart weakened by a childhood bout with rheumatic fever. Soon he had another Wehrmacht officer and priest join him, Major Theodore Leovenich, who began the same extracurricular actions as Stock. Eventually, Stock's religious co-conspirator—who hid candy, notes, pencils, paper, indeed a whole variety store, in his large empty pistol holster—was exposed by a prison snitch, fired as chaplain, and sent to the Eastern Front. His fate remains unknown. Stock found himself once again alone in his work.

Stock believed that anyone who died without the Catholic sacraments was doomed to purgatory at best, and hell at worst. So his job was not only to relieve the condemned of their anxieties about dying but to assure that their afterlife would be as bountiful as that of any dedicated Christian. (Stock was confident that he was saving souls; his sadness at not being able to convert, even at the last moment, Jews and communists is evident in his writings.) The Frenchmen with whom Stock spent time, especially the youngest ones, thinking of their mothers' deep faith, would confess their sins, and some would ask for last communion. Not a few asked to be rebaptized. Stock would often receive or visit with the families of the young men who had been shot, reassuring them that their sons had died as Catholics.

Yet in his entries, he avoids questioning why so many civilians, a good number of them in their teens and early twenties (he mentions their youth several times), were being stood up against poles driven into the ground and shot by five to twelve German soldiers. Possessing such a journal meant that Stock had to be continuously aware that it could be found or seized by police authorities, so he maintained his studiously objective "descriptions." There is never even a hint of criticism of the authority that would put young men to death for minor acts of sabotage, never a whisper of embarrassment that he was working for such a bloodless—and bloody—regime. For instance:

> We left for Fresnes at 6 a.m. Five Jews shot in reprisal for attacks: the Commandant of Paris requested that I attend. Ordinary people. Buried in the Nanterre cemetery. . . . [Visited first] at the Cherche-Midi, death sentence for possession of arms, 22-year-old Catholic, confessed and took communion calmly; then departure for La Santé Prison, where two terrorists [here, he uses automatically the German term for the prisoners], condemned to death for some time, were totally distant.[12]

All the same, some of his jottings do reveal a sensitive man, one who admired courage and sensed the presence of God in the prisons of Paris. He respectfully lets us know, in some detail, which resisters raised their hands in a communist salute, which ones sang "La Marseillaise" as they died, and which refused to be tied to the post or to wear a blindfold. He describes, for instance, the execution of twenty-one prisoners on April 17, 1942:

> Friday, April 17, 1942

> 21 EXECUTIONS
> Morning, visit to Fresnes [largest prison in Paris region]. The communists and terrorists [here he uses the official terminology] condemned Tuesday must be shot in the afternoon. After a brief lunch break, go to La Santé. . . . 21 shot. In their cells, useless attempts at

getting them to accept help from a priest! Not one wants anything.
The young ones speak about the ideal for which they are ready to die,
communism. . . . They [arrive at] the execution site, singing the first
verse of La Marseillaise.[13]

Reading entries that relentlessly recount fear, anxiety, sorrow, and death, one can perhaps gauge his charity and compassion between the lines of this journal of wasted blood and indifferent murder.

Little Maurice, 21 years old, came in an ambulance, and was the
only believer. Confessed earlier and took communion. Was with him
in ambulance—he had tried to escape and fell off the walls of Santé,
breaking a leg and vertebrae, lying down, encased in plaster. Had the
soul of a child, but he never lost his smile, despite his suffering. . . . He
hid his pain, didn't let out a single moan. He was shot, alone, the last
one. When his sentence was read, he said "That's fair." I went to his
side, [to give him the] last benediction, "Adieu"! Then he gave a good
handshake to Ernst, the guard who had carried him on a stretcher
every day during the trial, saying "merci, Ernst, and au revoir."[14]

Stock was a deeply Christian man who managed somehow to separate his status as a Wehrmacht priest from his pastoral service. Whether or not that conflict caused him angst or regret or self-doubt, we do not know, for all we have are the dry accounts of his diary entries. Stock was nothing if not a proper German soldier. In his daily notes, there is a macabre juxtaposition of the quotidian and the exceptional, the events, meetings, and meals that he had every day recorded alongside the details of his almost normalized attendance at the murder of so many youngsters. Still, despite his Wehrmacht role, Stock recognized the humanity of the "terrorists," the "communists," and, of course, the Jews (though, as noted, their defiant refusal to convert upset him).

From time to time, Stock does express incredulity about the courage of his charges. Why, he wonders, if a person has nothing else to
lose, including his life, would he not take the famous wager of Blaise
Pascal, the seventeenth-century philosopher and theologian: I am
not ready to say I believe, but just in case I am wrong and there is
an afterlife, why not live—and die—as if there were? Nothing lost,
and a lot to gain. But Stock fails to pierce the indomitable spirit and
idealism of most of these young people. Even if they wanted to tell
their parents that they were believers, that they had died with the
rites bestowed upon them, many of them had higher ideals that they
did not have the time or means to explain to others. These were the
ideals that had encouraged them to resist in the first place: a sturdy
belief in the difference between right and wrong; a desire to protect
those who were not able to protect themselves; a sense of solidarity
with their generation; anger at those, both domestic and foreign,
who had betrayed them; and a deeper, more profoundly felt patriotism than what they had been taught in their schools or by their
elders. We have few such powerful witnesses as Stock of the methods used by the Germans to cow civilians, nor of the courage of the
condemned.*

After the Liberation, the very success of Franz Stock's attempts at
keeping the survivors informed about those executed drew attention
from the Free French Army, which wanted to garner the important
information they thought he held. Rather than congratulate him on
his courage, they sought to plumb the secrets he held. The result was
one of those horribly comic moments in history when the tables are
not only turned, but so are the chairs:

---

* Over a thousand executions were carried out at Mont-Valérien between 1940
and 1944. Today there are monuments there to the executed in a memorial park
visited by thousands each year. In front of the main memorial is a square named
for Franz Stock, in recognition of his pastoral and clandestine support for
French—and German—prisoners.

*They demanded information [about what had happened in] the
Parisian prisons, the tortures, . . . etc. Above all, they demanded he
provide names: [of] those executed; [of] their betrayers; [of] prison
administrators, guards, etc. "They tried to force me to return to
Paris with them," Stock writes, "under pretense of informing the
families of those executed as well as serving the best interests of
humanity by helping them track down the ones responsible for these
crimes." . . .*

*[He] coldly advised his questioners that whatever information
he might possess, he had gained because he was a priest. Under no
circumstance would he allow himself to be used as an instrument of
revenge. Furious, the interrogators . . . returned to Paris leaving [a]
quietly defiant, stubborn Westphalian POW.*[15]

After the war, Stock would continue to work with young Germans, veterans of the Wehrmacht who wanted to become priests.
He fostered an attitude of rapprochement between Germans and
the French, but with his damaged heart, his work continued to exhaust him. He died from exhaustion at the age of forty-three and was
buried in France. In 1963, his body was exhumed to be entombed in
a new, small Catholic church near Chartres. Religious and political
leaders of France and Germany came to pay their respects, and the
last letter that Pope John XXIII sent before his own death was one
honoring Father Stock's work. Students of the Vatican predict that,
like John Paul himself, Stock will eventually be beatified.

Stock was a German, a soldier, and a priest, and at any given time
one of these identities would dominate. He ran the danger of being
discovered, removed from his duties, or transferred, but he was never
really threatened by the prospect of prison, execution, or excommunication. So why celebrate, whether officially and unofficially, this man's
actions during the long Occupation? Because his example shows the
complexity of the reactions of many German soldiers and bureaucrats

to the nasty repression enforced by their comrades-in-arms. They might not have put their lives on the line—Stock, for example, might have deeply believed that, as their belt buckles bragged, *Gott mit uns* (God is with us)—but thousands went up to that line and ignored the brutish orders of their superiors. Besides, Stock has provided us with one of the most precise chronicles that we have from the German side of the processes of imprisonment and execution of those who resisted. Objective to the point of blandness, uncritical of his comrades, his journal nevertheless opens a door to the intimacy of death, the last act of resistance on the part of young French patriots.

||||||||||||||||||||

Avoiding execution after arrest and judgment was not, for many, a respite. Deportation and internment in concentration camps in Germany or Poland were executions under another name. In such places, there were worse enemies than beatings and insults: freezing temperatures, meager rations, physical exhaustion, untreated illness, and constant fear required a concentration of luck, inner strength, and human solidarity that could be far more demanding than even the most courageous acts of resistance against an armed enemy.

After months of imprisonment in and around Paris, Jacques Lusseyran was finally sent to Konzenstrationlager Buchenwald, a massive collection of prison camps created by the Nazi regime in the 1930s. Buchenwald was near Weimar, in eastern Germany; one of the country's cultural capitals, Weimar was where Johann Wolfgang von Goethe had lived and written his scientific treatises, poetry, plays, and novels.* The camp was on a high hill, where it was more vulner-

---

* This camp in Goethe's backyard would hold some of Europe's most renowned inmates: Bruno Bettelheim, Maurice Halbwachs (who died a month before the camp's liberation), Léon Blum, Dietrich Bonhoeffer (hanged by the SS two weeks before the camp was liberated), Jorge Semprún, and a boy named Elie Wiesel.

able to the harsh winters of that part of Germany; Lusseyran's most frequently mentioned concern was the snow, rain, and bitter cold that surrounded the camp for six months a year. He estimated that of the two thousand French men and boys sent to Buchenwald between January 1944 and the camp's liberation by the U.S. army in April 1945, only thirty had survived. Unbelievably, the blind young man was one of them, though he had barely escaped death during the first months, so shocked was his system by the cold, the disease, and the slow starvation. He noticed too that boys and young men between the ages of twenty and twenty-five seemed to die as rapidly as the elderly. He suggests that the reason was the shock to their systems of such a sudden change in nutrition and exposure. Lusseyran himself had turned twenty only four months previously.

Lusseyran's guardian angel helped him on his first day. Each new inmate had to report his status to the record-happy SS bureaucracy. The clerks who took down the information were often inmates themselves. When asked by a Polish census-taker what his profession was, Jacques answered: "Student at the University of Paris." The clerk lowered his voice and whispered in German: "Don't let them know you are an intellectual. They hate intellectuals." Stubbornly, but cannily, Jacques instructed that his form show: "Profession: interpreter of French, Russian, and German," despite the fact that he knew no Russian (though he would quickly pick up the rudiments of the language within a few months). As it turned out, the life of prisoner number 41978 was most likely saved because of this fortuitous encounter.

The early weeks were probably the worst of Jacques's incarceration. First, he found that though his blindness kept him from being sent out daily on back-breaking work commandos, his fellow prisoners would steal his food or hide it from him. Without the reliable protection of his old friends, he was often pushed and shoved to the back of any line, whether for food or a comfortable place to sleep. Lusseyran had been assigned to the "Invalids Block," where those the Germans could not work to death were housed:

> *The one-legged, the one-armed, the trepanned, the deaf, the deaf-mute, the blind, the legless . . . , the aphasic, the ataxic, the epileptic, the gangrenous, the scrofulous, the tubercular, the cancerous, the syphilitic, old men over seventy, boys under sixteen, the kleptomaniacs, the tramps, the perverts, and last of all the flock of madmen. They were the only ones who didn't seem unhappy.*[16]

They all shared a common trait: not one was whole. Yet slowly, Jacques's belief in having an inner sight, gifted to him by his blindness, enabled him not only to survive but to become the same type of leader in camp as he had been as a seventeen-year-old Resistance organizer. He recited poetry—Rimbaud, Baudelaire—to inmates who did not understand French and inspired his new comrades—Russians, Poles, and others—to sing, dance, and laugh. "To forget was the law"—that is, to repress the restrictions and cruelties of the camp was the best way to remember past days of song and gentle revelry.

His reputation as a clear-spoken, direct, and transparent promoter of temporary happiness was augmented by his role as a trusted "spreader of the word." His German allowed him to listen carefully to the radio transmissions from Berlin that came across the loudspeakers, the same speakers that ordered the inmates to fulfill their minutely regulated tasks. He combined what he could gather from reading between the scripted lines of the radio broadcasters—what was omitted as much as what was said—with the news that came almost daily into the camp with the arrival of new internees. He interviewed newcomers, trying to coordinate stories, news, and rumors, and he recruited Dutch, Polish, Russian, Czech, and Hungarian native-speakers to spread his "newscast." (At one point he was stunned to learn of the Normandy invasion only a few weeks after it had happened, not from the Germans but from a new inmate.) In this way, information about the slow disintegration of the German front and the impending arrival of the American army reached the prisoners. Though the Germans tried to empty the camp with hastily prepared "death marches," eventually the inmates took matters into their own hands and attacked the few guards who remained, knowing that there would be massive Allied help coming up the road to Buchenwald.

And so Lusseyran survived. But the drama was not finished; after the camp was liberated, the inmates still had to wait, once again, to be counted and interrogated. Prisoners died daily, from overeating, from the shock of freedom, and from illnesses too far along for medical intervention. The retreating camp guards had poisoned the food stock, and starvation began to take lives:

> [Those] days . . . were days of stupefaction. We were drunk but with an evil drunkenness. . . . One doesn't pass over, all at once, from the idea of death to the idea of life. We listened to what they [the Americans] were saying to us, but we asked for a little time to believe in it. . . . Where was the joy of freedom, the joy of living? The camp was under an anesthetic, and it would take hours and hours to lay hold on life. Finally, all of a sudden, it burst upon you; blinding your eyes, stronger than your senses, stronger than reason. It came in great waves, every wave hurtling as it came in.[17]

||||||||||||||||||||

We are left with nagging questions about those who did not resist the Occupying Authority: How many Frenchmen who assisted in the punishment and murder of their own fellow citizens would live long lives of guilt, fearful at any moment that someone would remember

them or point them out? How many accepted responsibility for their
lapses in acting with common humanity? We write of the heroes and
the villains, but what of the other victims—those caught in between
absolute evil and ethical beneficence? Ever since the end of World
War II, the French have struggled with such questions. Perhaps
they—and we—always will.

CHAPTER EIGHT

Does Resistance Have a Gender?

Even if you doubted the effectiveness of your actions, you knew that you were not wrong.

—MARIE-MADELEINE FOURCADE, *RÉSISTANTE*

The Occupation historian Michèle Cointet states baldly in her latest book that "the Resistance is considered a virile act."[1] She then proceeds to debunk that claim. Still, the assertion continues to be argued today, and it is still considered necessary to correct this canard. The place of women and girls in the resistance to the Germans and their Vichy fellows remains an unsettled terrain of debate, despite such deeply substantiated studies as Cointet's. Research since the 1980s has vigorously argued that the Resistance's success might have been decisively impeded without the help of young women, women who put themselves in the same dangerous situations as their male companions. But after the war, men and boys garnered most of the attention, not to mention most of the medals, the role of women tending to become enveloped in, if not overwhelmed by, masculine exploits. And frankly, though many women and girls went to German prison camps to die or barely survive, the image of young men tied to stakes, blindfolded or not, being shot while singing "La Marseillaise" or shouting "Vive la France" captured more fascinated attention.

At the Musée de l'Ordre de la Libération at the Invalides in Paris, the portraits of the 1,038 members of the Ordre de la Libération include almost no women *compagnonnes*. Charles de Gaulle had established this decoration in 1940 to recognize extraordinary military and civil service to the liberation of France; only six women were awarded this highest distinction, and only one under the age of thirty.* Young women, recognized or not as major players, had often carried out dangerous assignments, and their exploits present examples of courage and decency that should fix their place firmly in the national narrative of resistance.

Today one can find important books about women who resisted, but far fewer than about male *résistants*. Yet women's voices continue to be heard; testimonies, formal as well as informal, have been presented and then repeated. One of the most tangible results of *résistantes'* postwar notoriety, no matter how hard-won, was that de Gaulle supported the right of women to have the vote, which was legalized before the war had ended.† He could not ignore the evidence of the important contributions of girls and women in the struggle on French territory that helped chase the Germans back across the Rhine.

Decades later, in May 2015, President François Hollande officiated at a ceremony at the Panthéon, burial site of some of France's greatest political, social, and cultural figures, as the remains of four *résistants*—Germaine Tillion, Geneviève de Gaulle-Anthonioz, and two men, Pierre Brossolette and Jean Zay—were transferred to lie

---

* About one hundred of the recipients of the Order were under age twenty, all male, and the youngest was only fourteen when shot by the Germans.

† In spite of its grand motto "Liberté, Égalité, Fraternité," France did not legalize women's suffrage until 1944 (women first voted in 1945); the right to vote came to France decades after it had been legalized in most other major European nations, including Italy, Spain, Germany, and the Soviet Union. (Switzerland would not permit women to vote until 1971.)

there.* For the first time in seventy years, widespread and massive public attention was paid to the women of the Resistance.

||||||||||||||||||||||

The role of girls and young women would present a recurring conundrum for the leaders of the PCF. The early 1920s had seen equal attention given to female youngsters, with photographs of them with fists raised assertively against fascism. But as the Front populaire tried to reassure the general public that their government was not ultra-radical, pressure was put on young women communists to resume their traditional role as intelligent and necessary, but still docile, members of the Party. As such, they were often assigned the mundane tasks of printing and typing, while otherwise keeping out of sight. At times they were even forbidden to pass leaflets out in the street, for fear of rousing the indignation of the center and right. Of course, the most outspoken communist females often defied these restrictions.

||||||||||||||||||||||

The sacrifice of the lives of almost two million Frenchmen in World War I had brought necessary attention to the crucial role that women played as single parents, house managers, workers in the war industry, and generally protectors of the ideal French family. The numerous youth movements of the 1930s had finally encouraged young women to leave home briefly, during the summer, to attend camps that would offer them a new independence from parental supervision. Through

---

* Jean Zay, education minister under the Front populaire, was a Jewish Freemason and socialist intellectual who was taken out of prison in June 1944 and shot dead by members of the Vichy Milice. Pierre Brossolette was a major socialist resistance organizer, also a Freemason, and close to de Gaulle. He was finally captured after years of clandestine service. In March 1944, under torture, he threw himself out of a window to his death.

vigorous physical exercise, they learned how to be more confident in public and in social activities. In these camps, they were able to make friends outside of their social class or neighborhood, even with immigrants. And they gained assurance in debating ideological positions. Cultural changes in the 1930s—the introduction of swing and jazz, the establishment of *bals* where boys and girls could enjoy each other's company without chaperones, the omnipresent new cinema depicting smart young women engaging with smart—and surprised—young men had transformed the popular image of what a young girl might become.

Still, traditional mores—secular and religious—as well as a deeply patriarchal legal system militated against too much independence. Girls had still to confront a consensus that they should be homemakers, that they were too emotional and fragile to enter the worlds of banking, engineering, or business. Men were legally the head of their family, and girls continued to be educated in single-sex schools. Still, the nation was filled with wives, sisters, and daughters who were caretakers for psychologically or physically wounded men. The same indomitability that had made females indispensable to the home front during the Great War did not leave them for long in the shadows of male-only resistance activities.

Germaine Tillion explained that there were three resistance activities for which young women and girls were immediately needed: to discover and distribute information; to help those trying to escape, especially POWs, Allied aviators, and Jews; and finally, to find ways to inform London and the Free French about what was happening in France. None of these tasks was danger-free. This work began immediately, even before the armistice was signed, for it was obvious that France had lost its war and that, many feared, the country would soon be under some sort of Nazi administration. Most girls and boys had no experience in such work, no organization, and no knowledge of how to distinguish between possible supporters and potential enemies. But both genders were already present on the thin line of resistance.

In her eminently researched study *A Train in Winter*, the historian Caroline Moorehead outlines how disorganized and chaotic women's earliest resistance efforts were. Through extensive interviews with surviving women resisters, she discovered that the earliest resisters had decided to participate on their own initiative, that is, they did not need the encouragement of their brothers, uncles, or fathers. Nonetheless, they often needed masculine permission to go out alone, especially at night, or to borrow a bicycle or spend unguarded time with men outside the family—that is, they had to "resist" the gender bias underlying male and female relationships in midcentury France while also figuring out how to resist the Occupier. At first, their activities, almost always nonviolent, often befuddled the German police and even their compatriots, the French police officers. It would take almost two years, until early 1942, before authorities realized how important young women were to the Resistance and how guilefully they did their jobs.

Still, for the average bourgeois girl (a term to distinghish those girls from their more worldly communist sisters), to resist was not at first a specifically ideological decision but a patriotic one—that is, one that emanated from an embarrassment that overshadowed their pride in being French. Of course, friends and boyfriends who bragged about writing "Vive de Gaulle!" on the walls or making fun of young German soldiers attracted the patriotic attention of the most confident of young women. But for the most part, the girls who did resist just slipped into those roles, often idiosyncratically, before and until the whole movement had had time to organize and direct their impulsive actions. Besides this emerging search for an answer to the question "what should I do?," girls were also continuously exposed to Vichy propaganda that women and girls were expected to have babies and care for the family. Newspapers, books, magazines, posters, radio announcements, school instruction—all repeatedly reminded girls of the domestic duties they were expected to fulfill. (The fact that men had failed to do their duty seemed to have escaped even the subtlest of the propagandists.)*

Another source of emulation that raised young women's awareness of the role they could play during the gray armistice period was found in their classrooms: their female teachers, at all levels, were often pacifists, leftists, and antifascists. Having their teachers explain in context what was happening in Europe (at least until they were fired by the Vichy educational establishment because of their assumed ideological prejudices), or hint at the weaknesses of the Vichy project, or ask students how they intended to live through the Occupation—all of these discussions demanded answers to questions that girls' families might not have been asking. Mothers and fathers were worried about their sons not following police regulations, being drafted, or remaining in POW camps. Girls, the culture assumed, were less vulnerable, saner, more cautious, and less spontaneous. This "invisibility" within their own families allowed some young women the freedom to make important decisions without parental interference.

At the beginning, there was an almost gay "cops-and-robbers" attitude toward interfering with German order. By this, I mean that adults did not take seriously the desire of young women to stand against what was happening. "What are you going to do?" they would ask patronizingly. "Run around whistling at German soldiers, defacing their vehicles, or tearing down posters? It will only get you—and us—into

---

* The vicious treatment of some women at the Liberation—most notably, the public shaving of their hair for supposedly having fraternized with Germans—has been interpreted by many scholars as a male reaction to the influential positions they had attained in a war lost by those very men.

trouble." But from the winter of 1940 until the summer of 1941, the game continued, as Moorehead explains:

> *There was yet no very clear goal to their activities, beyond the con-*
> *stant harassment of the Germans whose forces they hoped to keep in*
> *a perpetual state of uneasy alert. They also wanted to send a mes-*
> *sage to Vichy that collaboration was an odious affair, unacceptable*
> *to decent people, and that it would, when sanity and victory returned*
> *to France, be severely punished. . . . What none of them knew [the*
> *youngest as well as the oldest], . . . feeling oddly safe in a country*
> *where women were still not perceived to be active in the Resistance,*
> *was how lethal it was about to become.*[2]

Once the Gestapo and the SS had replaced the Wehrmacht as over-seer of the French police in mid-1942, arrests became increasingly public, security checks more frequent, and examination of IDs less cursory. Young women were now watched closely. They were not of-ten captured in the act of violence, but an arrest would lead back to those who had been instrumental in preparing false papers, finding lodging, hiding resisters, or passing information between resistance groups. Though they still could guilefully use their wholesome youth and apparent innocence to throw both Germans and Frenchmen off the scent, girls discovered that doing so had become more difficult to get away with. And not a few young women were arrested, if only to intimidate them rather than punish them.

As surveillance and betrayal became common, these girls and young women, often still living at home with their families, had to become more sophisticated about their activities. They rarely acted independently—that is, without support from adults, mostly male. There were no "all-girl" resistance groups, charged specifically with doing less onerous, less dangerous, or less significant acts. Maroussia Naïtchenko had a theory about why there were so few girls and young women in the active, or violent, resistance: "[The Resistance] had much difficulty in recruiting liaison agents. Families of sympathizers and even those of militants would not let their young daughters hang around, without supervision or surveillance, with a group of men."[3]

Then as now, girls were expected to write about their most private thoughts and dreams, especially as they approached puberty. We saw this in Micheline Bood's detailed recounting of her daily existence during the Occupation. Blank journals and diaries were given as gifts, some with locks and keys. Thanks to these records, much has been learned of daily life during the Occupation, and of the lives of young women in a repressive society; boys' diaries are rarer. During the Occupation, girls also wrote letters—to their absent fathers, boyfriends, husbands, and brothers—and to the BBC; they seemed to have an uncanny belief that, as Maroussia Naïtchenko exclaims toward the end of *Une Jeune Fille en guerre* (A girl at war), "If I escape, I will write! . . . My decision taken then was also a sort of psychological safeguard: a means of being able to support the increasing disappearances and my own suffering. . . . I would be the depository, a witness, having seen and remembered, these days of horror."[4] Micheline Bood called her notebooks *les années doubles*, "the double years": every rule, every expectation, every "normality" had a second meaning, a double expectation, an option. And so these documents continue to appear from the mists of history as children and grandchildren find them, stored in trunks and attics and old chifforobes.

⑊⑊⑊⑊⑊⑊⑊⑊⑊⑊⑊⑊⑊

Among the reasons that Maroussia Naïtchenko's memoir is affecting is because she not only remembers the anxiety of that period but never forgets that she was just a sixteen-year-old teenager. After the Germans arrived in the capital on June 14, 1940, she recounts, she and her friends had a brilliant idea: they wanted to go to the top of the Eiffel Tower, a short walk from the Invalides, and see Occupied Paris from above. Arriving there, they found that the elevators were not working, possibly having been sabotaged. So, being sixteen and with strong legs, they climbed the 1,700 steps. By late June 1940, Paris, almost overnight, was full of Germans. Again, with her friends, Maroussia decided to go to the grand parade ground in front of the Invalides, not far from her grandmother's apartment, to watch as enemy forces marched before Napoleon's tomb.

> *The German tanks . . . filed by in well-ordered ranks that covered the width of the esplanade. It was imposing, almost unimaginable, this tranquil power that, rolling along with a deep, but regular sound, crossed "our" asphalt. . . . I had lost all thought, all feeling, felt emptied, in a stupor. Thus had Nazism won, and now trampled on the soil of my childhood, of my very neighborhood!*
>
> *. . . The soldiers who drove these tanks and trucks, with their impeccable belts, appeared young and in excellent form. Nothing like our poor men, in faded uniforms, clumsy, exhausted. . . . Never would one have believed that this blond youth who paraded impassively by us had been successful in defeating us in such a short time. Against this hated army, what would we be able to do? In a single instant, I finally understood the word "Occupation."* [5]

In another telling anecdote that casually describes what must have been an important adjunct to the growth of a more violent resistance in later months, Maroussia recounts that her grandmother was afraid to give up an old pistol, as ordered by the authorities. The French police, advised by the Wehrmacht, had issued the early injunction to Parisians that they should surrender all personal arms by taking them to the nearest police station. Maroussia's grandmother was too nervous to comply, so she offered her small pistol to one of Maroussia's comrades and asked him to throw it into the sewer. Later, Maroussia learned that many had done the same and that communist sewer workers collecting them were slowly building an arsenal against the Occupiers.

Naïtchenko's captivating memoir might be the most intimate remembrance we have of not only the bigger questions that led adolescents to challenge authority, but the day-to-day preoccupations of courageous but nervous youngsters who, unlike their often-guarded parents, wanted to actively confront the Occupier. They itched to express how angry they were about the betrayal of their nation. The brilliantly provocative interaction of Maroussia's conservative grandmother and faithfully communist mother made the teenager a sensitive, always inquisitive fighter against the "new revolution" that was endeavoring to replace her pride in the French Republic.

After the exodus, Maroussia's account recalls, with youngsters returning to the capital, amateur posters and wall scribblings began to reappear. At first, the authorities had not been too severe toward the young miscreants, who were typically taken to the nearest police station, where they were scared to death by the cops and their parents were called. But, as Maroussia writes, "we were not aware that the Gestapo was working away in the shadows." Lists were being compiled, and foreign Jews, communists, and Freemasons were quietly being arrested. The homes of Jewish merchants were being looted, and "undesirables" were filling the concentration camps that had popped up all over France to handle Spanish refugees; though not death camps, they were still unpleasant. "Silently, the traps that would close in on us were being quietly set up."[6] Nevertheless, Maroussia and her young comrades fearlessly continued their timid harassment of both the Germans and the French police. They learned which street markets were the safest for the distribution of their tracts; which streets were dead ends; and which seemed to be dead ends, but in fact opened onto other avenues of escape. They found out where and how to hide their bikes.

And then a miracle occurred: Maroussia's mother found a job at the Kommandantur, headquarters for the Occupying Authority, situated on the Place de l'Opéra. (In applying, she had used her maiden name, de Guilhermy, and the particle "de" probably impressed German snobs.) She was hired as a professor and interpreter of French, and most important she had access to an official *Ausweis,* the pass that allowed her to go anywhere in Paris, enter all the finest hotels that the Germans had occupied, use public transit for free, and be out after curfew. This "cover" would be of inestimable use to her daughter, the young *résistante.*

It was during this time that Naïtchenko befriended the three boys whose names would become synonymous with youthful resistance: Guy Môquet, Thomas Elek, and André Kirschen. As was often the case among teens and students in the underground, their bonds, though often brief, were intense. Adult leaders were few, and the spontaneity and fearlessness of these youth often led them to unforeseen danger they had not anticipated. They could not always protect their parents from learning about their activities, nor prevent the family arguments that often ensued when they were found with incriminating evidence in their rooms or on their persons. One young warrior recalls that a friend's father had found, hidden under his son's mattress, not sexy magazines but dozens of pages of anti-German leaflets. Furious, the father threw them out of the window—onto the busy Avenue Bosquet. Mortified at his own spontaneous stupidity (which happily had no repercussions), he made sure his eighteen-year-old son was locked in his room at night, and he was forbidden to go anywhere but to school and back.

If she lacked patience in the classroom, Maroussia had spirit, a sense of humor, and a readily displayed impatience with cant. Pretty and popular, she was a "normal" youngster who had to grow up quickly. Soon, with her girlfriends, she acted illegally for the first time. All posters on Parisian walls had to have official stamps applied to them. Cautiously, she and a friend began delicately removing the expensive stamps, hoping that the Jeunesse communiste could use them for their own signs. When stopped by a policeman and warned that she was breaking a law, she and her friends giggled, acting as though they had been playing a game; the policeman smiled and walked away. It was not the first time she would use her girlishness as camouflage.

Maroussia learned several important lessons while acting out her romantic fantasies as a young communist: she observed that solidarity in a group was similar to belonging to a family; she learned to express her ideas in an environment where they might be questioned, but not ridiculed; she felt comfortable interacting with boys and young men, as her equals; and she realized that one's life plans could suddenly be changed by external events. She also came to recognize that internal fractures, even among the most committed, could suddenly make another suspicious, and that one could mysteriously become herself an object of suspicion. Even after the German invasion of the Soviet Union had freed French communists to act aggressively, the French Communist Party was divided between those who supported Stalin, with his belief that the Soviet Union should represent the ideal totalizing socialist state, and Trotsky, a close ally of Lenin, who emphasized the responsibility to promulgate international socialism. Arguments among her fellow Party members led to resignations and caused enmity among the most passionate. Young Maroussia often wondered if her comrades were forgetting the larger picture as they disputed each other's claims to be the most loyal communist.

Once she had thoroughly committed herself to action against the Occupier, Maroussia proudly describes her first golden moment, which would be remembered for four years by all who were there, or who were there in spirit:

That day, we entered the main court [of the Sorbonne] shouting: "Free Langevin!" The doors of the great auditorium, opening onto

the courtyard, were closed, so we had to wait on the steps shouting
our protest. . . . The small group of protesters then went to the
Collège de France [the elite institution of higher learning adjacent
to the Sorbonne]. There were not many of us and our intervention
certainly did not make the administration tremble, but this handful
of protesters had showed this venerable establishment that we were
present. We lit then the first torch of student resistance.[7]

This was, of course, her memory of the first major demonstration
against the Occupier, on November 11, 1940, discussed earlier in
Chapter Six.

Naïtchenko and her young friends continued to find ways to resist the orders of the higher-ups in the Party during the winter of
1940–1941 while the Hitler–Stalin pact was still in force. They im-
pudently printed tracts and distributed them; they played havoc
with the hundreds of German and Vichy propaganda posters that
littered Paris; and they regularly met in small groups to bemoan the
pusillanimity of the Soviet Union and its shameful non-aggression
treaty with Hitler. The youngsters also searched high and low for
ronéotype machines and even printing presses; found isolated locations to do the noisy work of printing; taught themselves to discern
whether they were being followed; and learned how to avoid being
stopped for ID checks. These kids were still living at home and still
hearing their parents, who were also communists for the most part,
complain about the noose the Russians had put around their efforts.
Yet the adventure of doing something, of showing one's solidarity, if
not with the Party then at least with their generation, was addictive.
They knew they needed to be especially careful: they were being
watched by a multitude of suspicious entities—the Germans, the Vichy police, the hierarchy of the PCF, and anticommunist resistance
cadres.

Certainly, they were cautious when asked where their fealty lay. They were careful not to mention anything about their surreptitious gatherings, not even to their parents, and they astutely avoided fights with students who had nothing but disdain for communists, Jews, and Gaullists. All the while they were hearing about youngsters like themselves who were being rounded up, held indefinitely, and, like Môquet, sometimes executed.

These young communists were defined by their solidarity with each other, by their commitment to freedom (innocent as they were of Stalin's vicious dictatorship), and by respect for what each of them—girls as well as boys—could bring to the cause. Girls especially were welcomed and recruited, for they had attributes, skills, and a cultural camouflage that would prove useful in the later struggles. During this gray period, Maroussia often served as a lookout for youngsters, communist and other, who would suddenly make a brief speech in a market, throw leaflets into a crowd, or pass to people leaving a church tickets that said "Join us in our fight against fascism." She and her friends were careful not to identify themselves as communist—so as to avoid conflict with their Party's obedient hierarchy—but they did not sit still while adults dickered over international politics and Jews, Roma, and political refugees were being rounded up and often deported.

"We were clandestine," Maroussia writes simply—hidden, under cover, subversive, silently antagonistic, obsessively secretive.[8] And it was not only young communists who were clandestinely subversive; a range of students, from the far right to the pacifist center to the noncommunist left, formed groups based on friendship and politics. For about a year, even though a few youngsters were caught and punished, the authorities were more concerned about their elders. As a result of this inattention, these youth were allowed time and space to become confident in their activities, but they also became less and less careful about making sure that they went unnoticed.

Not surprisingly, the strain of operating under so much surveillance began to show its effects. Maroussia, the teen who had wanted to climb the Eiffel Tower, was now short of breath after repeatedly going up five or six floors of apartment house stairs. Her fatigue and undernourished figure made her look harried to observers and suggested that she was perhaps on some clandestine mission. She had to worry about where to leave her bicycle while she distributed the tracts; a stolen bicycle was a crisis almost as serious as an arrest for anti-German activity: "I would come home wiped out by these activities. . . . I was always out of breath, and dizzy. Obviously, not having enough to eat made the least effort almost impossible. I began to have brief moments of deafness . . . in metro stairways. All of this would have been supportable had I not been the only one doing most of this work, feeling alone, exhausted."[9]

Released from their leashes by the German invasion of the Soviet Union in June 1941, communist resistance teams began to be organized. Maroussia now had two boys accompany her wherever she was distributing tracts, to warn her if they saw cops or plainclothesmen approaching. She regained her confidence, and her morale rose. Almost immediately, the activities of these teenagers became more serious, and more respected by the Party. She was told, in the deepest secrecy, that the loosely organized groups of the Jeunesse communiste would now take up sabotage of railroads, electrical pylons, and German warehouses.

Maroussia was surprised at how well led this new *Organisation spéciale* was, and she reluctantly supported it, though she knew nothing about arms. She learned of the effectiveness of these clandestine attacks, as did other Parisians, not through the newspapers, which tried to keep them quiet, but through the red posters "announcing the execution of hostages as reprisals for actions committed in Paris against the German army. On the walls of the capital these [red] posters . . . were like a smear of blood spattered on the stone."[10]

It was soon after Maroussia's eighteenth birthday that the Germans executed twenty-seven young communists in a camp in Brittany, including her comrade Guy Môquet, in reprisal for resistance actions. The ethical questions that violent resistance raised increasingly tormented her. Her cadre had to do all within their power to let the Germans know and feel that they were illegal occupants of a free nation, but what if, in doing so, they put some of their comrades in danger? If the Germans chose willy-nilly Jews and communists to be shot when violence occurred, how were they not responsible for their deaths? Such was the ethical web in which these youngsters lived and operated.

Naïtchenko repeatedly put her life on the line. She was caught up not only in a sense of party and patriotic passion but also in a sense of solidarity, friendship, and family as she worked with others to protect the young men who were living undercover lives.

Ah! No, they did not appear to be heroes! For the most part, they weren't even old enough to be drafted. They lived far from their families, without girlfriends, without a cent in their pocket, with shoes always in need of repair, wearing worn-out clothes, not even having enough money to pay for a metro ticket to get them to the next rendezvous. Some older militants, those who had fought in the International Brigades in the Spanish Civil War, gave them a few lessons in guerrilla warfare. They practiced in the fields, risking capture and death, even though they were still uneasy about killing. Our only strength was the very strong affection that linked us, that solidarity which led each of us to gamble our own lives to help the other, for the common goal. I had for my comrades an affection that only exists in extreme conditions.

And self-doubt comes up often: "Guerrilla war was not made for sensitive young girls, but I had no choice. I had to support my comrades. One didn't just quit like that."[11]

The mental fatigue that would set in was debilitating; it came not only from constant work but also from the sense of being constantly surveilled. Still, sometimes a bit of humor could be found. At one point, a Party member recommended a doctor to her, a woman sympathetic to the left. Maroussia made an appointment about a stubborn bronchitis that had been weakening her. The day before, her friend Robert had confided to her that in their work, "one can only expect a life of about two months, as if he were talking about preparing an oral exam." He too was exhausted, so he accompanied her to the physician's office. Once there, Maroussia asked the doctor if she might check him out also. She gave the young man prescriptions for his blood pressure, which she had found to be quite elevated. She also advised him to "lead a calm and well-regulated daily regime; no agitation, no emotion; go to bed early."[12] The two resisters laughed all the way down the stairs.

Naïtchenko's loyalty to her Party and to her nation closed off some of her ideological concerns about Stalinism, and if she thought too much about her growing disenchantment with the Party's beliefs, the brutality of the Germans always brought her quickly back to the fold. The names of the executed continued to be published on posters and in newspapers. Sometimes even their photos were made available for all to see how young they were. As 1943 rolled over to 1944, there was no longer any doubt that the authorities were much better at controlling the resisters than vice versa. "During this period, . . . more comrades fell than German soldiers."[13]

A reader of Maroussia's memoirs marvels at how fortunate she and her comrades were as they skirted the deadly zones of police control. She realized that even the best planning could be undone in an instant: "An arrest, liberty, or death depended on what during those days? On a handshake with a friend met by chance, in a garden in the spring? . . . All was nothing but chance and coincidence."[14] It was an increasingly stressful period for this intelligent young woman as she struggled to distinguish between orthodoxy and loyalty to friends. No matter how much the *résistants* and *résistantes* professed not to have any other ideology than ridding France of a foreign Occupier and an illicit government, preoccupations often surfaced. How important would the Parti communiste français be after the war? Which communist factions would dominate? Was de Gaulle but another Pétain—conservative, military, and autocratic?

New recruits often knew no more than a few members of their group, not only because they might be arrested and made to reveal secrets, but also so that the organizers of their cadres could use secrecy to retain their own influence and authority. This social isolation weighed on the gregarious girl. Maroussia details how she became caught up in Party factionialism and was made persona non grata in some quarters of the city because she was not trusted by a faction of the Party:*

> Up until then, I had always believed in the Party's message, but given its conduct [against some of its most loyal members], I realized that it was no longer possible for me to adhere to it. Fortunately, many solid comrades had surrounded my adolescence, had inculcated in me a conscience, and had armed me well enough so that I did not fall into any delinquency. I too found it completely incapable to denounce my friends. I might disapprove of their views, but condemn them, no. I too shared their disappointments.[15]

She succeeded in maintaining her activities even after she became pregnant by a fellow *résistant* and bore a son whom she named Guy, after the martyred Môquet. (Sadly, Georges Grünenberger,

---

* The history of infighting among national and international Communist Parties has been well told. Suspicion of fellow Party members, betrayals, and even violence against those who might disagree about Stalin or Trotsky or about whether national Parties should be independent or subservient to Moscow were frequent. Occasionally resistance efforts against the Germans failed because of this mutual distrust and enmity.

Maroussia's lover and later husband, had been caught by the Germans. While he would survive the war, he did not meet his son until little Guy was two and a half years old.)

After Guy's birth, Naïtchenko was encouraged to begin participating again in the Party's activities, but this time in the provinces, where she became an important member of *Inter 7*, a group operating in the *départements* immediately surrounding Paris. Her mother had agreed to take care of her baby, and she was adamant about returning to the confrontation with the Occupier. Maroussia led a more dangerous life there than she had in the city. Since there were only a handful of members of the network, her activities were more diverse and expansive. She had to type codes one day and on another practice riding a bicycle over unpaved roads and through fields; acting as a courier another day, she would turn to transporting weapons on the next.

Maroussia did finally uncover that her troubles within the Party had resulted from her having casually signed a petition regarding the reappearance of *L'Humanité* in 1940, while the German-Soviet pact was still in force. Such petty criticisms, and the lack of recognition for what she and Georges had done to resist the Occupation, forced her after the war not only to leave the Party but to leave communism in general. Nevertheless, she affirms that she felt fortunate to have joined the Jeunesse communiste while only a child: "I received from them an exceptional education, a civic morality, an ability to adapt, a sense of responsibility, and an entrepreneurial expertise, all of which have never left me."[16]

One of the subtlest memoirs—one that examines not only active confrontation but the psychology of those who chose to do so—is Annie Kriegel's *Ce que j'ai cru comprendre* (What I thought I knew), published a few years before she passed away in 1995. A fervent communist during the Occupation, Kriegel left the Party after the war. She wrote histories and critiques of the Party and was consistently and vehemently criticized by her former colleagues. But that was later. Swept up into the battle against fascism, Annie was not as ideologically confused as young Maroussia. She was only thirteen when the Germans invaded Poland, and since she was from an Alsatian-Jewish family, she was more aware than most of the threat of Nazi politics. Living in Paris, in the Marais, *quartier juif par excellence*, Annie learned early of the socio-religious split between poor Catholics and Jews, as well as of the tensions between Jews of different regions of Europe. But these differences became less important as the laws of Vichy and the Germans themselves failed to distinguish between types of Jews in rounding them up for deportation.

Because of her father's leanings in 1938–1939, Annie went to a leftist camp, where she heard the *Internationale* for the first time. Still, camp was camp: activities included hikes, bonfires, singing matches, and marches through the country. Before the world changed, Annie took full advantage of this organized adolescent freedom:

> *That September 1, 1939, the weather was still beautiful. Legs and feet bare in my sandals, my shoulders uncovered too, I sped on my bike in front of the Halle aux poissons. There, before a large white poster with two crossed French flags at its stop was a small group, especially women, . . . that drew my attention. I braked quickly, and jumped off my bike. It said "general mobilization." At 4 a.m., without declaring war, the German army had invaded Poland. After two days of indecisiveness, the 3rd September, Great Britain and France declared war on Germany, the first at 11 a.m., the second at 5 p.m.*[17]

Having heard her father bemoan the antisemitism of the Germans for years, she sensed that this event would mean more to her than to the women reading the poster. She was definitely French, but she was also Jewish.

With the invasion of the Low Countries and France, Annie's father tried to get his family to Saint-Nazaire on the Atlantic coast and over to England, but by the time they arrived the harbor had been ruined by the German air force. They were trapped in France. "Occupied France closes over us like an oyster. . . . We are Jews," her desperate father intoned.[18] They had no choice but to return to Paris.

Late one evening, returning from a mission, Kriegel found herself in the Jewish quarter after curfew. She remembered the address of gentiles in the Marais who hid Jews seeking temporary refuge and knocked at the door of one of them, who welcomed her. She was shown to a room filled, for the most part, with other Jews, all waiting until dawn and the lifting of the curfew. When she peeped out of the apartment house's large door, she saw, coming toward her, a French policeman carrying two large suitcases, tears streaming down his middle-aged, weathered face. Following him, carrying small bags of belongings, was a group of children, women, and old folk. (By this time, Jewish men had learned not to spend the night at home, thinking they alone were arrestable.) "It was a roundup," she recognized. Kriegel heard the screams of mothers being separated from their children—an unforgettable wailing that she never forgot. Annie knew not to go home; her mother had warned her about that. Finally, as dawn broke, she decided to walk to her new job, near the Avenue de l'Opéra, where she was an underpaid typist. Just act as if all is normal, she reasoned. That evening she returned home to find that her mother had left the apartment with her little sister until the arrests calmed down. They were safe, but not for long, her father insisted.

Annie was stricken by her parents' fear. Why run? They were French. They belonged in France. They had done nothing illegal. Had not Joan of Arc stood proudly against the English? Why not the Becker (Kriegel's maiden name) family against the Germans? She kept these thoughts to herself, but her anger and passion moved her closer to the shadows of clandestinity. Her family snuck out of Paris the next day, taking a train from the Gare de Lyon to Grenoble in the Unoccupied Zone. (This was before November 1942, when the Germans invaded the Unoccupied Zone.)

In Grenoble, Annie made her first contact with an organized resistance network. Instead of making her confident, her minor experiences in clandestine activities in Paris had intimidated her; she did not know what frightened her more—Germans, French police, administrators, or her parents. When asked to distribute larger and larger numbers of leaflets in Paris, she had done so, and then had vomited from fear. Now, in Grenoble, when she thought back on it, Annie realized what had terrified her: it was the fact that she had entered the underground world and new rules had to be learned for a life in the shadows. She writes of a difference between "clandestinity" and "resistance." This subtle distinction reveals how exquisite some of the rationales were for those moving deeper into the world of dangerous action:

> *The passage into clandestinity differed according to whether one lived alone, or was involved [in an organization with its own rules and regulations]. . . . One could not just wave a magic wand and cause all of one's [social obligations] to disappear. . . . It was a slow process of submersion, the process of weakening [though leaving unbroken] former social ties. . . . This is what marked the years 1940–1942. . . . It was the passage from thought to action, from the permitted to the forbidden, from the public to the clandestine. Not everyone is made for transgressions, no matter the kind or the motive. I was less so than most. I do not easily become a rebel.*[19]

In Grenoble, Annie soon learned that the group she became affiliated with was from the Jeunesse communiste and thus had the patience and respect for young women that most groups lacked. Her decision to join was almost casual. She knew that the communists were being constantly hunted, but they knew how to live secretly and were not afraid to confront the Germans. But just associating with young communists was considered dangerous, so what drew this timid girl in? There was a familiarity remembered from her summers in leftist camps. But more compelling was an impulse to act, rather than just complain about the situation.

These cadres of young communists used first names only, and most often not their own. This was another protection against inadvertently revealing information to spies or traitors. Even beyond names, most of the youngsters adopted a complete clandestine identity, which enabled them to establish social relations as blank slates: no class distinction, no geographical distinction, no ethnic distinction. For specific missions, an additional onetime layer of false identity was assigned, and after the mission that name and biography had to be forgotten for it would be used again by underground colleagues. This play with and interchange of identities, which noncommunist groups came also to use late in the war, may have unconsciously reminded the youthful miscreants of their own still-evolving selves. The continuous need to hide one's identity must have been both exhilarating and exhausting.

Soon, Annie was assigned to a working-class Jewish network. This brought her to consider, once again, why she was resisting. "Perhaps no one has measured the irreparable rip in the fragile tissue of our souls [when we found ourselves] from one day to the next brusquely rejected, thrown out of the national community, and even more, out of our social worlds."[20] She had concluded that Jews had little choice, but, she wondered, why did non-Jews join in resistance too? They had nothing to fear; they were not to be separated from their parents. Why would a sixteen-year-old girl worry herself about the outcome of the war unless she was Jewish? These were naive questions, of course, but the answers eventually brought young Jews to admire their gentile brothers and sisters.

Annie's adventures made her bolder and more confident, though like most youngsters her age, she was occasionally somewhat scatterbrained as well. Once, while carrying incriminating materials in the saddlebags of her bike, she jumped off, leaned her bike against the wall of a store, and went in quickly to buy a comb. Her hair was a mess, and she did not want her father to ask questions about where she had been. Leaving the store, she found her bike gone—stolen!—as would have been almost any bike in those days that had been left unlocked and unattended. She was terrified, not only that police or Gestapo officers had found it, but also at what her teammates would say. The next day, when she arrived at an agreed-upon rendezvous, she was verbally thrashed by her leader. Then, miraculously, he brought the bike in! It had been taken by one of the young "followers"—girls and boys assigned to keep an eye on the couriers— and brought to headquarters. Relieved beyond expression, she also realized then and there that the Jeunesse communiste organization was a well-maintained machine.

It was also, as mentioned before, a machine that in most cases treated its workers equally, whether girls or boys. Annie had noticed in her courier rides around the countryside that most of the members of the groups hiding in the mountains and valleys of southeastern France were boys and young men; there were very few girls and young women. But in the city there were as many girls as boys in clandestine work, with similar tasks to perform. This fact would become publicly important after the war, when women would argue that the men were receiving the great majority of the honors and benefits of the Resistance, while little was done to acknowledge the contributions of women beyond thanking them. The rural Maquis had been made out to be a network of attractive, virile heroes only.

"The concept of clandestinity evokes, in those who have not practiced it, a sense of the fictional, even the romantic. . . . Clandestinity during the years of 1940–1944 was in and of itself, defiance against a ferocious force. [It] was not a game."[21] The popular images of untold numbers of brave Frenchmen taking up arms to harass the Germans and their Vichy supporters was a postwar fantasy that undermined the truth: being clandestine was tedious, often seemingly fruitless work. Most of the activities of this increasingly large group of young people centered on printing and distributing tracts—newspapers, warnings, and propaganda. The fabrication of false ID papers—passes, *cartes d'identité*, food tickets, metro tickets—occupied much of their time. They could not casually walk into a stationery store and purchase colored ink, different types of paper, and pens; they had to visit different stores, buying paper a few sheets at a time and purchasing one color of ink in one store and another in the one down the street—or better yet, in a completely different neighborhood or town. In the end, these monotonous routines, not the more "romantic" work of lobbing a grenade into a parade of German soldiers, defined most of the resistance work. Nevertheless, carrying out such banal tasks could also end perilously for the resisters.

Secret networks did not encourage the relationships that teenagers seek at that age; of course, there were episodes of illicit sexual relations—after all, rules had been bent by everyone, *n'est-ce pas*? But for those who were most serious about their work, one of the primary fascinations of teenagers, sexually intimate connection, lost some of its luster as they all sought to succeed in their resistance and avoid being caught.

For young women who offered their intelligence, energy, and imagination to the Resistance—some of whom were married, pregnant, or mothers—the fear must have been corrosive. In the 1940s, French society still upheld nineteenth-century norms for what girls and women should be doing with their talents. Women were still legally minors: they could not vote; they could not open personal bank accounts; and their financial affairs were kept in the hands of their fathers or husbands. Yet post–World War I society had seen some major advances for women in employment, brought more freedom in dress, and opened up new liberties in socializing with men. Still, a woman had to work three times as hard to make her mark in the company of men.

‖‖‖‖‖‖‖‖‖‖‖‖‖‖‖‖‖‖‖

Women resisters were not spared the horrors of the concentration camps. The niece of Charles de Gaulle, Geneviève, twenty-two, was arrested in Paris on July 20, 1943, caught in a dragnet by the Bonny-Lafont gang (the *Gestapo française*). She had been performing the same undercover work as Annie Kriegel and Maroussia Naïtchenko—passing information and messages, helping Jews and others to escape. After her arrest, she spent six months in French jails and finally, in February 1944, was sent to Ravensbrück. Located north of Berlin, this concentration camp was established especially for women political prisoners. Geneviève de Gaulle never tried to hide her relationship to her uncle, even after she joined the Resistance at the age of twenty. The Germans knew they had a prize.

Geneviève understood and spoke German, which allowed her to hear bits of information in camp that could make her life and those of her fellow inmates a bit better. She remained a resister, undermining as much as she could the rigorous rules and routines of a hellish existence. When her name was called in the interminable roll calls every morning and evening, the crowd of women prisoners would shout "Vive de Gaulle!" She thus provided intangible succor to a psychologically famished population. Many French *résistantes* were sent there, including Germaine Tillion. "I am no longer alone when the door closes. My comrades reminded me of that fraternal chain which unites us, one and all."[22] Doubtless she feared being alone, not only for survival's sake, but for her own mental health. As with Jacques Lusseyran's blindness in Buchenwald, Geneviève's notoriety provided both advantages and drawbacks at Ravensbrück.

She is exceptionally attentive to detail in her memoirs. Vittorio de Sica, the Italian film director, is reported to have observed that "there are no small events in the lives of the poor." And the same is true in the lives of camp inmates—no detail, even a large roach crossing the dirt floor of a hut, is ignored. She writes too of the inmate's preoccupation with her body, for it is a gauge of time passing in a camp and a prediction of the future. Her memoir of despair persistently repeats her conviction that she was living in an alternative universe, a place of fractured time. She writes that "the days pass astoundingly fast, while every moment seems interminable." And further: "Time exists no more; there is no frontier between dream, or nightmare, and reality."[23] The arbitrary behavior of her guardians, both the Nazis and the inmates who had taken on the role of proctors, added even more unpredictability, preventing any psychological certainty and creating permanent stress for the suffering human body and hallucinating mind.

Yet there is a reliable clarity and observational sobriety in her depiction of the qualities of others who had been in the Resistance. "I found great diversity among these women, of age, of social milieu, of geographical origin. Most of them having been arrested for resistance, but with differing motives, were alike in their refusal of the defeat and of Nazism. . . . Odette told us of how her son, sixteen years old, had cried out to her [at her 'trial']: 'Mama, don't talk; Mama!'"[24] And other small portraits constellate her memoir, illuminating those remarkably brave women and girls who had threatened—and frightened—the enemy. This sorority of shared anger and shared pain represented the best that France could offer against an implacable regime. The guards called them *Stücke* (pieces, things), but they were women, and proved themselves to be.

Fortunately, Geneviève de Gaulle-Anthonioz (her postwar married name) survived her incarceration, and fortunately also for posterity, through her descriptions we can gather an inkling of the daily, never-ending exhaustion of living in a place reeking of hatred and cruelty. Geneviève's memoir, along with others, such as Charlotte Delbo's *Auschwitz et après: Aucun de nous ne reviendra* (Auschwitz and after: Not one of us will return), reflect how courageous young women were, in camps as well as on the streets where they served as couriers and planners before their capture. The Germans had separated the genders, but their methods in handling incarcerated women and men were equally cruel, both for those who resisted and those who did not.

Also in Ravensbrück was Anise Postel-Vinay, born in 1922 in the Jura region of eastern France. Her mother was an intellectual who wanted her daughters to learn about the complex cultural and philosophical ramifications of faith and religion, not devotion to a particular denomination. She also ensured that her daughters learned German, given their home's proximity to their Teutonic neighbor; this skill would be crucial to Anise's survival in Ravensbrück.[*] While there, she befriended both Geneviève de Gaulle and Germaine Tillion.

Anise was sent to the camp after being arrested as a spy. The description in her memoir of her brief career as a member of the underground reveals how confused, disorganized, and even incompetent the early resisters were. Like most teenagers, she had not known where to turn to "do something" (*faire quelque chose*, the term commonly used for resisting). She had participated in the march up the Champs-Élysées on November 11, 1940, barely escaping arrest, but had concluded then that marching in demonstrations was not going to undermine the German presence. Anise thought that her knowledge of the language and culture of the enemy state would surely be useful to some activist group, but she did not know where to find

---

[*] In 2015, Anise published a brief memoir, *Vivre* (To live), recalling in supple prose her own and others' travails as a concentration camp inmate.

them. "We had all decided that we must do something against the Occupier, but what? How? With whom? From time to time, pamphlets fell into our hands, but they were never signed; there was no address: it was impossible to track down who had printed them. It was quite difficult to penetrate Resistance networks."[25] As noted, this was the experience of most young people who wanted "to do something," except for members of communist organizations, which had begun organizing as early as the late 1930s.

Anise then decided to try to reach England, but her mother forbade her leaving without a friend to accompany her. Not one of the young women she asked accepted her request; most people wanted to wait out the war, without causing trouble. Finally, through friends of friends, she contacted a woman professor connected to the English intelligence service. Immediately, she was recruited and put to work locating and identifying major armaments of the Wehrmacht, despite a near total lack of expertise:

> *I knew absolutely nothing about military affairs; it seemed folly to give me such a mission; moreover, I was petrified that I could not complete them. To ask a nineteen-year-old girl to tell the difference between one tank and another! . . . I could barely distinguish a machine gun from a tank! For me a corporal was the same as a colonel!* [26]

But intrepidly, when assigned to count and identify German tanks leaving the Vincennes fort on the outskirts of Paris, she took with her a seamstress's tape measure for cleverly gauging the difference in tank treads. She sent this information to England, relying on the intelligence services there to figure out which tanks were in Occupied France. Soon she was tasked with a variety of new duties, among them mapping bomb blasts and identifying German bunkers and the anti-aircraft balloons that surrounded Paris. She became quite adept at pinpointing these sites and photographing them, then sending the information through Le Havre to England.[*]

Of course, Anise's luck ran out. In August 1942, she traveled from Le Havre, where she had been gathering information for the English for a map that would pinpoint damage and possible targets, to Paris, where she was to deliver the information. The only clandestine contact she had in Paris was the same professor who had recruited her two years previously. Arriving at this woman's address, she noticed a large black car parked in front of the apartment house, with its official ID—*Ausweis*—proudly displayed. Something felt wrong—*Don't go up there*, her gut said—but she figured that it could be a medical doctor's automobile, like her father's, as they also had passes like the one she saw. She climbed to the fifth floor and knocked on the door, expecting to see the face of her mentor, but instead encountered that of a young German in shirtsleeves. The apartment had been identified and was being searched by the Gestapo. Anise had walked into a trap, and to make matters worse, she carried the photographed maps of Le Havre in her backpack.

This was the beginning of three years of incarceration for the young girl, first a year in Paris's La Santé prison, then a stint in Fresnes; finally she was taken to a transit camp at Romainville.[†] She was kept in isolation for most of the time; though she was not tortured, the threat of execution hung over her for thirteen months. In October 1943, the Germans suddenly ordered her to gather her belongings

---

[*] It was not until this century that she learned the identity of one of the translators of those documents: none other than the Irish writer and Nobel laureate Samuel Beckett, an active member of the Resistance, who had translated them from French to English.

[†] France had had "internment camps" for years, especially during the First World War, but with the Spanish Civil War and then the Occupation, they had proliferated. Over two dozen could be found spread throughout France. Romainville was very near Paris.

and get on a train headed east, to Ravensbrück. For the next eighteen months, until the camp's liberation in late April 1945, she managed to survive in a satanic universe. Not everyone else was as lucky: by war's end, the number of women and children murdered in the camp could not be accurately determined, but was at least ninety thousand, and perhaps more.

After the war, she married another *résistant*, André Postel-Vinay, but a profound sadness appears to have become part of her identity, not only because of the loss of her sister, who died in deportation, but because her return did not seem to have brought any feeling of closure: "We were coming back to a country that had been liberated for some time, but that had forgotten its [returning] prisoners."[27] One finds variations of this sentiment in numerous memoirs that describe what it was like to come back from the concentration and death camps in Germany and Poland; and so felt many POWs who had been held in Germany for five years. It was as if their very presence reminded the French of the mistakes and moral failures that had enabled their defeat and the Occupation. The wounded nation needed time to heal, to forget, now that the Nazis had been crushed. But for those who could not forget, coming home caused a different type of festering wound.

Much is owed to those young women who would not let prejudice keep them from confronting a vicious enemy and its Vichy minions. And thanks to their commitment to remembering, to witnessing, they have left for us narratives that still resonate with their passion for justice. Their desire to remind subsequent generations of their honest service, even when afraid or confused, is another manifestation of their resistance to injustices that never quite vanish.

Conclusion

————

It is my sense that . . . memory [of the Occupation] . . . has to struggle
ceaselessly against amnesia and forgetfulness. Because of this layer,
this mass, of the forgotten that covers everything, we can only glimpse
fragments of [that] past, intermittent traces of the shadowy, almost
ungraspable human lives of [the period].

—PATRICK MODIANO, NOBEL PRIZE IN
LITERATURE ACCEPTANCE SPEECH, 2015

Writing this book has caused me to question so many bromides—
about coming of age, about the differences between male and female
adolescence, about the relationship between those leaving childhood and
their elders, not to mention about what constitutes "resistance"—that I
have occasionally rubbed my eyes and decided it was time for another
glass of Médoc.

It was short, this tragic interlude, a bit less than five years of intense
confrontation among four distinct populations: German Occupiers,
Vichy bureaucrats and supporters, those who resisted, and those who
just wanted to get on with their lives. That last group was the prize:
each of the other three groups endeavored to move them to offer support, or at least to remain neutral while the struggle continued. It was
not an easy time for anyone. But those few who resisted—either violently or subtly—had the most difficult task. To refer again to Michael
Walzer's complex but helpful study about the moral demands and expectations of warfare, guerrilla action—and this term essentially defines the Resistance, in all of its guises—is by its nature deceptive and
ethically corrosive. But without such activity, options for the defeated

are few. "The guerrillas mobilize only a small part of the nation—a very small part, when they first begin their attacks. They depend upon the counter-attacks of their enemies to mobilize the rest. . . . They seek to place the onus of indiscriminate warfare on the opposing army."[1]

Though the harassment of the German Occupation by French youth may not have been militarily decisive, these youngsters definitely had an effect on the mood, the psychology, and the pride of those in France who waited for a happier outcome. Alya Aglan has suggested that "resistance" is like a temporal place-holder that occupies the space between defeat and victory.[2] The act of resisting is as important as the results of that action, if not more so. Keeping morale up, reminding bewildered citizens that they have been victims of a crime, and suggesting just a bit of optimism for a better future are some of the most salient benefits of a visible political and quasi-military resistance.

One constant reinforced the sudden decision of French men and women to confront injustice. Perhaps too easily we use the term "courage" to describe any exemplary act by an individual that may bring humiliation, harm, expulsion, or death, rendering the term banal and overused. Yet the sudden courage showed by most of the young people described in this book was a rare quality, brought on by events that forced them to make decisions quickly, barely considering their possible outcomes.

There were millions of young folks in France during the Occupation who did not join resistance networks. Some, we have seen, expressed their revulsion toward the German Occupier in less dangerous ways. And we must not forget that there were also numberless young people who were resistant to resistance itself, for a variety of reasons: because of their parents' beliefs; because they were impressed by omnipresent shows of force; because they felt that those of their demographic cohort who resisted were show-offs; or because they were entranced by the example of a resurgent Reich. Some of those in this last group immediately signed up in 1942 when the légion des volontaires français contre le bolchévisme was created, or in 1943 when the Milice was established. These male adolescents were not very ideologically sophisticated (nor, to be fair, were many of those who supported de Gaulle and the communists), but they had an innate sense of the importance of supporting the status quo, or working to create a "new" Europe. And they were recruited and armed by the only established French government, L'État Français. They too have stories, but they are not my subject.

Then there were those who knew that life had radically changed, but who remained confused about how to respond. Young Micheline Bood was just that sort of teenager. At the end of the final chapter of her journal, she summarized what it had been like, growing from fourteen to eighteen while waiting for some relief from the suffocating presence of the Germans' gray-green uniforms. One entry is dated August 16, 1944, nine days before the Liberation of Paris:

> *For four years we have been waiting for this moment! When I think back over different periods of my life [under the Occupation], I see myself, every six months, sustained by this single hope: deliverance. If we had thought that it would have taken four years to arrive, would we have had the courage to live, and to wait? We are all exhausted.*[3]

As the word spread in late summer of 1944 that the Normandy invasion had been an Allied success, many French citizens remained in the dark about who might "win" the war—or peace—and still half-believed that another armistice might be signed that could send Germans away, or keep a quasi-fascist French state in power. Could it even be that a communist government would be established? Would the Republic survive? Even though average French citizens may have had no deeply held political beliefs other than the primacy of their own safety, they longed for a predictable life.

The result of this continuing confusion was that, during the last ten months of the war (from August 1944 to May 1945), more and more young people were compelled to make decisions while growing up. There was almost a comedy of changing identities. Recent archival documents have revealed how young *Miliciens*—anti-Gaullist, anticommunist, but not all Vichy fanatics—schemed to maintain a foot in each camp: they carried German ID cards, but also forged IDs from underground groups, or even from the newly arrived Free French Army. Some even went so far as to find and join Maquis camps so as to prove their bona fides in case things turned out differently than they had first bet, as it was increasingly obvious they might. The covert British Special Operations Executive (SOE) even tried to recruit young *Miliciens* as armed members of the FFI. The SOE provided these young *truands* with a couple of other ID cards besides the necessary German *Ausweis* that gave them freedom of movement; some even tried to pass as Red Cross workers. They were ready to jump to whichever side seemed to be winning. Writes the historian Marc Berlière in his study of this desperate last period: "A large fringe of the population [was] multi-carded, and played double and even triple games of deception. . . . And while still working for their own behalf . . . , they served at the same time their different masters and protectors: the German security services, the Milice, but also the Resistance."[4]

Therein lies the other narrative I mentioned of how some adolescents in France confronted the Occupation, and it deserves attention. The historian Valerie Deacon notes that those from the far right who initially had fought to suppress the Front populiare of Léon Blum and its leftist surge, and who then had supported Maréchal Pétain, were often the most militant at the end in their rejection of that very government. A good number of these "reborn," politically inconsistent young men and women did become—briefly—*résistants*.

The participation ... of all these [far-right-wing] men in the Re-
sistance suggests several things. . . . There was simply no way to
determine in advance what course of action men and women would
take in a time of great crisis. The question [of] who would or who
would not join the resistance can only be answered in retrospect ...
and cannot be answered with simple generalizations. Sociological
studies of résistants ... can tell us that young people were more
inclined to join the clandestine interior resistance [where perhaps
they felt they had more freedom of action], while exterior resistance
[de Gaulle's Free French] was staffed by older men and women. . . .
But these studies will never be able to tell us that action during the
war was determined by these factors.[5]

This book's examples, of course, are about those less calculating,
less selfish young people, the ones worthy of admiration by lovers of
political liberty. Yet we must not forget that, despite de Gaulle's in-
sistency, there was never a monolithic, bureaucratically governed
resistance, despite efforts by de Gaulle and his agent, Jean Moulin.
Also, *résistants* were always in the minority, and that even today, after
major archives have been opened and witnesses have spoken or written, the motives and identities of many remain unknown.[*] Dispersed
throughout France, fiercely independent, suspicious of other groups
similar to their own, often driven ideologically, young resisters nevertheless managed to persist in an immediate, and common mission: to
undermine Germany's vaunted forces, and to intimidate Vichy's most
egregious collaborators.

---

[*] It is a fact that still amazes, but it was not until December 2015 that President
François Hollande finally opened all of the files pertaining to World War II held by
the French government, including the Quai d'Orsay (foreign office), the Préfecture
de police, and the Archives nationales.

The history of adolescent participation in resistance—as with those who continued to support the other side, or those who only wanted to wait and see—was also driven by events, such as sudden changes in military fortune, and by the passage of time, an especially delicate matter for adolescents. To suggest that the youth who resisted were less successful than they are thought to be is to ignore the courage—sometimes blind, but often passionate—of a significant segment of adolescents in France during the Occupation. We must not confuse the disparity of their reasons for engagement with a lack of purposefulness, for their judgments did lead to relevant actions. Each event cracked open access to a future that had until that moment been darkly clouded. Some had had enough and wanted to return home after the exode; others wanted to join before it was too late; still others, especially Jews, had no other option. Youth in resistance in France during this era had many excuses and reasons for challenging two brutal regimes. They were clandestine operators, but their courage was not invisible.

||||||||||||||||||||

Collective and institutional memories have established a strong mythology that World War II was a clear example of good overcoming evil—the last real victory for American wars in the twentieth, and so far, in the twenty-first centuries. This is a powerful conceit that sustains our personal and communal confidence in some ethical order. Yet we know deep down that it is only a myth, a collective reassurance, for no human conflict ends with one side having been completely good and the other totally evil. What did the Allies have to do in order to defeat the Axis powers and their hateful ideologies? Were our actions justified? What exactly are "war crimes"? Are they only vicious acts committed by our enemies? Was World War II unequivocally a "good" war? Such questions continue to be raised, and answers sought.

The majority of American and European citizens seek to establish and maintain a rational, fair, and just template for societal and governmental performance. Yet, as I write, there remain many in our "first world" who would impose noncompromising definitions of nationhood, religious certainty, and racial purity; consequently, millions have been drawn once again to the great experiments of communism and nationalist fascism that dominated most of the twentieth century. If we succeeded in ending those threats in the second half of that century, or at least in containing them, then why are they recurring? What is different this time? If the average Italian or German or American is anxious about the immigrant, how do we relieve this anxiety without falling back on the same propositions that sustained fascism? Are remedies from the past applicable to the present? Does history count anymore? Why can we not remember, or learn how to recall?

Another question insistently arises: would there have been, in France then, effective resistance to arbitrary power without the active participation of youth? Indeed, many of the leaders and victims of the early resistance against the Germans were adults in their thirties, forties, fifties, and older. Some were veterans of the First World War. Their social prestige and contacts in business and government were great advantages to early networks. That is a given that perhaps I have not emphasized enough, but then others have done so, and extensively. On the other hand, every resistant activity needs foot soldiers, just as does every army. Adolescents are emotionally and psychologically malleable; they search for approval and are ready to try out their only recently opened wings. But the best among them are not weak followers of popular cant. In times of crisis, many youth see an opportunity to define their future, to depart from the paths that elders have mapped for them. So they are attracted to resistance to any threatening ideology, no matter the source; they rush to challenge those who have undermined their developing beliefs. For teenagers and those in their early twenties, decisions are easier—not easy, but easier—to make than when they will be a decade later. More intimately attached to their generational contacts, adolescents are often easily detached—whether in truth or for the sake of appearance—from parents' experiences and judgments. The ethical world is much clearer to them: moral certainty is a characteristic, not an aberration.

There is no argument that what happened in France during the first half of the 1940s was unique. But the responses of young and old to those events should have been somewhat predictable. Older challengers to authority may have well-defined principles, but they may also have much to lose: families, careers, and good reputations. Consequently, they often lack the energy or the psychological strength needed to change comfortable and demanding habits. Adolescents are less socially and morally inconvenienced. Typically, they rely on the support of their families and their mentors and expect that protection to extend to their frustration with norms. Some parents support them; others will not. Yet even the most timid adolescents can find some courage to thread this labyrinth of obligation and desire.

My research and conversations have led me to believe that the dominant characteristic of many of those youth who fought against the German Occupation of France in the early 1940s was a strongly felt *moral certainty*. Indeed, most of those who did not take umbrage or take up arms against the Germans may also have felt certain of their own ethical choices. Yet dig one layer below their apparent conviction, and one finds myriad reasons that substantiate what in effect was a philosophical and ideological question these adolescents had to ask: *How am I intended to lead my life to protect my family? What sort of citizen will I be? Is my own well-being the only consideration?*

The adolescents I have presented in this book surprised themselves when events led them to become committed to a better future. Realizing that there were values larger than tribal or familial affection, some of them even transcended the constraints of nationalism to work for a more expansive idea of what it was to be politically and socially free. They involved themselves deeply—on all sides—in the events of these dark years as they attempted to have some effect on the present in order to ensure a clearer future. They may not have understood that their decisions to act in the often dangerous public sphere would affect future youthful generations, who would look back and ask: *What would I have done? How courageous would I have been?* This idea—that there is a better future—is not new, nor is it limited to the "progressive" or to the "reactionary." It is almost every citizen's dream, even if that dream has been inflected by the prejudices of those in power. Many of us, no matter the imperatives of the present, have what the Irish call a nostalgia for the future. And we must work hard to reject the air-brushed version of a selectively remembered past.

This passion for freedom from violence, from feckless politics, and from a virulent and official racism did not end in France with the defeat of the Third Reich and the melting of the Vichy regime. An example will explain: Following the war, and for the next forty years, Adolpho Kaminsky continued to forge documents for anyone who was fighting against colonialism, or dictatorships, or unjust persecution. He became known the world over—in South America, sub-Saharan Africa, northern Africa, the Middle East, even in the United States, where he helped those trying to evade the Vietnam War draft. And he was never discovered or arrested. Fearing his luck would run out, however, and wishing to lead a normal life, he finally gave up his forger's tools in the 1970s and began a new career as a

---

* In 2013, the French essayist Pierre Bayard wrote *Aurais-je été résistant ou bourreau?* (Would I have been a resister or an executioner?), in which he muses about the pressures on youngsters during this period. He concludes that though he would never have collaborated, he might have quietly sat out the Occupation, unless a best friend or a lover had nudged him to join. In effect, he suggests that his "moral certainty" would have remained unsure.

talented photographer. From darkness to darkroom, he engaged the world, reproducing memory.

||||||||||||||||||||||

Youngsters in dangerous and demanding times rarely consider the most far-reaching results of their actions. *I will act, for action is called for. I will act because I believe deeply in something. I will act to establish who I am, and what I believe. I will act to change my world.* They rarely go so far as to say that *I will act though it may cause my death,* or *I will act even though it may put my family in danger.* Such bravado in the face of the personal costs of taking a noble action defines the adventures of young people both then and now. Adolescents do break rules, and some take their punishment well, while others are inflamed by the unfairness of a world that does not take into account their "specialness." But when the whole edifice of morality cracks or falls down, when adolescents see their elders angry, befuddled, and frightened by changes in those very rules, they are uncertain, since the rule-makers had protected them. But there is also an excitement caused by a new taste of freedom, a freedom to misbehave. So it was in France between 1940 and 1945.

Annie Kriegel argues that there is a difference between what she and her group were doing in those years and what young people have done since when they go to the streets to break laws in order to embarrass their government. Postwar students, she says, no matter how bravely they withstand police beatings, tear gas, and short arrests, are not having to put their lives on the line. (Of course, in some societies, outspoken young people do risk grave harm.) Annie and her communist and Jewish contemporaries, faced with little choice, were almost compelled to act; for them, there were no protections. Hiding was the only alternative. Age and gender no longer mattered. What was important was to offer one's life for values that had simply disappeared from the nation's horizon, and from their own. Kriegel has a point:

there is a huge difference between standing up to an absolutist, violently insecure state and criticizing one that is only hardheaded or hard-hearted. She and her comrades lied to their families; they made and just as quickly ended intimate contacts with their comrades; and they always had to be *sur le qui-vive* (on the lookout):

> *Danger and fear surrounded us. . . . I thought of it constantly, this terror, derived I think from an interrupted childhood, when the night falls, and there is no light. Please understand me: courage is not the absence of fear when everything signals danger; it is to calmly do what must be done to ensure [every success], and to do the same for your partners. Courage forces you to make constraining and repetitive actions. . . . Courage is self-control, pleasurable if possible, seasoned with a touch of irony and humor that causes the soufflé to rise.*[6]

I know of no better definition of the courage that these young people felt. Fear was always present—fear of the police, of course, but also fear of failure, of letting comrades down, of inadvertently releasing information, of betraying trust. Being followed by the police was not as scary as being found out by your friends as having been careless or paralyzed by fear.

Are we to conclude, then, that we will always need—even count on—youthful enthusiasm emboldened by an unencumbered innocence to push those who are no longer young to be bolder? There is much in this book that should remind experienced readers that the transition from childhood to adulthood takes place in a gray area and that the physical markers of that transition explain only part of it. Each adolescent grows up differently, depending on his or her class, family structure, location, religious and political formation, and so much more. Growing up is not only hard to do, but almost impossible to explain in any precise way. Studies of how adolescents mature in chaotic, disastrous, or violent environments reveal that some of the characteristics that we generally attribute to them—moodiness, rudeness, a hypersensitive desire for privacy, emotional turmoil—fade in comparison with their sense of responsibility when decisive action is needed. As someone has said, being an adolescent means not knowing what you cannot or should not do. Of course you have been told what the rules are, but they have to be tested, or else you risk fading into the forest and becoming another invisible tree.

Today's newspapers and social media are filled with stories of the passionate stubbornness of youth around the world as they confront a frightening future.* Climate change, the rise of authoritarian governments, gun violence in the United States, stark racism in even the most tolerant nations, the sexual and gender inequality of women, and, now again, the shadow of nuclear destruction have energized a whole generation. They are called post-millennials, or Generation Z (they were born from the mid- and late 1990s to the early 2000s), and they take stands, in voices loud enough to be heard by those who control the political sphere. As I pointed out in my introduction, the cynical admire them but patronizingly. "Things will calm down when examination time arrives," say these observers, "or when summer comes, or after they graduate and become employees." Privately, however, many of us, their elders, hope that they will light a fire that intimidates both us and those who control our lives. We respect their integrity and forthrightness, but rarely enough to leave our own jobs, careers, or social positions to join them in the streets.

---

* While I was finishing this book, France was commemorating—strangely enough—the quasi-revolution known as the *évènements de mai* that occurred in May–June 1968 and eventually brought down the presidency of Charles de Gaulle. And at the end of 2018 and into 2019, another popular revolt was in progress, that of the *gilets jaunes* (yellow vests), led by those in the French middle and lower economic classes who have felt left behind in an unequal society.

I began this book by noting how difficult it has been for France to reckon with what happened inside its borders during the German Occupation. This is not a judgment but a fact, and it is equally a fact that substantial progress toward transparency and forthrightness has marked the last few decades in that country. When I asked Claude Weill if he had been recognized by the French government after the war for his two-plus years fighting the Germans, he looked surprised. "No," he answered. "Why would I have been?" He obviously did not see himself as a hero, but only as a small cog in what turned out to be a victorious war for liberty. He returned to Paris, took over his father's business, and prospered.

All of us envy the unselfish courage of the young—and their modest refusal to be considered exceptional—a courage that suddenly arises in response to unexpected events and unanticipated tears in the fabric of their lives, be they undocumented immigrants or comfortably situated Americans. As someone who has been teaching for decades, who has met voters when they were still teenagers, and who has been continuously in awe of their enthusiasm and curiosity and decency, I ask myself: What will happen to that moral enthusiasm when they get older? In our search for social and political stability, is it the very nature of our democratic systems to level political enthusiasm, to keep things steady? If so, what do we do when angry factions and immoral leaders endanger the values that we are proudest of? Who will resist the temptation to acquiesce to a radical return to those earlier, sterile, and more merciless times? Only the kids?

Acknowledgments

———

This is always the most intimidating part of writing a book, for an author cannot just check his notes, go to the library, or scan the internet. He must rely on his memory to recall each and every one of those who have helped make his book possible. And we know what an unreliable tool one's memory is. I have done my best here.

The three people to whom I have dedicated this work cannot know in full how helpful they have been. This book is far better than it would have been without their support. Stacy Schiff, an intuitive biographer and gifted writer, has been my ready therapist at every moment. English Showalter continues to read with a laser eye, as he did when he was my dissertation director decades ago. Philippe Rochefort, himself a scholar of history, was pleased and amused in equal measure at my treatment of France. To you three, I offer my affection and my respect.

Geoff Shandler of Custom House has been an editor sans pareil, and deserves my deepest appreciation for having guided me through yet another work on nasty Nazis and gutsy French men and women. He had faith in this project before it was a project. This book is as much his as mine.

At HarperCollins/William Morrow/Custom House, I thank the following colleagues for their early and continuing confidence in my work: Liate Stehlik (William Morrow's publisher), Kelly Rudolph, Maureen Cole (director of publicity), Nyamekye Waliyaya, Andrea Molitor, Evangelos Vasilakis, Owen Corrigan (who designed the striking cover), Lynn Grady, Ben Steinberg, Kayleigh George, Andy

LeCount (this is the second book of mine he has enhanced), Molly Gendell, and the punctilious Vedika Khanna, who kept me on track and on time. I was fortunate to have Cynthia Buck as my copyeditor. She was meticulous, diplomatic, and persistent. If you find any typos or garbled sentences in this work, they are mine, not hers.

Geri Thoma has been a faithful and provocative agent for two books now, and still answers my calls with wit and warmth. She is an unerring source of common sense.

For thirty years, Amherst College has been my professional home, and has provided an ideal environment for a teacher and scholar. Not only has it permitted me to engage intellectually adventurous students, its administration has also been unselfish in supporting the sort of research that demands time, technology, and travel. My many trips to France have been made possible by generous grants and awards, most recently from the office of Dean of the Faculty Catherine Epstein, herself an expert on Nazi Germany. As well, the generosity of an admirable alumnus, Axel Schupf, has supported for years research and teaching for Amherst faculty and students.

The research and technological facilities at Amherst keep us all seamlessly productive. Jayne Lovett in Information Technology has maintained my sanity by nursing my Mac, always with patience and humor. Dunstan McNutt, Susan Sheridan, Judy Lively, Susan Kimball, and Steven Heim are superb librarians and researchers who made my constant quest for more and more information always productive, and never a chore. And the incomparable sisters Hanley, Rachel, and Julia, who keep trying to teach me how to use social media.

For my faculty colleagues, here at Amherst and everywhere, I offer my gratitude for having listened to, queried, and supported my project. I have been fortunate in having such bright, generous, and deadly critical friends to correct, encourage, and support my effort: Catherine Lafarge; Judith Mayne; Sara Brenneis; my fellows in the formidable Amherst French department, Laure Katsaros, Rosalina de la Carrera, Paul Rockwell, Raphaël Sigal, Sanam Nader-Esfahani, Raina Uhden, and our indispensable Academic Coordinator, Elizabeth Eddy, whose eagerness to help is legend.

And I am grateful as well to others who have been supportive, in large ways and small, as I worked on this project: Sidne Koenigsberg, Ruda Dauphin, Sue Talbott, Harriett Rochefort, John Katzenbach, Madeline Blais, Joe Ellis, William Cooley, James Young, Lisa Ades, Guy and Brigitte Bizot, Monique Lajournade, Michèle Lajournade, Marc Schulz, the late Richard Beban, Tom Schwab, Michael Neiberg, Alan Marty, and Jean Salomon.

Claude Weill, now ninety years old, welcomed me to his home more than once, and shared fascinating stories about his life in France during the Occupation. His openness, integrity, and directness encouraged me to be faithful to the sacrifices of so many young people who lent their light to a dark time.

To all those who read *When Paris Went Dark* and encouraged me to write another book on this dismal period, I am deeply indebted.

The Mémorial de la Shoah in Paris is one of the most pleasant, accommodating, and fruitful archives I have worked in. I am especially grateful for the help of Madame Lior Lalieu-Smadja, who introduced me to the rich photographic archives of the research center.

Much of this book was written with the inestimable commitment of Amherst students, who dedicated generous amounts of time to helping me produce this work. Terry Lee was a grand help, both here and in Paris, at the beginning of this project, and Patrick Frenett taught me much about virtual maps.

Two young men have been with *Sudden Courage* since their first months at Amherst: Jacob Schulz and Henry Newton. Intuition told me these eager guys were intellectual dynamos, and thirsty to learn more than what they were studying in their regular courses. Henry Newton, a sophomore, hit the ground running when he joined this team as a freshman. He is diligent, smart as a whip, and unflappable whenever crises arise. Jacob, a senior, has been for four years a patient and indefatigable researcher, even during his junior term in Bordeaux, at the Institut d'études politiques. His imagination and deep sense of history are reflected throughout this book. He has also become a good friend, and a calming influence whenever I thought this project would never end. I cannot thank him enough.

Finally, but really not, I offer a deep gratitude to Betty, my wife, companion, and friend since we were youths in Paris. Her love is by far my strongest asset; her impatience with phoniness and bloviation, my most useful guide. And her sharp eye continues to improve my writing. My son, Michael, and his wife, Heidi, are always standing behind me. And, my grandchildren, Edie and Griffin, often remind me of the courage, honesty, and loyalty that characterized the young people whom you have read about here.

January 2019
Amherst and Paris

Bibliography

Agence-France Presse. "Marine Le Pen Denies French Role in Wartime Roundup of Paris Jews." *Guardian*. April 9, 2017. https://www.theguardian.com/world/2017/apr/09/marine-le-pen-denies-french-role-wartime-roundup-paris-jews.

Aglan, Alya. *La Résistance sacrifiée: Histoire du mouvement*. Paris: Flammarion, 2005.

———. *Le Temps de la Résistance* [Time in the Resistance]. Arles: Actes Sud, 2008.

———. *La France défaite 1940–1945: La Documentation photographique*. Dossier 8120 (November–December 2017). Paris: Documentation Française, 2017.

Alary, Éric. *Un Procès sous l'Occupation au Palais-Bourbon: Mars 1942* [A trial during the occupation at the Palais-Bourbon: March 1942]. Preface by Jean-Pierre Azéma. Paris: Assemblée Nationale, 2000.

Alary, Éric, Gilles Gauvin, and Bénédicte Vergez-Chaignon. *Les Français au quotidien, 1939–1949*. Paris: Tempus Perrin, 2009.

Albertelli, Sébastien. *Atlas de la France libre: De Gaulle et la France libre: Une Aventure politique* [Atlas of Free France: De Gaulle and Free France: A political adventure]. Paris: Éditions Autrement, 2010.

Amis de la Commission centrale de l'enfance. *Les Juifs ont résisté en France, 1940–1945*. Paris: AACCE, 2009.

Amouroux, Henri. *Vie des Français sous l'Occupation*. Paris: Arthème Fayard, 1961.

Andrieu, Claire. "Women in the French Resistance: Revisiting the Historical Record." *French Politics, Culture, and Society* 18, no. 1 (Summer 2000): 13–27.

Assouline, Pierre, et al. *Les Collabos*. Paris: Arthème Fayard, 2011.

Aubrac, Lucie. *La Résistance expliquée à mes petits-enfants*. Paris: Éditions du Seuil, 2000.

Audiat, Pierre. *Paris pendant la guerre: Juin 1940–août 1944*. Paris: Librairie Hachette, 1946.

Azéma, Jean-Pierre. *1940: L'Année noire*. Paris: Points, 2012.

———. *L'Occupation expliquée à mon petit-fils*. Paris: Éditions du Seuil, 2012.

Balvet, Dominique, with Bruno Leroux and Christine Levisse-Touzé. *Dictionnaire historique de la Résistance*. Paris: Robert Laffont, 2006.

Baronnet, Jean. *Les Parisiens sous l'Occupation: Photographies en couleurs d'André Zucca*. Paris: Gallimard, 2000.

Baruch, Marc Olivier. *Le Régime de Vichy*. Paris: La Découverte, 1996.

Basse, Pierre-Louis. *Guy Môquet, une enfance fusillée* [Guy Môquet, an executed childhood]. Paris: Stock, 2000.

Baumel, Jacques. *Résister: Histoire secrète des années d'Occupation*. Paris: Albin Michel, 1999.

Bayard, Pierre. *Aurais-je été résistant ou bourreau?* [Would I have been a resister or an executioner?]. Paris: Éditions de Minuit, 2013.

Bazin, André. *French Cinema of the Occupation and Resistance: Birth of a Critical Aesthetic.* Translated by S. Hochman. New York: Frederick Ungar, 1982.

Belot, Robert, ed., with Éric Alary and Bénédicte Vergez-Chagnon. *Les Résistants: L'Histoire de ceux qui réfusèrent.* Paris: Larousse, 2015.

Benoit, Floriane, and Charles Silvestre. *Les Inconnus de la Résistance: Livre d'un témoignage collectif.* Paris: Éditions Messidor, 1984.

Bensoussan, Georges, ed. *Atlas de la Shoah.* Paris: Autrement, 2014.

Berlière, Jean-Marc de. *Policiers français sous l'Occupation* [The French police under the Occupation]. Paris: Perrin, 2001.

Berlière, Jean-Marc de, and François Le Goarant de Tromelin. *Liaisons dangereuses: Miliciens, truands, résistants, Paris 1944* [Dangerous liaisons: *Miliciens*, truants, resisters, Paris 1944]. Paris: Perrin, 2013.

Berlière, Jean-Marc, and Franck Liaigre. *L'Affaire Guy Môquet: Enquête sur une mystification officielle* [The Guy Môquet affair: An official hoax]. Paris: Larousse, 2009.

Besse, Jean-Pierre, and Thomas Pouty. *Les Fusillés: Répression et exécutions pendant l'Occupation, 1940–1944* [The executed: Repression and executions during the Occupation, 1940–1944]. Paris: Éditions de l'Atelier, 2006.

Béthouart, Antoine. *Cinq Années d'espérance: Mémoires de guerre 1939–1945.* Paris: Plon, 1968.

Birnbaum, Pierre. *Léon Blum: Prime Minister, Socialist, Zionist.* Translated by Arthur Goldhammer. New Haven, CT: Yale University Press, 2015.

Bloch, Marc. *L'Étrange défaite: Témoignage écrit en 1940* [A strange defeat: Eyewitness account, written in 1940]. Paris: Gallimard, 1990.

Bohec, Jeanne. "La Plastiqueuse à bicyclette." *Vingtième Siècle: Revue d'histoire* 66, no. 1 (2000): 181–182.

Boiry, Philippe, and Jacques Baumel. *Les Jeunes dans la Résistance.* Périgueux: Pilote 24, 1996.

Bood, Micheline. *Les Années doubles: Journal d'une lycéenne sous l'Occupation.* [The double years: Journal of a high school girl under the Occupation]. Introduction by Jacques Labib. Paris: Robert Laffont, 1974.

Bourdais, Henri. *La JOC sous l'Occupation allemande: Témoignages et souvenirs d'Henri Bourdais.* Paris: Les Éditions de l'Atelier—Éditions Ouvrières, 1995.

Bourdieu, Pierre. "La 'Jeunesse' n'est qu'un mot." In *Questions de sociologie.* Paris: Éditions de Minuit, 1984.

Boursier, Jean-Yves. *La Politique du PCF, 1939–1945: Le Parti communiste français et la question nationale.* Collection Chemins de la Mémoire. Paris: L'Harmattan, 1992.

Bowers, Paige. *The General's Niece: The Little-known de Gaulle Who Fought to Free Occupied France.* Chicago: Chicago Review Presss, 2017.

Bragança, Manuel, and Fransiska Louwagie. *Ego-Histories of France and the Second World War: Writing Vichy.* New York: Springer International Publishing, 2018.

Broche, François. *Dictionnaire de la Collaboration: Collaborations, compromissions, contradictions.* Paris: Belin, 2014.

———. *Où était la France? Vél d'Hiv, juillet 1942.* Paris: Pierre-Guillaume de Roux, 2017.

Broche, François, and Jean-François Muracciole. *Histoire de la Collaboration (1940–1945).* Paris: Tallandier, 2017.

Browning, Christopher R. *Ordinary Men: Reserve Police Battalion 101 and the Final Solution in Poland*. New York: Harper Perennial, 1998.

Bruneau, Antone. *Journal d'un collabo ordinaire*. Paris: Éditions Jourdan, 2018.

Buisson, Patrick. *1940–1945, Années érotiques*, vol. 1, *Vichy, ou, Les Infortunes de la vertu*. Paris: Librairie Générale Française, 2011.

———. *1940–1945, Années érotiques*, vol. 2, *De la Grande Prostituée à la revanche des mâles*. Paris: Librairie Générale Française, 2011.

Burrin, Philippe. *La France à l'heure allemande: 1940–1944*. Paris: Éditions du Seuil, 1995.

Bynner, John. "Rethinking the Youth Phase of the Life-Course: The Case for Emerging Adulthood?" *Journal of Youth Studies* 8, no. 4 (December 2005): 367–384. https://doi.org/10.1080/13676260500431628.

Cabanel, Patrick. *Chère mademoiselle: Alice Ferrières et les ende Murat, 1941–1944*. Preface by Mona Ouzof. Paris: Calmann-Lévy/Mémorial de la Shoah, 2010

———. *Histoire des Justes en France*. Paris: Armand Colin, 2012.

———, ed. *La Montagne refuge: Accueil et sauvetage des Juifs autour du Chambon-sur-Lignon*. Paris: Albin Michel, 2013.

———. *Résister: Voix protestantes*. Nîmes: Alcide, 2014.

———. *De la Paix aux résistances: Les Protestants français de 1930 à 1945*. Paris: Arthème Fayard, 2015.

Capdevila, Luc, ed. *Hommes et femmes dans la France en guerre: 1914–1945*. Paris: Payot, 2003.

Carrard, Philippe. *The French Who Fought for Hitler: Memories from the Outcasts*. Cambridge: Cambridge University Press, 2010.

Cauchy, Pascal. *Les Six Miliciens de Grenoble*. Paris: Vendémiaire, 2015.

Cera, Jean-François. "Les Raisons de l'engagement de volontaires français sous l'uniforme allemande." Thesis, University of Nice Sophia Antipolis, 1992.

Chamboredon, Jean-Claude. "La Délinquance juvénile: Essai de construction d'objet." *Revue française de sociologie* 12, no. 3 (1971): 335–377.

Charles, François. *Vie et mort de Poil de Carotte: Robert Lynen, acteur et résistant* [Life and death of Carrot-top: Robert Lynen, actor and resister]. Strasbourg: La Nuée Bleue, 2002.

Chemla, Véronique. *Les Juifs ont résisté en France: 1940–1945*. Paris: Association des Amis de la Commission Centrale de l'Enfance, 2009.

Christophe, Francine. *Une Petite Fille privilégiée: Une Enfant dans le monde des camps, 1942–1945*. Paris: L'Harmattan, 1996.

Cloonan, William J. *The Writing of War: French and German Fiction and World War II*. Gainesville: University Press of Florida, 1999.

Cobb, Richard. *French and Germans, Germans and French: A Personal Interpretation of France under Occupations, 1914–1918/1940–1945*. Hanover, NH: University Press of New England, 1983.

Cohen, Asher. *Persécutions et sauvetages: Juifs et Français sous l'Occupation et sous Vichy*. Paris: Éditions du Cerf, 1993.

Cointet, Jean-Paul. *Paris 40–44*. Paris: Perrin, 2001.

Cointet, Michèle. *Marie-Madeleine Fourcade: Un Chef de la Résistance*. Paris: Perrin, 2006.

———. *Les Françaises dans la guerre et l'Occupation* [French women at war and during the Occupation]. Paris: Arthème Fayard, 2018.

Collectif, and Agnes Blondel. *Manuel de résistance*. Paris: Des Équateurs, 2015.

Collet, Jean. *A 20 ans dans la Résistance 1940–1944*. Paris: Graphein, 1999.

Collette, Paul. *J'ai tiré sur Laval* [I shot at Laval]. Caen: Ozanne & Compagnie, 1946.

Collin, Claude. *Jeune Combat: Les Jeunes Juifs de la MOI dans la Résistance*. Grenoble: Presses Universitaires de Grenoble, 1998.

Combès, Gustave. *Lève-toi et marche: Les Conditions du relèvement français*. Toulouse: Édouard Privat, Libraire-Éditeur, 1941.

Corday, Pauline. *J'ai vécu dans Paris occupé* [I lived in Occupied Paris]. Montréal: Éditions de l'Arbre, 1943.

Cordier, Daniel. *Alias Caracalla*. Paris: Gallimard, 2007.

Cortanze, Gérard de. *Zazous*. Paris: Albin Michel, 2016.

Courtois, Stéphane, Denis Peschanski, and Adam Rayski. *Le Sang de l'étranger: Les Immigrés de la MOI dans la Résistance* [Blood of the foreigner: The immigrants of the MOI (Immigrant Workers) in the Resistance]. Paris: Arthème Fayard, 1989.

Crémieux-Brilhac, Jean-Louis. *La France libre: De l'Appel du 18 juin à la Libération.* [Free France: From the speech of 18 June (1940) until the liberation]. Paris: Gallimard, 1996.

———. *De Gaulle, la République, et la France libre*. Paris: Tempus Perrin, 2014.

Cyrulnik, Boris. *Sauve-toi, la vie t'appelle*. Paris: Odile Jacob, 2012.

Deacon, Valerie. *The Extreme Right in the French Resistance: Members of the Cagoule and Corvignolles in the Second World War*. Baton Rouge, LA: Louisiana State University Press, 2016.

Delbo, Charlotte. *Auschwitz et après: Aucun de nous ne reviendra* [Auschwitz and after: Not one of us will return]. Paris: Éditions de Minuit, 1970.

Déreymez, Jean-William, ed. *Être jeune en France (1939–1945)* [To be young in France (1939–1945)]. Paris: L'Harmattan, 2001.

Desprairies, Cécile, and Serge Klarsfeld. *Paris dans la Collaboration*. Paris: Éditions du Seuil, 2009.

Diamant, David. *250 Combattants de la Résistance témoignent*. Paris: L'Harmattan, 1991.

———. *Jeune Combat: La Jeunesse juive dans la Résistance*. Paris: L'Harmattan, 1993.

Domenach-Lallich, Denise. *Demain il fera beau: Journal d'une adolescente (5 novembre 1939–septembre 1944)*. Lyon: Éditions BGA Permezel, 2001.

Douzou, Laurent. *La Résistance française: Une Histoire périlleuse*. Paris: Éditions du Seuil, 2005.

———. "La Résistance: Une Affaire d'hommes?" *Cahiers de l'IHIP* 31 (October 1995): 11–24.

Drapac, Vesna, and Gareth Pritchard. *Resistance and Collaboration in Hitler's Empire*. Studies in European History. London: Palgrave, 2017.

Dreyfus-Armand, Geneviève. "L'Émigration politique espagnole en France après 1939." *Matériaux pour l'histoire de notre temps* (July–December 1985): 82–89. https://doi.org/10.3406/mat.1985.403925.

Druckerman, Pamela. "'If I Sleep for an Hour, 30 People Will Die.'" *New York Times*, October 2, 2016. https://www.nytimes.com/2016/10/02/opinion/sunday/if-i-sleep-for-an-hour-30-people-will-die.html?smprod=nytcore-ipad&smid=nytcore-ipad-share.

Duranton-Cabrol, Anne-Marie. Review of Ralph Schor, « *L'Antisémitisme en France pendant les années trente.* » *Vingtième Siècle: Revue d'histoire* 36, no. 1 (1992): 112–115.

Eismann, Gaël. *Hôtel Majestic: Ordre et sécurité en France occupée (1940–1944)* [Hotel Majestic: Order and security in Occupied France (1940–1944)]. Paris: Éditions Tallandier, 2010.

Elek, Hélène. *La Mémoire d'Hélène.* Paris: F. Maspero, 1977.

Endewelt, Robert. "L'Engagement dans la Résistance des jeunes Juifs parisiens avec la MOI (1940–1945)." *Cahiers d'histoire* 129 (October 2015): 139–150.

Éparvier, Jean. *À Paris sous la botte des nazis.* Paris: Le Cherche Midi, 2014.

Fauxbras, César. *Le Théâtre de l'Occupation: Journal, 1939–1944.* Paris: Allia, 2012.

Fichtenberg, Roger. *Journal d'un résistant juif dans le sud-ouest.* [Journal of a Jewish resister in the southwest]. Paris: Éditions le Manuscrit, 2015.

Fishman, Sarah. *The Battle for Children: World War II, Youth Crime, and Juvenile Justice in Twentieth-Century France.* Cambridge, MA: Harvard University Press, 2002.

———. *We Will Wait: Wives of French Prisoners of War, 1940–1945.* New Haven, CT: Yale University Press, 1991.

Fiss, Karen. *Grand Illusion: The Third Reich, the Paris Exposition, and the Cultural Seduction of France.* Chicago: University of Chicago Press, 2009.

———. "Cinema in the 1930s: Exile as Experience and Metaphor." In *Encounters with the 1930s* (exhibition catalog): 251–264. Edited by MNCARS Publications Department and La Fábrica. Madrid: La Fábrica, 2012 .

Fogg, Shannon Lee. *The Politics of Everyday Life in Vichy, France: Foreigners, Undesirables, and Strangers.* Cambridge: Cambridge University Press, 2009.

Fontaine, Thomas, and Denis Peschanski, eds. *La Collaboration: Vichy, Paris, Berlin, 1940–1945.* Exposition catalog. Paris: Tallandier, 2018.

Foulon, Charles-Louis, Christine Levisse-Touzé, and Jean-Noël Jeanneney. *Les Résistants,* vol. 1, *Jean Moulin et les soutiers de la gloire.* Paris: Société Éditrice du Monde, 2012.

Foulon, Charles-Louis, Christine Levisse-Touzé, and Grégoire Kauffmann. *Les Résistants,* vol. 2, *Lucie Aubrac et l'armée des ombres.* Paris: Société Éditrice du Monde, 2012.

Fourcade, Marie-Madeleine. *L'Arche de Noé* [Noah's Ark]. Paris: Fayard, 1968.

Fussell, Paul. *The Boys' Crusade: The American Infantry in Northwestern Europe, 1944–1945.* New York: Modern Library, 2003.

Garcin, Jérôme. *Le Voyant* [The seer]. Paris: Gallimard, 2016.

Gaulle, Charles de. *Mémoires de guerre: L'Appel, 1940–1942.* Paris: Plon, 1954.

Gaulle-Anthonioz de, Geneviève. *La Traversée de la nuit* [Crossing the night]. Paris: Éditions du Seuil, 2001.

Gensburger, Sarah, and Collectif. *C'étaient des enfants: Déportation et sauvetage des enfants juifs à Paris.* Paris: Skira, 2012.

Gildea, Robert. *Marianne in Chains: Everyday Life in the French Heartland under the German Occupation.* New York: Metropolitan Books, 2003.

———. "Resistance, Reprisals, and Community in Occupied France." *Transactions of the Royal Historical Society* 13 (December 2003): 163–185.

———. *Fighters in the Shadows: A New History of the French Resistance.* Cambridge, MA: Belknap Press of Harvard University Press, 2015.

Gilzmer, Mechtild, Christine Levisse-Touzé, and Stefan Martens. *Actes du colloque international de Berlin, 8–10 octobre: Les Femmes dans la Résistance en France.* Paris: Tallandier, 2003.

Giolitto, Pierre. *Histoire de la jeunesse sous Vichy.* Paris: Perrin, 1991.

———. *Histoire de la Milice.* Paris: Perrin, 1997, 2002.

Girard, Claire. *Lettres de Claire Girard: Fusillée par les Allemands le 17 août 1944.* Paris: Roger Lescaret, 1954.

Glass, Charles. *Americans in Paris: Life and Death under Nazi Occupation.* New York: Penguin Press, 2010.

Goldhagen, Daniel Jonah. *Hitler's Willing Executioners: Ordinary Germans and the Holocaust.* New York: Alfred A. Knopf, 1996.

Goldman, Pierre. *Souvenirs obscurs d'un Juif polonais né en France.* Paris: Éditions du Seuil, 1975.

Granet, Marie. *Les Jeunes dans la Résistance.* Paris: France Empire, 1996.

Grenard, Fabrice, with Jean-Pierre Azéma. *Les Français sous l'Occupation en 100 questions* [The French under Occupation in 100 questions]. Paris: Tallandier, 2016.

Guéhenno, Jean. *Journal des années noires, 1940–1944.* Paris: Gallimard, 2002.

———. *Diary of the Dark Years, 1940–1944: Collaboration, Resistance, and Daily Life in Occupied Paris.* Translated by David Ball. New York and Oxford: Oxford University Press, 2016.

Guéno, Jean-Pierre, ed. *Paroles d'étoiles: Mémoire d'enfants cachés.* Paris: Radio France, 2002.

———, ed. *Paroles de l'ombre: Lettres, carnets, et récits des Français sous l'Occupation, 1939–1945.* Paris: E. J. L., 2009.

———, ed. *Paroles d'exode, mai–juin 1940: Lettres et témoignages des Français sur les routes.* Paris: E. J. L., 2015.

Guérin, Alain, Marie-Madeleine Fourcade, and Henri Rol-Tanguy. *Chronique de la Résistance.* Paris: Omnibus, 2000.

Guidez, Guylaine. *Femmes dans la guerre, 1939–1945.* Paris: Perrin, 1989.

Halls, W. D. *The Youth of Vichy France.* Oxford: Clarendon Press, 1981.

Hanley, Boniface. *The Last Human Face: Franz Stock, A Priest in Hitler's Army.* Self-published, 2010.

Hervet, Robert. *Les Chantiers de la jeunesse.* Paris: Éditions France-Empire, 1962.

Hirsch, Jean-Raphaël. *Réveille-toi papa, c'est fini!* [Wake up papa, it's over!]. Paris: Albin Michel, 2014.

L'Histoire. Les Collabos. Paris: Arthème Fayard, 2011.

Holban, Boris. *Testament: Après quarante-cinq ans de silence, le chef militaire des FTP-MOI de Paris parle.* Paris: Calmann-Lévy, 1989.

Humbert, Agnes. *Resistance: A Frenchwoman's Journal of the War.* Translated by Barbara Mellor. New York: Bloomsbury USA, 2008.

Huot, Paul. *J'avais 20 ans en 1943: Les Chantiers de [la] Jeunesse, le Maquis, le Commando de Cluny . . .* [I was 20 years old in 1943]. Bayonne: Éditions Jakin, 1996.

Hyman, Paula. *De Dreyfus à Vichy.* Paris: Arthème Fayard, 1985.

Jackson, Jeffrey H. *Making Jazz French: Music and Modern Life in Interwar Paris.* Durham, NC: Duke University Press, 2003.

Jackson, Julian. *The Popular Front in France: Defending Democracy, 1934–38.* Cambridge: Cambridge University Press, 1988.

——. *France: The Dark Years, 1940–1944.* Oxford: Oxford University Press, 2001.

——. *De Gaulle.* Cambridge, MA: Belknap Press of Harvard University Press, 2018.

Jamet, Dominique. *Un Petit Parisien, 1941–1945.* Paris: Flammarion, 2000.

Josephson, Hannah, and Malcolm Cowley, eds. *Aragon: Poet of the French Resistance.* New York: Duell, Sloan and Pearce, 1945.

Jouhandeau, Marcel. *Journal sous l'Occupation,* followed by *La Courbe de nos angoisses.* Paris: Gallimard, 1980.

Kaiser, Charles. *The Cost of Courage.* New York: Other Press, 2015.

Kaminsky, Sarah. *Adolfo Kaminsky: Une Vie de faussaire.* Paris: Calmann-Lévy, 2009.

——. *Adolfo Kaminsky: A Forger's Life.* Translated by Mike Mitchell. Los Angeles: Doppel House Press, 2016.

Kaufmann, J. E., and H. W. Kaufmann. *Fortress France: The Maginot Line and French Defenses in World War II.* Westport, CT: Praeger Security International, 2006.

Kedward, H.R. *In Search of the Maquis: Rural Resistance in Southern France, 1942–1944.* Oxford: Oxford University Press, 1993.

——. *Occupation and Resistance During World War II.* Oxford: Oxford University Press, 2005.

Kersaudy, François. *De Gaulle et Churchill.* Paris: Perrin, 2003.

Kershaw, Ian. *Hitler, 1889–1936: Hubris.* New York: W. W. Norton, 1999.

——. *Hitler, 1936–1945: Nemesis.* New York: W. W. Norton, 2000.

Klarsfeld, Beate, and Serge Klarsfeld. *Mémoires.* Paris: Flammarion/Arthème Fayard, 2015.

Kofman, Sarah. *Rue Ordener, rue Labat.* Paris: Galilée, 1994.

——. *Rue Ordener, Rue Labat.* Translated by Ann Smock. Lincoln, NE: University of Nebraska Press, 1996.

Kriegel, Annie. *Résistants communistes et Juifs persécutés: Réflexion sur les questions juives.* Paris: Hachette, 1984.

——. *Adolescente dans la Résistance communiste juive: Grenoble 1942–1944.* Paris: Éditions de la Fondation Nationale des Sciences Politiques, 1989.

——. *Ce que j'ai cru comprendre* [What I thought I knew]. Paris: Robert Laffont, 1991.

Krivopissco, Guy. *Les Fusillés de la Cascade du Bois de Boulogne, 16 août 1944.* Paris: Mairie de Paris, 2000.

——. *La Vie à en mourir: Lettres de fusillés (1941–1944)* [To love life to death: Letters from the executed, 1941–1944]. Paris: Tallandier, 2006.

Kupferman, Fred. *Pierre Laval.* Paris: Tallandier, 2016.

Laborie, Pierre. *L'Opinion française sous Vichy.* Paris: Éditions du Seuil, 2001.

——. *Les Français des années troubles: De la Guerre d'Espagne à la Libération.* Paris: Desclée de Brouwer, 2001.

——. *Les Mots de 39–45.* Toulouse: Presses Universitaires du Mirail, 2006.

——. *Le Chagrin et le venin: La France sous l'Occupation, mémoire et idées reçues.* Montrouge: Bayard, 2011.

Lajournade, Michèle. "[Jean] Lajournade Biography." Unpublished manuscript, n.d.

Laqueur, Walter, and Judith Tydor Baumel-Schwartz. *The Holocaust Encyclopedia*. New Haven, CT: Yale University Press, 2001.

Latour, Anny. *La Résistance juive en France (1940–1944)*. Paris: Stock, 1970.

Lefébure, Antoine. *Les Conversations secrètes des Français sous l'Occupation*. Paris: Plon, 1993.

Legrand, Freddy, and Antoine Bruneau. *Journal d'un collabo ordinaire*. Paris: Éditions Jourdan, 2018.

Lehr, Johanna. *De l'École au maquis: La Résistance juive en France*. Paris: Éditions Vendémiaire, 2014.

Leleu, Jean-Luc, Françoise Passera, and Jean Quellien. *La France pendant la Seconde Guerre Mondiale: Atlas historique*. Paris: Arthème Fayard, 2010.

Lévy, Claude. *Les Parias de la Résistance* [The Pariahs of the Resistance]. Paris: Calmann-Lévy, 1970.

Lévy, Claude, Paul Tillard, and Joseph Kessel. *La Grande rafle du Vél d'Hiv*. Paris: Tallandier, 2010.

L'Humanité. "50 otages fusillés à Nantes et 50 à Bordeaux par les Allemands." *L'Humanité* 135 (November 1941), http://archive.wikiwix.com/cache/?url=http%3A%2F%2Fitinerairesdecitoyennete.org%2Fjournees%2F22_oct%2Fimages%2Fhumanite.jpg.

Lloyd, Christopher. *Collaboration and Resistance in Occupied France: Representing Treason and Sacrifice*. New York: Palgrave Macmillan, 2004.

Loiseau, Jean-Claude. *Les Zazous*. Paris: Le Sagittaire, 1977.

Lottman, Herbert R. *The Fall of Paris: June 1940*. New York: HarperCollins, 1992.

Loubes, Olivier, Frédérique Neau-Dufour, Guillaume Piketty, and Tzvetan Todorov. *Pierre Brossolette, Geneviève de Gaulle Anthonioz, Germaine Tillion, et Jean Zay au Panthéon*. Preface by Mona Ozouf. Paris: Textuel, 2015.

Luneau, Aurélie, and Jean-Louis Crémieux-Brilhac. *Radio Londres*. Paris: Tempus Perrin, 2010.

———. *Je vous écris de France: Lettres inédites à la BBC, 1940–1944*. Paris: Points, 2016.

Lusseyran, Jacques. *Ce que l'on voit sans les yeux*. Paris: Cahiers de l'Unitisme, 1958.

———. *And There Was Light: Autobiography of Jacques Lusseyran, Blind Hero of the French Resistance*. New York: Parabola, 1998.

———. *What One Sees without Eyes: Selected Writings of Jacques Lusseyran*. Edinburgh: Floris Books, 1999.

———. *Against the Pollution of the I: Selected Writings*. Introduction by Christopher Bamford. Sandpoint, ID: Morning Light Press, 2006.

———. *Le Monde commence aujourd'hui*. 1959; reprint, Paris: Silène, 2012.

———. *Et la lumière fut*. Preface by Jacqueline Pardon. Paris: Folio, 2016.

Mairie de Paris. *Les 11,400 enfants juifs déportés de France, juin 1942–août 1944*. Paris: Mairie de Paris, 2007.

Malraux, André. *Entre ici, Jean Moulin: Discours d'André Malraux, Ministre d'état chargé des affaires culturelles, lors du transfert des cendres de Jean Moulin au Panthéon, 19 décembre 1964*. Paris: Éditions Points, 2010.

Marcot, François, with Bruno Leroux and Christine Levisse-Touzé. *Dictionnaire historique de la Résistance: Résistance intérieure et France libre*. Paris: Robert Laffont, 2006.

Marianne. "Les Résistances juives durant la Seconde Guerre Mondiale." *Marianne* (May 2015).

Marrus, Michael Robert, and Robert O. Paxton. *Vichy France and the Jews*. New York: Basic Books, 1981.

Martin, Jeanne-Marie. *Portraits de résistants*. Paris: J'ai Lu, 2015.

Martinez, Gilles, and Gilles Scotto di Covella. *La France de 1939 à 1945: Le Régime de Vichy, l'Occupation, la Libération*. Paris: Éditions du Seuil, 1997.

Matot, Bertrand. *La Guerre des cancres: Un Lycée au coeur de la Résistance et de la Collaboration* [War of the dunces: A high school at the heart of the Resistance and the Collaboration]. Preface by Patrick Modiano. Paris: Perrin, 2010.

May, Ernest R. *Strange Victory: Hitler's Conquest of France*. New York: Hill and Wang, 2000.

McCauley, Clark, and Sophia Moskalenko. "Understanding Political Radicalization: The Two-Pyramids Model." *American Psychologist* 72, no. 3 (April 2017): 205–216.

Meyers, Mark. "Feminizing Fascist Men: Crowd Psychology, Gender, and Sexuality in French Antifascism, 1929–1945." *French Historical Studies* 29, no. 1 (February 1, 2006): 109–142.

Mitchell, Allan. *Nazi Paris: The History of an Occupation, 1940–1944*. New York: Berghahn Books, 2008.

Modern Mechanix. "France Builds World's Greatest Defense System." *Modern Mechanix* (March 1931): 58–59. Archived and posted March 23, 2011, at: http://blog .modernmechanix.com/france-builds-worlds-greatest-defense-system/ (accessed March 27, 2018).

Modiano, Patrick. *Dora Bruder*. Paris: Gallimard, 1997.

——. *Dora Bruder*. Translated by Joanna Komartin. Berkeley, CA: University of California Press, 1999.

——. *Discours à l'Académie suédoise* (Nobel lecture, December 7, 2014). Paris: Gallimard, 2015.

Monod, Alain. *Le Réseau du Museé de l'Homme: Une Résistance pionnière, 1940–1942*. Paris: Riveneuve Éditions, 2015.

Moorehead, Caroline. *A Train in Winter: An Extraordinary Story of Women, Friendship, and Resistance in Occupied France*. New York: Harper Perennial, 2012.

Mosier, John. *The Blitzkrieg Myth: How Hitler and the Allies Misread the Strategic Realities of World War II*. New York: HarperCollins, 2003.

Muller, Annette. *La Petite Fille du Vél d'Hiv*. Paris: Livre de Poche Jeunesse, 2014.

Muracciole, Jean-François, and Guillaume Piketty. *Encyclopédie de la Seconde Guerre mondiale*. Paris: Bouquins, 2015.

Naïtchenko, Maroussia. *Une Jeune Fille en guerre: La Lutte antifasciste d'une génération* [A girl at war: The antifascist struggle of a generation]. Preface by Gilles Perrault. Paris: Imago, 2003.

Noguères, Henri. *En France au temps du Front populaire: 1935–1938*. Paris: Hachette, 1977.

——. *La Vie quotidienne en France au temps du Front populaire, 1935–1938*. Paris: Hachette, 1977.

——. *La Vie quotidienne des résistants de l'armistice à la Libération, 1940–1945*. Paris: Hachette, 1984.

Oberski, Jona, and Jim Shepard. *Childhood.* Translated by Ralph Manheim. New York: Penguin Classics, 2014.

Oeuvre, L'. "Avis." *L'Oeuvre.* October 23, 1941.

Olson, Lynne. *Last Hope Island.* New York: Random House, 2017.

——. *Madame Fourcade's Secret War: The Daring Young Women Who Led France's Largest Spy Network Against Hitler.* New York: Random House, 2019.

Ophuls, Marcel, dir. *Le Chagrin et la pitié: Chronique d'une ville française sous l'Occupation.* Film. 1971.

Oppenheim, Daniel. *Des Adolescences au cœur de la Shoah.* Lormont: Le Bord de l'Eau, 2016.

Ory, Pascal. *Villes sous l'Occupation: L'Histoire des Français au quotidien.* Paris: Express Roularta, 2012.

Ousby, Ian. *Occupation: The Ordeal of France, 1940–1944.* New York: Cooper Square Press, 2000.

Ouzoulias, Albert. *Les Bataillons de la jeunesse* [The Youth Battalions]. Paris: Éditions Sociales, 1969.

Paris-Musées. *1940: L'Année de tous les destins.* Paris: Paris-Musées, 2000.

Passera, Françoise. *Les Affiches de propagande: 1939–1945.* Caen: Mémorial de Caen, 2005.

Paxton, Robert O. *Parades and Politics at Vichy: The French Officer Corps under Marshal Pétain.* Princeton, NJ: Princeton University Press, 1966.

——. *Vichy France: Old Guard and New Order, 1940–1944.* New York: Alfred A. Knopf, 1972.

——. *The Anatomy of Fascism.* New York: Alfred A. Knopf, 2004.

Pearson, Chris. *Scarred Landscapes: War and Nature in Vichy France.* New York: Palgrave Macmillan, 2008.

Perrault, Gilles. *Dictionnaire amoureux de la Résistance.* Paris: Plon, 2014.

—— and Pierre Azéma. *Paris under the Occupation.* New York: Vendome Press, 1989.

Piketty, Guillaume. *Français en résistance: Carnets de guerre, correspondances, journaux personnels.* Paris: Robert Laffont, 2009.

Poliakov, Léon. *L'Étoile jaune.* Paris: Grancher, 1999.

Postel-Vinay, Anise. *Vivre* [To live]. Paris: Grasset, 2015.

Poznanski, Renée. "Reflections on Jewish Resistance and Jewish Resistants in France." *Jewish Social Studies* 1 (1995): 124–158.

——. *Jews in France during World War II.* Hanover, NH: Brandeis University Press/US Holocaust Memorial Museum, 2002.

——. *Propagandes et persécutions: La Résistance et le "problème juif," 1940–1944.* Paris: Arthème Fayard, 2008.

Preston, Paul. *The Spanish Civil War, 1936–39.* New York: Grove Press, 1986.

Prost, Antoine. "Jeunesse et société dans la France de l'entre-deux-guerres." *Vingtième Siècle: Revue d'histoire* 13, no. 1 (1987): 35–44.

Pryce-Jones, David. *Paris in the Third Reich: A History of the German Occupation, 1940–1944.* New York: Holt, Rinehart and Winston, 1981.

Rajsfus, Maurice. *La Rafle du Vél d'Hiv.* Paris: Presses Universitaires de France, 2002.

——. *Opération Étoile jaune,* followed by *Jeudi noir.* Paris: Cherche Midi, 2002.

——. *Operation Yellow Star*, followed by *Black Thursday: The Roundup of July 16, 1942.* Translated by Phyllis Aronoff and Mike Mitchell. Los Angeles: Doppel House Press, 2017.

Rancé, Christiane. *Simone Weil: Le Courage de l'impossible* [Simone Weil: Impossible courage]. Paris: Éditions du Seuil, 2009.

Rayski, Adam. *L'Affiche rouge: Une Victoire posthume.* Paris: Délégation à la Mémoire et à l'Information Historique, 1999.

Rearick, Charles. *The French in Love and War: Popular Culture in the Era of the World Wars.* New Haven, CT: Yale University Press, 1997.

Recchia, Holly E., and Cecilia Wainryb. "Youths Making Sense of Political Conflict: Considering Protective and Maladaptive Possibilities." *Human Development* 54, no. 1 (2011): 49–59.

Richert, Philippe, et al., eds. *Lettres de Malgré-nous: Témoignages d'incorporés de force alsaciens.* Strasbourg: La Nuée Bleue, 2012.

Riedweg, Eugène. *Les "Malgré-nous": Histoire de l'incorporation de force des Alsaciens-Mosellans dans l'armée allemande* [The "against our will": The history of the Alsatians-Mossellans forced to join the German army]. Strasbourg: La Nuée Bleue, 2008.

——. *Lettres de Malgrés-nous: Témoignages d'incorporés de force alsaciens.* Strasbourg: La Nuée Bleue, 2012.

Robrieux, Philippe. *L'Affaire Manouchian: Vie et mort d'un héros communiste.* Paris: Arthème Fayard, 1986.

Rosbottom, Ronald C. *When Paris Went Dark: The City of Light under German Occupation, 1940–1944.* New York: Little, Brown and Co., 2014.

Rossel-Kirschen, André, and Gilles Perrault. *Le Procès de la Maison de la Chimie (7 au 14 avril 1942): Contribution à l'histoire des débuts de la Résistance armée en France* [The trial at the Chemistry Palace (7 to 14 April 1942): Contibution to the history of the beginning of the armed resistance in France]. Paris: L'Harmattan, 2002.

——. *La Mort à quinze ans: Entretiens avec Gilles Perrault* [Death at fifteen: Interviews with Gilles Perrault]. Paris: Arthème Fayard, 2005.

Roussel, Eric. *Le Naufrage: 16 juin 1940.* Paris: Gallimard, 2009.

——. *Pierre Brossolette.* Paris: Arthème Fayard, 2011.

Rousso, Henry. *Le Syndrome de Vichy: 1944–198–.* Paris: Éditions du Seuil, 1987.

——. *The Vichy Syndrome: History and Memory in France since 1944.* Cambridge, MA: Harvard University Press, 1991.

——. *La Seconde Guerre Mondiale expliquée à ma fille.* Paris: Éditions du Seuil, 2013.

Rousso, Henry, and Henri Michel. *Le Régime de Vichy.* Paris: Presses Universitaires de France, 2007.

Ruffin, Raymond. *Journal d'un J3* [Journal of a J3 adolescent]. Paris: Presses de la Cité, 1979.

Sabbagh, Antoine. *Lettres de Drancy.* Paris: Tallandier, 2002.

Sainclivier, Jacqueline, et al. *La Résistance et les Français: Enjeux stratégiques et environnement social.* Proceedings of the symposium "La Résistance et les Français: Le Poids de la stratégie, résistance, et société." Rennes: Presses Universitaires de Rennes, 1995.

Saint-Exupéry, Antoine de. *Pilote de guerre.* Paris: Gallimard, 1972.

Sajer, Guy. *The Forgotten Soldier.* New York: Harper & Row, 1971.

Salat-Baroux, Frédéric. *De Gaulle–Pétain: Le Destin, la blessure, la leçon*. Paris: Tallandier, 2013.

Sartre, Jean-Paul, and Chris Turner. *The Aftermath of War (Situations III)*. London and New York: Seagull Books, 2008.

Schiff, Stacy. *Saint-Exupéry: A Biography*. New York: Henry Holt, 2006.

Schroeder, Liliane. *Journal d'occupation, Paris, 1940–1944: Chronique au jour le jour d'une époque oubliée*. Paris: François-Xavier de Guibert, 2000.

Schwab, Thomas J. *Experiences of My French Jewish Family under German Occupation 1940–1944*. Unpublished manuscript, 2002.

Semelin, Jacques. *Persécutions et entraides dans la France occupée: Comment 75% des Juifs de France ont échappé à la mort*. Paris: Éditions du Seuil/Éditions des Arènes, 2013.

———. *The Survival of the Jews in France, 1940–1944*. Preface by Serge Klarsfeld. Oxford: Oxford University Press, 2019.

Snyder, Timothy. *On Tyranny: Twenty Lessons from the Twentieth Century*. New York: Tim Duggan Books, 2017.

Soo, Scott. *The Routes to Exile: France and the Spanish Civil War Refugees, 1939–2009*. Studies in Modern French History. Manchester: Manchester University Press, 2013.

Soucy, Robert. *French Fascism: The Second Wave, 1933–1939*. New Haven, CT: Yale University Press, 1995.

Soudagne, Jean-Pascal. *L'Histoire de la Ligne Maginot* [The story of the Maginot Line]. Rennes, Lille: Éditions Ouest-France, 2016.

Stern, Thomas. *Thomas et son ombre* [Thomas and his ghost]. Paris: Grasset, 2015.

Stock, Franz. *Journal de guerre: Écrits inédits de l'aumônier du Mont Valérien* [War journal: Unpublished writings of the priest of Mont Valérien]. Translated (from the German) by Valentine Meunier, preface by Étienne François. Paris: Éditions du Cerf, 2017.

Stovall, Tyler. *Paris Noir: African Americans in the City of Light*. Boston: Houghton Mifflin, 1996.

Sudey, Robert. *Ma Guerre à moi: Résistant et maquisard en Dordogne* [My own war: Resister and member of the Maquis in Dordogne]. Périgueux: Décal'âge Productions Éditions, 2013.

Suleiman, Susan Rubin. *The Némirovsky Question: The Life, Death, and Legacy of a Jewish Writer in 20th-Century France*. New Haven, CT: Yale University Press, 2016.

Sullerot, Évelyne. *Nous avions 15 ans en 1940* [We were 15 in 1940]. Paris: Arthème Fayard, 2010.

Taflinger, Nicole H. *Season of Suffering: Coming of Age in Occupied France, 1940–45*. Pullman, WA: Washington State University Press, 2010.

Taïeb, Karen, and Tatiana de Rosnay. *Je vous écris du Vél d'Hiv: Les Lettres retrouvées*. Paris: J'ai Lu, 2012.

Tandonnet, Maxime. *1940: Un autre 11 novembre* [1940: Another November 11]. Tallandier, 2009.

Texcier, Jean. *Écrit dans la nuit*. Paris: La Nouvelle Édition, 1945.

Thibault, Laurence, and Jean-Marie Delabre. *Les Jeunes et la Résistance*. Cahiers de la Résistance. Paris: La Documentation Française, 2007.

Thoraval, Anne. *Paris, les lieux de la Résistance: La Vie quotidienne de l'armée des ombres dans la capitale*. Paris: Parigramme, 2007.

Todorov, Tzvetan, and René Sadrin. *Une Tragédie française: Été 44: Scènes de guerre civile*, followed by *Souvenirs d'un maire*. Paris: Éditions du Seuil, 1994.

Torgovnick, Marianna. *The War Complex: World War II in Our Time*. Chicago: University of Chicago Press, 2005.

Torrès, Tereska. *Une Française libre: Journal 1939–1945*. Paris: France Loisirs, 2002.

Triboit, Philippe, dir. *Un Village français*. Television series, 2009–2017.

Tumblety, Joan. *Remaking the Male Body: Masculinity and the Uses of Physical Culture in Interwar and Vichy France*. Oxford: Oxford University Press, 2012.

Union des Femmes Françaises. "Les Femmes dans la Résistance." Symposium proceedings, Paris, La Sorbonne, 22–23 November 1975. Monaco: Éditions du Rocher, 1977.

Vegh, Claudine, and Bruno Bettelheim. *Je ne lui ai pas dit au revoir: Des Enfants de déportés parlent*. Paris: Gallimard, 1996.

Veil, Simone. *Une Vie, une jeunesse au temps de la Shoah*. Paris: Le Livre de Poche, 2010.

Vergez-Chaignon, Bénédicte. *Les Vichysto-résistants*. Paris: Perrin, 2008.

——. *La Résistance*. Paris: Éditions Métive, 2016.

Verny, Françoise. *Serons-nous vivantes le 2 janvier 1950?* Paris: Grasset, 2005.

Vincenot, Alain. *Les Larmes de la rue des Rosiers*. Paris: Éditions des Syrtes, 2010.

Vinen, Richard. *The Unfree French: Life under the Occupation*. New Haven, CT: Yale University Press, 2006.

Walzer, Michael. *Just and Unjust Wars: A Moral Argument with Historical Illustrations*. 1977; 5th ed., New York: Basic Books, 2015.

Weber, Eugen Joseph. *The Hollow Years: France in the 1930s*. New York: W. W. Norton, 1996.

Weinberg, David H. *Les Juifs à Paris de 1933 à 1939*. Paris: Calmann-Lévy, 1974.

Weisman, Joseph, and Caroline Andrieu. *Après la rafle*. Paris: J'ai Lu, 2013.

Weitz, Margaret Collins. *Sisters in the Resistance: How Women Fought to Free France, 1940–1945*. New York: John Wiley & Sons, 1995.

Whitney, Susan B. "Embracing the Status Quo: French Communists, Young Women, and the Popular Front." *Journal of Social History* 30, no. 1 (1996): 29–53.

——. *Mobilizing Youth: Communists and Catholics in Interwar France*. Durham, NC: Duke University Press, 2009.

Wieder, Thomas. "Daniel Cordier: De Jean Moulin à la jeunesse d'aujourd'hui, la leçon de vie d'un homme libre." *Le Monde*, May 9, 2018, https://www.lemonde.fr/idees /article/2018/05/09/daniel-cordier-il-faut-etre-optimiste_5296372_3232.html.

Wieviorka, Annette. *Ils étaient Juifs, résistants, communistes* [They were Jews, resisters, Communists]. Paris: Perrin, 1986.

——. *Auschwitz expliqué à ma fille*. Paris: Éditions du Seuil, 1999.

Wieviorka, Olivier. *Une Certaine idée de la Résistance*. Paris: Éditions du Seuil, 1995.

——. "*La Résistance: Une Affaire de jeunes?*" [The Resistance: A youthful business?]. In *Être jeune en France*, edited by Jean-William Déreymez. Paris: L'Harmattan, 2001, 241–253.

——. *La Mémoire désunie: Le Souvenir politique des années sombres, de la Libération à nos jours*. Paris: Éditions du Seuil, 2010.

——. *Divided Memory: French Recollections of World War II, from the Liberation until the Present.* Translated by George Holoch. Stanford, CA: Stanford University Press, 2012.

——. *Histoire de la Résistance, 1940–1945.* Paris: Perrin, 2013.

Wieviorka, Olivier, and Jean Lopez. *Les Mythes de la Seconde Guerre Mondiale.* Paris: Perrin, 2015.

Wlasskikoff, Michel, and Philippe Delangle. *Signes de la Collaboration et de la Résistance.* Preface by Jean-Pierre Azéma, presentation by Jean-Pierre Greff. Paris: Éditions Autrement, 2002.

Wohl, Robert. *The Spectacle of Flight: Aviation and the Western Imagination, 1920–1950.* New Haven, CT: Yale University Press, 2005.

Young, James Edward. *The Texture of Memory: Holocaust Memorials and Meaning.* New Haven, CT: Yale University Press, 1993.

——. *At Memory's Edge: After-Images of the Holocaust in Contemporary Art and Architecture.* New Haven, CT: Yale University Press, 2000.

Zaidman, Annette. *Mémoire d'une enfance volée: 1938–1948.* Paris: Ramsay, 2002.

Zajde, Nathalie. *Les Enfants cachés en France.* Paris: Odile Jacob, 2012.

Zwerin, Mike. *Swing under the Nazis: Jazz as a Metaphor for Freedom.* New York: Cooper Square Press, 2000.

EPIGRAPHS

Introduction: Jay Falk, quoted in reference to an American high school shooting in which seventeen students and staff were killed. Matt Flegenheimer and Jess Bidgood, "After Gun Control Marches, 'It'll Go Away' vs. 'We Are Not Cynical Yet,'" in *New York Times*, April 2, 2018, A10.

Chapter 1: Jean Paulhan, *The Bee*. This first appeared in a clandestine paper called *Les Cahiers de Libération* in February of 1944 in a piece called "The Bee," written under the codename "Juste."

Chapter 2: Eugen Weber, *The Hollow Years*

Chapter 3: Évelyne Sullerot, *Nous avions 15 ans in 1940*

Chapter 4: Jacques Lusseyran, *And There Was Light*

Chapter 5: Raymond Ruffin, *Journal d'un J3*

Chapter 6: Guy Sajer, *The Forgotten Soldier*

Chapter 7: Timothy Snyder, *On Tyranny*

Chapter 8: Marie-Madeleine Fourcade, *L'Arche de Noé* (Noah's Ark)

Conclusion: Patrick Modiano, Nobel Prize in Literature acceptance speech, 2015

Notes

INTRODUCTION

1. Jay Falk, quoted in reference to an American high school shooting in which seventeen students and staff were killed. Matt Flegenheimer and Jess Bidgood, "After Gun Control Marches, 'It'll Go Away' vs. 'We Are Not Cynical Yet," in *New York Times*, April 2, 2018, A10.

2. Agence-France Presse, "Marine Le Pen Denies French Role in Wartime Roundup of Paris Jews," *Guardian*, April 9, 2017, https://www.theguardian.com/world/2017/apr/09/marine-le-pen-denies-french-role-wartime-roundup-paris-jews.

3. François Broche, *Où était la France? Vél d'Hiv, juillet 1942* (Paris: Pierre-Guillaume de Roux, 2017), 157–158. All translations from the French in this book are mine, unless otherwise noted.

4. Alya Aglan, *Le Temps de la Résistance* (Arles: Actes Sud, 2008).

5. For this and other statistics about the Free French, see the excellent illustrated "atlas" of wartime France by Sébastien Albertelli, *Atlas de la France libre: De Gaulle et la France libre: Une Aventure politique* (Paris: Éditions Autrement, 2011). Figures cited here are found on pp. 12, 16.

6. Timothy Snyder, *On Tyranny: Twenty Lessons from the Twentieth Century* (New York: Tim Duggan Books, 2017), 84.

7. Holly E. Recchia and Cecilia Wainryb, "Youths Making Sense of Political Conflict: Considering Protective and Maladaptive Possibilities," *Human Development* 54, no. 1 (2011): 51.

CHAPTER ONE: "PRESENT!"

1. For a detailed history of this complex period, see Julian Jackson, *The Popular Front in France: Defending Democracy, 1934–1938* (Cambridge: Cambridge University Press, 1988).

2. For a remarkable description of how persistent and successful the Brigades were, see Annette Wieviorka, *Ils étaient Juifs, résistants, communistes* (Paris: Perrin, 2018), esp. 211–236.

3. Some of this information has come from the punctiliously detailed study by Jean-Marc Berlière and Franck Liaigre, *L'Affaire Guy Môquet: Enquête sur une mystification officielle* (Paris: Larousse, 2009).

4. Ibid., 113.

5. Gaël Eismann, *Hôtel Majestic: Ordre et sécurité en France occupée (1940–1944)* (Paris: Tallandier, 2010), 311.

6. Berlière and Liaigre, *L'Affaire Guy Môquet*, 114.

7. Ibid., 122.

8. Pierre-Louis Basse, *Guy Môquet, une enfance fusillée* (Paris: Éditions Stock, 2000), 148–149.

9. Hannah Josephson and Malcolm Cowley, eds., *Aragon: Poet of the French Resistance* (New York: Duell, Sloan and Pearce, 1945), 137.

10. Ibid., 139.

11. Ibid., 68.

12. Basse, *Guy Môquet*, 27.

13. Albert Ouzoulias, *Les Bataillons de la jeunesse* (Paris: Éditions Sociales, 1969), 345.

14. "Maurice Druon: 'Pourquoi je lirai cette lettre,'" *Figaro*, October 22, 2001, http://www.lefigaro.fr/actualites/2007/10/22/01001-20071022ARTFIG90088-maurice_druon_pourquoi_je_lirai_cette_lettre.php.

CHAPTER TWO: COMING OF AGE IN THE 1930s

1. Boniface Hanley, *The Last Human Face: Franz Stock, A Priest in Hitler's Army* (privately published, 2010), 61.

2. Robert Wohl, *The Spectacle of Flight: Aviation and the Western Imagination, 1920–1950* (New Haven, CT: Yale University Press, 2005), 2–4.

3. Karen Fiss, "Cinema in the 1930s: Exile as Experience and Metaphor," in *Encounters with the 1930s* (exhibition catalog), ed. MNCARS Publications Department and La Fábrica (Madrid: La Fábrica, 2012), 251–264.

4. Charles Rearick, *The French in Love and War: Popular Culture in the Era of the World Wars* (New Haven, CT: Yale University Press, 1997), 142.

5. Eugen Joseph Weber, *The Hollow Years: France in the 1930s* (New York: W. W. Norton, 1996), 64.

6. Jean-Pascal Soudagne, *L'Histoire de la Ligne Maginot* (Rennes, Lille: Éditions Ouest-France, 2016), 26.

7. *Modern Mechanix*, "France Builds World's Greatest Defense System," *Modern Mechanix* (March 1931): 58–59.

8. Christiane Rancé, *Simone Weil: Le Courage de l'impossible* (Paris: Éditions du Seuil, 2009), 49.

9. Fred Kupferman, in his excellent biography of Laval, recounts in detail the political and diplomatic confusion that Hitler caused by his impudent invasion. See Kupferman, *Pierre Laval* (Paris: Tallandier, 2016), 193–194.

10. There is much information about this "militarization" of the Latin Quarter in Henri Noguères, *La Vie quotidienne en France au temps du Front populaire, 1935–1938* (Paris: Hachette, 1977).

11. Robert Sudey, *Ma Guerre à moi: Résistant et maquisard en Dordogne* (Périgueux: Décal'âge Productions Éditions, 2013), 10.

12. Weber, *The Hollow Years*, 64–65.

13. Radio allocution, June 10, 1936, *Sport* (17 June 1936): 3.

14. Joan Tumblety, *Remaking the Male Body: Masculinity and the Uses of Physical Culture in Interwar and Vichy France* (Oxford: Oxford University Press, 2012), 79.

15. Ibid.

CHAPTER THREE: WHAT THE HELL HAPPENED?

1. Évelyne Sullerot, *Nous avions 15 ans en 1940* (Paris: Arthème Fayard, 2010), 30.

2. Ibid., 72.

3. Ibid., 75.

4. Michèle Lajournade, "[Jean] Lajournade Biography" (unpublished typescript), 19.

5. Marc Bloch, *L'Étrange défaite: Témoignage écrit en 1940* (Paris: Gallimard, 1990), 55.

6. Ibid., 67.

7. John Mosier, *The Blitzkrieg Myth: How Hitler and the Allies Misread the Strategic Realities of World War II* (New York: HarperCollins, 2003), 284, 287.

8. See Lynne Olson, *Last Hope Island* (New York: Random House, 2017), an absorbing narrative about those exiled governments and their effectiveness during the war.

9. Jean-Louis Crémieux-Brilhac, *La France libre: De l'Appel du 18 juin à la Libération* (Paris: Gallimard, 1996), 98, 101.

10. Sullerot, *Nous avions 15 ans en 1940*, 85.

11. See Robert O. Paxton, *Parades and Politics at Vichy: The French Officer Corps under Marshal Pétain* (Princeton, NJ: Princeton University Press, 1966), 23.

12. Fabrice Grenard, with Jean-Pierre Azéma, *Les Français sous l'Occupation en 100 questions* (Paris: Tallandier, 2016), 81.

13. See a fuller account of the Napoleon II fiasco in my *When Paris Went Dark: The City of Light under German Occupation, 1940–1944* (New York: Little, Brown and Co., 2014), 113–116.

CHAPTER FOUR: A BLIND RESISTANCE

1. Jacques Lusseyran, *And There Was Light: Autobiography of Jacques Lusseyran, Blind Hero of the French Resistance* (New York: Parabola, 1998), 15.

2. Jacques Lusseyran, *Against the Pollution of the I: Selected Writings*, introduction by Christopher Bamford (Sandpoint, ID: Morning Light Press, 2006), 13.

3. Lusseyran, *And There Was Light*, 59.

4. Lusseyran, *Against the Pollution of the I*, 84.

5. Lusseyran, *And There Was Light*, 147.

6. Ibid., 61.

7. Ibid., 106.

8. Ibid., 110.

9. Ibid., 160.

10. Lusseyran, *Against the Pollution of the I*, 34.

11. Lusseyran, *And There Was Light*, 145.

12. Annie Kriegel, *Ce que j'ai cru comprendre* (Paris: Robert Laffont, 1991), 178.

13. Bernard Matot, *La Guerre des cancres: Un Lycée au coeur de la Résistance et la Collaboration* (Paris: Perrin, 2010), 40–41.

14. Lusseyran, *And There Was Light*, 151.

15. Jérôme Garcin, *Le Voyant* (Paris: Gallimard, 2016), 62.

16. Lusseyran, *And There Was Light*, 145.

17. Ibid., 164

18. Ibid., 163.

19. Lusseyran, *Against the Pollution of the I*, 43.

20. Lusseyran, *And There Was Light*, 161.

21. For more on the impact of this new music, especially in France, see Tyler Stovall, *Paris Noir: African Americans in the City of Light* (Boston: Houghton Mifflin, 1996), 21–22.

22. Mike Zwerin, *Swing under the Nazis: Jazz as a Metaphor for Freedom* (New York: Cooper Square Press, 2000), 86.

23. Jeffrey H. Jackson, *Making Jazz French: Music and Modern Life in Interwar Paris* (Durham, NC: Duke University Press, 2003).

24. Jean-Claude Loiseau, *Les Zazous* (Paris: Le Sagittaire, 1977), 61.

25. Lusseyran, *And There Was Light*, 169.

26. Lusseyran, *Against the Pollution of the I*, 33.

27. Ibid.

28. Lusseyran, *And There Was Light*, 170.

29. Ibid., 171.

30. Ouzoulias, *Les Bataillons de la jeunesse*, 98.

31. Lusseyran, *And There Was Light*, 173.

32. Ibid., 225.

33. Ibid., 230.

34. Ibid., 181.

35. Ibid., 248.

36. Ibid., 251.

37. Ibid., 263.

38. Ibid., 267.

39. Ibid.

CHAPTER FIVE: LIFE AS A J3 DURING THE DARK YEARS

1. Raymond Ruffin, *Journal d'un J3* (Paris: Presses de la Cité, 1979), 250.

2. Jean-William Déreymez, ed., *Être jeune en France (1939–1945)* (Paris: L'Harmattan, 2001), 22–23.

3. Ruffin, *Journal d'un J3*, 11–13.

4. Ibid., 32.

5. Ibid., 54–55.

6. André Rossel-Kirschen and Gilles Perrault, *La Mort à quinze ans: Entretiens avec Gilles Perrault* (Paris: Arthème Fayard, 2005), 14. After the war, Kirschen used the pseudonym Rossel for his publishing and artistic ventures; later he adopted it permanently.

7. Ibid., 73.

8. Ibid., 37–38.

9. Maroussia Naïtchenko, *Une Jeune Fille en guerre: La Lutte antifasciste d'une génération*, preface by Gilles Perrault (Paris: Imago, 2003), 108.

10. Ibid., 127.

11. Ibid., 128.

12. Ibid., 151.

13. Eisman, *Hôtel Majestic*, 274.

14. Micheline Bood, *Les Années doubles: Journal d'une lycéenne sous l'Occupation*, introduction by Jacques Labib (Paris: Robert Laffont, 1974).

15. Ibid., 126.

16. Ibid., 118.

17. Ibid., 157.

18. Susan B. Whitney, *Mobilizing Youth: Communists and Catholics in Interwar France* (Durham, NC: Duke University Press, 2009), 243.

19. Matot, *La Guerre des cancres*, 84–85.

20. François Broche and Jean-François Muracciole, *Histoire de la Collaboration (1940–1945)* (Paris: Tallandier, 2017), 254.

21. This and other pertinent information about a rarely studied phenomenon may be found in Eugène Riedweg, *Les "Malgré-nous": Histoire de l'incorporation de force des Alsaciens-Mosellans dans l'armée allemande* (Strasbourg: La Nuée Bleue, 2008).

22. Ibid., 42.

23. Pauline Corday, *J'ai vécu dans Paris occupé* (Montréal: Éditions de l'Arbre, 1943), 193.

24. Paul Huot, *J'avais 20 ans en 1943: Les Chantiers de jeunesse, le Maquis, le Commando de Cluny* (Bayonne: Éditions Jakin, 1996), 38.

25. Roger Fichtenberg, *Journal d'un résistant juif dans le sud-ouest* (Paris: Éditions le Manuscrit, 2015), 43.

26. Ibid., 51–52.

27. Ibid., 63.

28. Ibid., 71.

29. Corday, *J'ai vécu dans Paris occupé*, 102.

30. This anecdote and the one about the Alsatian family named Muller were found in a fascinating exposition about women who lived through World War II and related their stories late in life. Composed of texts, photographs, and videos, the show was curated by Maureen Ragoucy, documentary photographer and videographer. "Rappelle-toi, Barbara" was shown January 2–22, 2019, at the town hall of the eighth arrondissement in Paris.

31. Claude Lévy, *Les Parias de la Résistance* (Paris: Calmann-Lévy, 1970), 65–66.

32. Ibid, 67.

33. Fichtenberg, *Journal d'un résistant juif dans le sud-ouest*, 73.

34. Ibid.

35. Olivier Wieviorka, "La Résistance, une affaire de jeunes?," in Déreymez, *Être jeune en France*, 245.

36. Ruffin, *Journal d'un J3*, 72–74.

37. Ibid., 136.

38. Ibid., 137.

CHAPTER SIX: SUDDEN COURAGE

1. Maxime Tandonnet, *1940: un autre 11 novembre* (Paris: Tallandier, 2009), 64.

2. Ibid., 90.

3. Jean Guéhenno, *Diary of the Dark Years, 1940–1944: Collaboration, Resistance, and Daily Life in Occupied Paris*, trans. David Ball (New York: Oxford University Press, 2015; first published as *Journal des anneés noires, 1940–1944* [Paris: Gallimard, 1947]), 34.

4. Ibid.

5. Rossel-Kirschen and Perrault, *La Mort à quinze ans*, 97.

6. Ibid., 98.

7. Ibid., 51.

8. Ibid., 54.

9. Paul Collette, *J'ai tiré sur Laval* (Caen: Ozanne & Compagnie, 1946), 13.

10. Ibid., 18.

11. Ibid., 27.

12. Ibid., 32.

13. Ibid., 50–51.

14. Robert Gildea, *Fighters in the Shadows: A New History of the French Resistance* (Cambridge, MA: Belknap Press of Harvard University Press, 2015), 45.

15. Much of the information in this section comes from Sarah Kaminsky's book, *Adolpho Kaminsky: Une Vie de faussaire* (Paris: Calmann-Lévy, 2009), published in the United States as *Adolpho Kaminsky: A Forger's Life*, trans. Mike Mitchell (Los Angeles: Doppel House Press, 2016). For a brief documentary of Kaminsky's career, see Pamela Druckerman, "'If I Sleep for an Hour, 30 People Will Die,'" *New York Times*, October 2, 2016, https://www.nytimes.com/2016/10/02/opinion/sunday/if-i-sleep-for-an-hour-30-people-will-die.html?smprod=nytcore-ipad&smid=nytcore-ipad-share.

16. Kaminsky, *Adolpho Kaminsky: A Forger's Life*, 23–24.

17. Ibid., 25.

18. Ibid., 34.

19. Jean-Raphaël Hirsch, *Réveille-toi papa, c'est fini!* (Paris: Albin Michel, 2014), 242.

20. Ibid., 292.

21. Ibid., 241.

22. Ibid., 200–201.

23. Ibid., 442.

24. François Charles, *Vie et mort de Poil de Carotte: Robert Lynen, acteur et résistant* (Strasbourg: La Nuée Bleue, 2002), 138.

25. Ibid., 89.

26. Ibid., 201.

27. Quite precise information has been gathered by Jean-Pierre Besse and Thomas Pouty in their *Les Fusillés: Répression et exécutions pendant l'Occupation, 1940–1944* (Paris: Les Éditions de l'Atelier, 2006). See especially pp. 181, 185–186.

28. Guy Krivopissko, ed., *La Vie à en mourir: Lettres de fusillés (1941–1944)* (Paris: Tallandier, 2006), 88–89.

29. Ibid., 88–91.

30. Ibid., 45.

31. Ibid., 47.

32. Ibid., 126–127.

33. Ibid., 164.

CHAPTER SEVEN: RESISTING THE RESISTANCE

1. Jean-Marc Berlière, *Policiers français sous l'Occupation* (Paris: Perrin, 2001, 2009), 7.

2. Michael Walzer, *Just and Unjust Wars: A Moral Argument with Historical Illustrations* (1977; 5th ed., New York: Basic Books, 2015), 178, 179.

3. Éric Alary, *Un Procès sous l'Occupation au Palais-Bourbon: Mars 1942* (Paris: Assemblée Nationale, 2000), 71.

4. André Rossel-Kirschen, *Le Procès de la Maison de la Chimie (7 au 14 avril 1942): Contribution à l'histoire des débuts de la Résistance armée en France* (Paris: L'Harmattan, 2002), 28.

5. Ibid.

6. Thomas Stern, *Thomas et son ombre* (Paris: Grasset, 2015), 199, 200. Thomas Elek has been the subject of another novel, *Le Tombeau de Tommy*, by Alain Blottière (Paris: Gallimard, 2009), about an actor who plays Elek in a film on his life.

7. Stéphane Courtois, Denis Peschanski, and Adam Rayski, *Le Sang de l'étranger: Les Immigrés de la MOI dans la Résistance* (Paris: Arthème Fayard, 1989), 363–364.

8. Hanley, *The Last Human Face*, 84.

9. Ibid., 140.

10. Christopher Browning, *Ordinary Men: Reserve Police Battalion 101 and the Final Solution in Poland* (New York: Harper Perennial, 1998), 182.

11. Ibid., 74, 76.

12. Franz Stock, *Journal de guerre: Écrits inédits de l'aumônier du Mont Valérien*, trans. Valentine Meunier, préface by Étienne François (Paris: Éditions du Cerf, 2017), 85–86.

13. Ibid., 80.

14. Ibid., 80–81.

15. Hanley, *The Last Human Face*, 235–236.

16. Lusseyran, *And There Was Light*, 278–279.

17. Ibid., 306–307.

CHAPTER EIGHT: DOES RESISTANCE HAVE A GENDER?

1. Michèle Cointet, *Les Françaises dans la guerre et l'Occupation* (Paris: Arthème Fayard, 2018), 160.

2. Caroline Moorehead, *A Train in Winter: An Extraordinary Story of Women, Friendship, and Resistance in Occupied France* (New York: Harper Perennial, 2011), 54.

3. Naïtchenko, *Une Jeune Fille en guerre*, 344.

4. Ibid., 325.

5. Ibid., 163.

6. Ibid., 173.

7. Ibid., 186.

8. Ibid., 214.

9. Ibid., 216.

10. Ibid., 241.

11. Ibid., 254, 216.

12. Ibid., 255.

13. Ibid., 345.

14. Ibid., 297.

15. Ibid., 382.

16. Ibid., 416.

17. Kriegel, *Ce que j'ai cru comprendre*, 103.

18. Ibid.

19. Ibid., 128, 179.

20. Ibid., 195.

21. Ibid., 227–228.

22. Geneviève de Gaulle-Anthonioz, *La Traversée de la nuit* (Paris: Éditions du Seuil, 1998), 42.

23. Ibid., 41, 48.

24. Ibid., 65–66.

25. Anise Postel-Vinay, *Vivre* (Paris: Grasset, 2015), 17.

26. Ibid., 20.

27. Ibid., 106.

CONCLUSION

1. Walzer, *Just and Unjust Wars*, 180.

2. Aglan, *La France défaite*, 13-14.

3. Bood, *Les Années doubles*, 314.

4. Jean-Marc Berlière and François Le Goarant de Tromelin, *Liaisons dangereuses: Miliciens, truands, résistants, Paris, 1944* (Paris: Perrin, 2015), 14.

5. Valerie Deacon, *The Extreme Right in the French Resistance: Members of the Cagoule and Corvignolles in the Second World War* (Baton Rouge: Louisiana State University Press, 2016), 179.

6. Kriegel, *Ce que j'ai cru comprendre*, 240.

Index